AN ANTHOLOGY OF CATHOLIC POETS

AN ANTHOLOGY OF CATHOLIC POETS

ANTHOLOGY OF Catholic Poets

Joyce Kilmer

Fredonia Books
Amsterdam, The Netherlands

Anthology of Catholic Poets

by
Joyce Kilmer

ISBN: 1-4101-0281-5

Copyright © 2003 by Fredonia Books

Reprinted from the 1917 edition

Fredonia Books
Amsterdam, The Netherlands
http://www.fredoniabooks.com

All rights reserved, including the right to reproduce this book, or portions thereof, in any form.

In order to make original editions of historical works available to scholars at an economical price, this facsimile of the original edition of 1917 is reproduced from the best available copy and has been digitally enhanced to improve legibility, but the text remains unaltered to retain historical authenticity.

Nihil Obstat:

ARTHUR J. SCANLAN, S.T.D.
Censor Librorum

Imprimatur:

✠ STEPHEN J. DONAHUE, D.D.
Administrator, New York

New York, April 5, 1939

To
Rev. James J. Daly, S.J

ACKNOWLEDGMENTS

For advice and assistance in collecting and arranging these poems, I am grateful to many friends, especially to Mr. T. R. Smith, Miss Caroline Giltinan and Mr. John Bunker. The publishers, editors and authors who have kindly consented to let me use copyright material are numerous and I assure them of my deep sense of obligation. In particular I desire to thank the following publishers for their generous permission to use all that I required from their lists: Charles Scribner's Sons, John Lane Company, Small, Maynard Company, P. J. Kenedy Sons, Frederick A. Stokes Company, *The Catholic World,* Houghton Mifflin Company, The Encyclopaedia Press, Henry Holt & Company, The Devin-Adair Company, Little, Brown & Company, The Macmillan Company, Elkin Mathews, *The Ave Maria,* Laurence Gomme, and Wilfrid Meynell.

J. K.

Grateful acknowledgment for permission to use some of the supplementary material included in this anthology is made to the following publishers, publications and individuals: D. Appleton & Company, Harcourt, Brace & Company, Jonathan Cape, Ltd., B. W. Huebsch, Burns, Oates & Washbourne, *Spirit, America, The Irish Statesman, The Spectator,* London, *The Commonweal, Yale Review,* Edward J. O'Brien, Seumas O'Brien, A. M. Sullivan, Gerald Raftery.

ACKNOWLEDGMENTS

"Good Luck," "Verse," and "Non Dolet,' from Oliver Gogarty's Selected Poems, and "Celibacy," from Austin Clarke's Collected Poems, are used by permission of the Macmillan Company. "The Convert," by Gilbert K. Chesterton, is used by permission of Dodd, Mead & Co., Inc. "I Shall Not Be Afraid," is from Selected Poems, by Aline Kilmer, and "Olim Meminisse Juvabit" is from Candles That Burn, by Aline Kilmer, and both are used by permission of Doubleday, Doran & Company. "Pied Beauty," "The Windhover," and "At the Wedding March" by Gerard Hopkins are used with the permission of the poet's family and the Oxford University Press.

INTRODUCTION

This is not a collection of devotional poems. It is not an attempt to rival Orby Shipley's admirable "Carmina Mariana" or any other similar anthology. What I have tried to do is to bring together the poems in English that I like best that were written by Catholics since the middle of the Nineteenth Century. There are in this book poems religious in theme; there are also love-songs and war-songs. But I think that it may be called a book of Catholic poems. For a Catholic is not a Catholic only when he prays; he is a Catholic in all the thoughts and actions of his life. And when a Catholic attempts to reflect in words some of the Beauty of which as a poet he is conscious, he cannot be far from prayer and adoration.

The Church has never been without her great poets. And in the Nineteenth Century there was a splendid renascence of Catholic poetry written in English. It had already begun when Francis Thompson wrote his Essay on Shelley, in which he longed for the by-gone days when poetry was "the lesser sister and helpmate of the Church; the minister to the mind, as the Church to the soul." The members of the Pre-Raphaelite Brotherhood were not Catholics, but their movement was related to the renascence of Catholic poetry— it was an attempt to restore to art and letters some

INTRODUCTION

of the glory of the days before what is called the Reformation. Coventry Patmore carried the theories of the Pre-Raphaelite Brotherhood to their logical conclusion, as Newman did those of the Tractarians. Coventry Patmore became a Catholic, and found in his Faith his inspiration and his theme. And his disciple Francis Thompson, born to the Faith which Patmore reached by way of the divine adventure of conversion, with art even greater than that of his master, made of the language of Protestant England an instrument of Catholic adoration.

A few of the poets represented in this book were not yet Catholics when they wrote the poems I have quoted. But I do not think that anyone will find fault with me for including Newman and Hawker among the Catholic poets. I am very sorry that the limitations of space have made me exclude many poems dear to me, many poems that are part of the world's literary heritage. There should be many Catholic anthologies.

The poet sees things hidden from other men, but he sees them only in dreams. A poet is (by the very origin of the word) a maker, but a maker of images, not a creator of life. This is a book of reflections of the Beauty which mortal eyes can see only in reflection, a book of dreams of that Truth which one day we shall waking understand. A book of images it is, too, containing representations carved by those who worked by the aid of memory, the strange memory of men living in Faith.

JOYCE KILMER.

August, 1917.
    165th Regiment, Camp Mills, Mineola, New York.

CONTENTS

Anonymous   PAGE
- Charm Against Enemies 289
- May the Sweet Name of Jesus 289
- A Night Prayer 290
- The Straying Sheep 290
- Prayer Before Going to Sleep 290
- I Rest with Thee, O Jesus 291
- The Sacred Trinity 292

Beardsley, Aubrey
- The Three Musicians 293

Belloc, Hilaire
- Our Lord and Lady 1
- To the Balliol Men Still in Africa 2
- The South Country 3
- The Early Morning 6
- The Prophet Lost in the Hills at Evening . . . 6
- The Birds 7
- Courtesy 8
- Noel 9

Benson, Robert Hugh
- After a Retreat 10
- The Teresian Contemplation 11

Blunt, Wilfred Scawen
- How Shall I Build 12
- Song 13
- The Desolate City 13

Brayton, Teresa
- A Christmas Song 16

CONTENTS

	PAGE
BREATHNACH, MICHAEL	
Man-Child	295
BRÉGY, KATHERINE	
Japanese Cherries	355
BRIDGES, MADELINE	
Wid Thady's Pipe Beside the Door	296
BRUNINI, JOHN GILLAND	
Silent Sufferer	355
BRYNE, WILLIAM A.	
The Bog Lands	296
CAMPBELL, JOSEPH	
Ciaran, the Master of Horses and Lands	298
I Am the Mountainy Singer	299
I Will Go with My Father A-Ploughing	300
The Shining Spaces of the South	301
CARBERY, ETHNA	
Mea Culpa	19
In Tir-na'n-Og	20
CARLIN, FRANCIS	
Wine	302
The Irish	302
Alchemy	303
The Solar Road	303
CARROLL, P. J.	
Lady Day in Ireland	22
St. Patrick's Treasure	23
CASEMENT, SIR ROGER	
Hamilcar Barca	304
Lost Youth	304
CASEY, D. A.	
The Spouse of Christ	24

CONTENTS

	PAGE
CASEY, JOHN KEEGAN	
Maire My Girl	305
CHESTERTON, GILBERT KEITH	
The Convert	356
CLARKE, AUSTIN	
Celibacy	357
CLARKE, JOSEPH I. C.	
The Fret of Father Carty	306
Bill Manning	308
CODD, GERTRUDE JANE	
Song Against Servants	358
COLUM, PADRAIC	
Christ the Comrade	25
An Old Woman of the Roads	25
CONNOLLY, MYLES E.	
Quo Vadis?	359
CORRIDAN, FRANCES O'CONNELL	
First Born	310
Strong Arms	311
COX, ELEANOR ROGERS	
Dreaming of Cities Dead	29
Death of Cuchulain	30
Gods and Heroes of the Gael	32
At Benediction	34
CUSTANCE, OLIVE	
Primrose Hill	34
Twilight	35
DALY, S.J., JAMES J.	
Nox Ignatiana	359

CONTENTS

	PAGE
DALY, THOMAS A.	
To a Thrush	36
To a Plain Sweetheart	40
To a Robin	40
The Poet	41
October	42
DE VERE, AUBREY	
Sorrow	43
Human Life	44
Cardinal Manning	45
Song	45
DOLLARD, JAMES B.	
The Sons of Patrick	46
Song of the Little Villages	48
The Soul of Kernaghan Buidhe	49
DONAHUE, D. J.	
The Angelic Chorus	51
DONNELLY, ELEANOR	
Ladye Chapel of Eden Hall	52
Mary Immaculate	52
DOUGLAS, LORD ALFRED	
Of a Dead Poet	311
A Summer Storm	312
A Prayer	312
A Song	313
DOWNING, ELEANOR	
The Pilgrim	53
On the Feast of the Assumption	54
Mary	55
DOWSON, ERNEST	
Extreme Unction	57
Benedictio Domini	58
Carthusians	58

CONTENTS

DRANE, AUGUSTA T.   PAGE
    Maris Stella 60

DUFF, JAMES L.
    Upon This Rock 360

DURWARD, BERNARD ISAAC
    Good Night 314
    To My Firstborn 315

DURWARD, REV. JOHN T.
    Missed Again 317

EARLS, S J., MICHAEL
    An Autumn Rose Tree 62
    To a Carmelite Postulant 63

EDEN, HELEN PARRY
    A Purpose of Amendment 64
    The Confessional 65
    An Elegy 66
    Sorrow 70

EDMUND, C. P., FATHER
    Our Lady's Death 71

EGAN, MAURICE FRANCIS
    Vigil of the Immaculate Conception . . . 71
    The Old Violin 72
    Maurice de Guerin 73
    He Made Us Free 73

ESSEX, EDWIN, FATHER
    Loneliness 361

FABER, FATHER
    Grandeur of Mary 75
    Right Must Win 77

FAHY, FRANCIS A.
    The Ould Plaid Shawl 317

CONTENTS

FEENEY, S.J., LEONARD   PAGE
    A Fledgling Robin 362

FITZPATRICK, JOHN
    Mater Dolorosa 79

FLEMING, MARY
    Two Kisses 319

FURLONG, ALICE
    Yuletide 79

GAFFNEY, O.P., FRANCIS A.
    Our Lady of the Rosary 81

GARESCHE, S. J., EDWARD F.
    At the Leap of the Waters 81
    Niagara 83

GILTINAN, CAROLINE
    Communion 85

GOGARTY, OLIVER
    Good Luck 363
    Non Dolet 364
    Verse 364

GRIFFIN, GERALD
    The Nightingale 86

GUINEY, LOUISE IMOGEN
    Tryste Noel 86
    The Wild Ride 87
    Ode for a Master Mariner Ashore 89
    Leinster 91

HACKETT, FRANCIS
    The Dead Aviator 319

HAWKER, ROBERT STEPHEN
    Aunt Mary 92
    King Arthur's Waes-hael 93

CONTENTS

HAYES, JAMES M. PAGE
   Old Nuns 94
   The Mother of the Rose 95
   Transfiguration 96

HICKEY, EMILY M.
   Beloved, It Is Morn 97
   A Sea Story 98

HOPKINS, J. G. E.
   To a Baffled Idealist 367

HOPKINS, S.J., GERARD
   The Starlight Night 99
   The Habit of Perfection 100
   Spring 101
   The Windhover 365
   Pied Beauty 366
   At the Wedding March 366

IRIS, SCHARMEL
   The Friar of Genoa 102

JOHNSON, LIONEL
   The Dark Angel 103
   Te Martyrum Candidatus 105
   Christmas and Ireland 106
   To My Patrons 108
   Our Lady of the Snows 109
   Cadgwith 111
   A Friend 112
   The Statue of King Charles at Charing Cross . . 113

JOYCE, ROBERT DWYER
   Fineen the Rover 321

CONTENTS

	PAGE
KELLEY, MGR. F. C.	
The Throne of the King	117
KELLY, BLANCHE MARY	
The Housewife's Prayer	115
Brother Juniper	116
KELLY, PATRICK	
Light Shoes	368
KETTLE, TOM	
The Lady of Life	322
Parnell's Memory	323
KICKHAM, CHARLES JOSEPH	
The Irish Peasant Girl	324
KILMER, ALINE	
I Shall Not Be Afraid	369
Olim Meminisse Juvabit	370
KILMER, JOYCE	
Main Street	326
A Blue Valentine	327
The Singing Girl	329
Trees	330
Dave Lilly	331
KING, ELEANOR HAMILTON	
The Garden of the Holy Souls	333
KOLARS, MARY	
If This Old Place	370
LATHROP, GEORGE PARSONS	
The Child's Wish Granted	127
Charity	128
LATHROP, ROSE HAWTHORNE	
A Song Before Grief	128
The Clock's Song	129

CONTENTS

	PAGE
LAUBE, CLIFFORD J.	
To Fear	371
LEAMY, SIR EDMUND	
Ireland	130
LEAMY, EDMUND (SENIOR)	
Music Magic	132
Gethsemane	133
My Lips Would Sing	134
My Ship	135
Visions	135
LEDWIDGE, FRANCIS	
Lament for the Poets: 1916	334
Had I a Golden Pound	335
LESLIE, SHANE	
Ireland, Mother of Priests	137
LINDSAY, RUTH TEMPLE	
The Hunters	138
LIVINGSTON, FATHER	
In Cherry Lane	140
M.S.M.	
Surrender	141
MACCARTHY, DENIS FLORENCE	
A Lament	335
MACDERMOTT, MARTIN	
Girl of the Red Mouth	338
MACDONOUGH, THOMAS	
What is White?	146
Wishes for My Son	147

CONTENTS

MacManus, Seumas   PAGE
    Resignation 148
    In Dark Hour 150

Sister M. Madeleva
    As One Finding Peace 372
    At Winter's End 374

Maguire, Francis
    The Root 374

Mallock, William H.
    Lines 339
    Human Life 339

Mangan, James Clarence
    Pentecost 142
    Dark Rosaleen 143

Sister Mary Angelita
    Dust 340
    Signum Cui Contradicetur 342

Sister Mary Benvenuta, O.P.
    A Song of White and Red 375
    Hawkesyard 376

Sister Mary of the Visitation
    As One Finding Peace 376

Maynard, Theodore
    A Song of Colours 151
    The World's Miser 152
    Cecidit, Cecidit, Babylon Magna 153
    A Song of Laughter 154
    Apocalypse 155

McCarthy, Denis A.
    St. Brigid 156
    Rosa Mystica 160
    The Poor Man's Daily Bread 161

CONTENTS

McGee, Thomas D'Arcy   PAGE
    To Ask Our Lady's Patronage 162

Meynell, Alice
    A General Communion 163
    The Shepherdess 163
    Christ in the Universe 164
    "I Am the Way" 165
    Via, et Veritas, et Vita 166
    Unto Us a Son is Given 166
    To a Daisy 167
    The Newer Vainglory 168

Meynell, Wilfrid
    The Folded Flock 168

Miller, J. Corson
    Hymn to the Guardian Angel 377

Moriarty, Helen L.
    Convent Echoes 169

Newman, John Henry
    England 170
    The Greek Fathers 171
    The Pillar of the Cloud 171
    Relics of Saints 172
    The Sign of the Cross 173

O'Brien, Edward J.
    Her Fairness, Wedded to a Star 378

O'Brien, Seumas
    The Poet 379

O'Daly, Murdoch
    Consecration 292

O'Donnell, C.S.C., Charles L.
    The Son of God 173

CONTENTS

	PAGE
To St. Joseph	174
The Dead Musician	175

O'HAGAN, THOMAS
  Giotto's Campanile 178

O'REILLY, JOHN BOYLE
  Name of Mary 179

O'REILLY, MARY A.
  A Christmas Carol 180

O'SHEEL, SHAEMAS
  Roma Mater Sempaeterna 182
  Mary's Baby 183
  They Went Forth to Battle 183
  He Whom a Dream Hath Possessed 184

PALLEN, CONDÉ BENOIST
  Maria Immaculata 186
  The Raising of the Flag 191
  The Babe of Bethlehem 194

PATMORE, COVENTRY
  The Toys 195
  "If I Were Dead" 197
  Departure 197
  Regina Coeli 199

PEARSE, P. H.
  Ideal 199

PHILLIPS, CHARLES
  Music 200

PIATT, MRS. SARAH M. B.
  A Word with a Skylark 343

PLUNKETT, JOSEPH M.
  I See His Blood Upon the Rose 202
  The Stars Sang in God's Garden 202

CONTENTS

PROBYN, MAY   PAGE
    Is It Nothing to You? 203
    The Bees of Myddleton Manor 204

PROCTOR, ADELAIDE ANNE
    A Legend 210
    The Sacred Heart 211
    The Annunciation 214
    Our Daily Bread 216

RAFTERY, GERALD
    On a Dead Teacher 379

RANDALL, JAMES RYDER
    My Maryland 217
    Magdalen 220
    Why the Robin's Breast Was Red 221

REPPLIER, AGNES
    Le Repos en Egypte—The Sphinx 221

SISTER RITA AGNES
    On Moving Into a Skylight Room 380

ROCHE, JAMES JEFFREY
    Andromeda 222
    Nature the False Goddess 223
    Three Doves 224
    The Way of the World 225

ROONEY, JOHN JEROME
    Ave Maria 225
    Revelation 227
    Marquette on the Shores of the Mississippi . . . 229
    The Empire Builder 230
    The Men Behind the Guns 233

ROONEY, WILLIAM
    Dear Dark Head 343
    The Poet 345

CONTENTS

RUSSELL, S.J., MATTHEW   PAGE
    A Thought from Cardinal Newman 234

RYAN, ABRAM J.
    The Conquered Banner 235
    A Child's Wish 237
    Sword of Robert E. Lee 238
    Song of the Mystic 239

RYAN, ANNE
    Mary Salome, Widow 381

SETON, E.
    Mary, Virgin and Mother 242

SHUSTER, GEORGE N.
    Newman 382

SIGERSON, DORA
    The Wind on the Hills 242

SIGERSON, GEORGE
    Far-Away 346
    The Calling 347

SPALDING, JOHN LANCASTER
    Believe and Take Heart 244

STERLING, GEORGE
    To Pain 383

STODDARD, CHARLES WARREN
    Ave Maria Bells 245
    Stigmata 246
    The Bells of San Gabriel 247

STRAHAN, C.S.C., SPEER
    The Poor 249
    The Promised Country 250
    Holy Communion 250

CONTENTS

STUART, HENRY LONGAN — PAGE
    Intempestiva 384

SULLIVAN, A. M.
    Avowal 384
    Plenitude 386

SULLIVAN, TIMOTHY DANIEL
    You and I 348

SWAN, CAROLINE D.
    Stars of Cheer 251

TABB, JOHN BANNISTER
    Christ and the Pagan 252
    Out of Bounds 253
    Father Damien 253
    Recognition 253
    "Is Thy Servant a Dog?" 254

SISTER MARGARET TERESA, S.S.J.
    Woodland 387

THOMPSON, FREDERIC
    Constant 388

THOMPSON, FRANCIS
    Lilium Regis 254
    To the English Martyrs 255
    The Hound of Heaven 261
    The Dread of Height 267
    To My Godchild 270

TORMEY, REV. MICHAEL
    The Ancient Race 349

TYNAN, KATHERINE
    Michael the Archangel 272
    Planting Bulbs 274
    Sheep and Lambs 275

CONTENTS

	PAGE
The Making of Birds	276
The Man of the House	278

WALSH, THOMAS
| Coelo et in Terra | 279 |
| Egidio of Coimbra | 281 |

WHITE, JOSEPH BLANCO
| Night | 351 |

WILDE, OSCAR
Sonnet on Holy Week	352
E Tenebris	353
Le Jardin Des Tuileries	353
Ave Maria Gratia Plena	354

AN ANTHOLOGY OF CATHOLIC POETS

AN ANTHOLOGY OF CATHOLIC POETS

OUR LORD AND OUR LADY

By Hilaire Belloc

They warned Our Lady for the Child
  That was Our Blessed Lord,
And She took Him into the desert wild
  Over the camel's ford.

And a long song She sang to Him
  And a short story told:
And She wrapped Him in a woolen cloak
  To keep Him from the cold.

But when Our Lord was grown a man
  The Rich they dragged Him down,
And they crucified Him in Golgotha,
  Out and beyond the Town.

They crucified Him on Calvary,
  Upon an April day;
And because He had been her little Son
  She followed Him all the way.

Our Lady stood beside the Cross,
  A little space apart,
And when She heard Our Lord cry out
  A sword went through Her Heart.

They laid Our Lord in a marble tomb,
  Dead, in a winding sheet.
But Our Lady stands above the world
  With the white Moon at Her feet.

TO THE BALLIOL MEN STILL IN AFRICA

By Hilaire Belloc

Years ago when I was at Balliol,
  Balliol men—and I was one—
Swam together in winter rivers,
  Wrestled together under the sun.
And still in the heart of us, Balliol, Balliol,
  Loved already, but hardly known,
Welded us each of us into the others:
  Called a levy and chose her own.

Here is a House that armours a man
  With the eyes of a boy and the heart of a ranger,
And a laughing way in the teeth of the world
  And a holy hunger and thirst for danger:
Balliol made me, Balliol fed me,
  Whatever I had she gave me again:
And the best of Balliol loved and led me,
  God be with you, Balliol men.

I have said it before, and I say it again,
  There was treason done, and a false word spoken,
And England under the dregs of men,
  And bribes about, and a treaty broken:
But angry, lonely, hating it still,
  I wished to be there in spite of the wrong.
My heart was heavy for Cumnor Hill
  And the hammer of galloping all day long.

Galloping outward into the weather,
  Hands a-ready and battle in all:
Words together and wine together
  And song together in Balliol Hall.
Rare and single! Noble and few! . . .
  Oh! they have wasted you over the sea!
The only brothers ever I knew,
  The men that laughed and quarrelled with me.

Balliol made me, Balliol fed me,
  Whatever I had she gave me again;
And the best of Balliol loved and led me,
  God be with you, Balliol men.

THE SOUTH COUNTRY

By Hilaire Belloc

When I am living in the Midlands
  That are sodden and unkind,
I light my lamp in the evening:
  My work is left behind;
And the great hills of the South Country
  Come back into my mind.

THE SOUTH COUNTRY

The great hills of the South Country
  They stand along the sea;
And it's there walking in the high woods
  That I could wish to be,
And the men that were boys when I was a boy
  Walking along with me.

The men that live in North England
  I saw them for a day·
Their hearts are set upon the waste fells,
  Their skies are fast and grey;
From their castle-walls a man may see;
  The mountains far away.
The men that live in West England

  They see the Severn strong,
A-rolling on rough water brown,
  Light aspen leaves along.
They have the secret of the Rocks,
  And the oldest kind of song.

But the men that live in the South Country
  Are the kindest and most wise,
They get their laughter from the loud surf,
  And the faith in their happy eyes
Comes surely from our Sister the Spring
  When over the sea she flies;
The violets suddenly bloom at her feet,
  She blesses us with surprise.

I never get between the pines
  But I smell the Sussex air;
Nor I never come on a belt of sand
  But my home is there.

And along the sky the line of Downs
  So noble and so bare.

A lost thing could I never find,
  Nor a broken thing mend:
And I fear I shall be all alone
  When I get towards the end.
Who will there be to comfort me
  Or who will be my friend?

I will gather and carefully make my friends
  Of the men of the Sussex Weald,
They watch the stars from silent folds,
  They stiffly plough the field.
By them and the God of the South Country
  My poor soul shall be healed.

If I ever become a rich man,
  Or if ever I grow to be old,
I will build a house with deep thatch
  To shelter me from the cold,
And there shall the Sussex songs be sung
  And the story of Sussex told.

I will hold my house in the high wood
  Within a walk of the sea,
And the men that were boys when I was a boy
  Shall sit and drink with me.

THE EARLY MORNING

By Hilaire Belloc

The moon on the one hand, the dawn on the other:
The moon is my sister, the dawn is my brother,
The moon on my left and the dawn on my right.
My brother, good morniing: my sister, good night.

THE PROPHET LOST IN THE HILLS
AT EVENING

By Hilaire Belloc

Strong God which made the topmost stars
   To circulate and keep their course,
Remember me; whom all the bars
   Of sense and dreadful fate enforce.

Above me in your heights and tall,
   Impassable the summits freeze,
Below the haunted waters call
   Impassable beyond the trees.

I hunger and I have no bread.
   My gourd is empty of the wine.
Surely the footsteps of the dead
   Are shuffling softly close to mine!

It darkens. I have lost the ford.
   There is a change on all things made.
The rocks have evil faces, Lord,
   And I am awfully afraid.

Remember me! the Voids of Hell
  Expand enormous all around.
Strong friend of souls, Emmanuel,
  Redeem me from accursed ground.

The long descent of wasted days,
  To these at last have led me down;
Remember that I filled with praise
The meaningless and doubtful ways
  That lead to an eternal town.

I challenged and I kept the Faith,
  The bleeding path alone I trod;
It darkens. Stands about my wraith,
  And harbour me—almighty God!

THE BIRDS

By Hilaire Belloc

When Jesus Christ was four years old,
The angels brought Him toys of gold,
Which no man ever had bought or sold.

And yet with these He would not play.
He made Him small fowl out of clay,
And blessed them till they flew away:
  Tu creasti Domine.

Jesus Christ, Thou child so wise,
Bless mine hands and fill mine eyes,
And bring my soul to Paradise.

COURTESY

By Hilaire Belloc

Of Courtesy, it is much less
Than Courage of Heart or Holiness,
Yet in my Walks it seems to me
That the Grace of God is in Courtesy.

On Monks I did in Storrington fall,
They took me straight into their Hall;
I saw Three Pictures on a wall,
And Courtesy was in them all.

The first Annunciation;
The second the Visitation;
The third the Consolation,
Of God that was Our Lady's Son.

The first was of Saint Gabriel;
On Wings a-flame from Heaven he fell
And as he went upon one knee
He shone with Heavenly Courtesy.

Our Lady out of Nazareth rode——
It was her month of heavy load;
Yet was Her face both great and kind,
For Courtesy was in Her Mind.

The third it was our Little Lord,
Whom all the Kings in arms adored;
He was so small you could not see
His large intent of Courtesy.

Our Lord, that was Our Lady's Son,
Go bless you, People, one by one;
My Rhyme is written, my work is done.

NOEL

By Hilaire Belloc

I

On a winter's night long time ago
  (*The bells ring loud and the bells ring low*),
When high howled wind, and down fell snow
  (Carillon, Carilla).
Saint Joseph he and Notre Dame,
Riding on an ass, full weary came
From Nazareth into Bethlehem,
  And the small child Jesus smile on you.

II

And Bethlehem inn they stood before
  (*The bells ring less and the bells ring more*),
The landlord bade them begone from his door
  (Carillon, Carilla).
"Poor folk" (says he), "must lie where they may,
For the Duke of Jewry comes this way,
With all his train on a Christmas Day."
  And the small child Jesus smile on you.

III

Poor folk that may my carol hear
  (*The bells ring single and the bells ring clear*),
See! God's one child had hardest cheer!
  (Carillon, Carilla).

Men grown hard on a Christmas morn;
The dumb beast by and a babe forlorn.
It was very, very cold when our Lord was born
  And the small child Jesus smile on you.

IV

Now these were Jews as Jews may be
  (*The bells ring merry and the bells ring free*).
But Christian men in a band are we
  (Carillon, Carilla).
Empty we go, and ill be-dight,
Singing Noel on a Winter's night.
Give us to sup by the warm firelight,
  And the small child Jesus smile on you.

AFTER A RETREAT

By ROBERT HUGH BENSON

WHAT hast thou learnt to-day?
Hast thou sounded awful mysteries,
Hast pierced the veiléd skies,
Climbed to the feet of God,
Trodden where saints have trod,
Fathomed the heights above?
    Nay,
This only have I learnt, that God is love.

What hast thou heard to-day?
Hast heard the Angel-trumpets cry,
And rippling harps reply;
  Heard from the Throne of flame

Whence God incarnate came
Some thund'rous message roll?
>   *Nay,*
This have I heard, His voice within my soul.

What hast thou felt to-day?
The pinions of the Angel-guide
That standeth at thy side
In rapturous ardours beat,
Glowing, from head to feet,
In ecstasy divine?
>   *Nay,*
This only have I felt, Christ's hand in mine.

THE TERESIAN CONTEMPLATIVE

By Robert Hugh Benson

She moves in tumult; round her lies
  The silence of the world of grace;
The twilight of our mysteries
  Shines like high noonday on her face;
Our piteous guesses, dim with fears,
She touches, handles, sees, and hears.

In her all longings mix and meet;
  Dumb souls through her are eloquent;
She feels the world beneath her feet
  Thrill in a passionate intent;
Through her our tides of feeling roll
And find their God within her soul.

Her faith and awful Face of God
  Brightens and blinds with utter light;
Her footsteps fall where late He trod;
  She sinks in roaring voids of night;
Cries to her Lord in black despair,
And knows, yet knows not, He is there.

A willing sacrifice she takes
  The burden of our fall within;
Holy she stands; while on her breaks
  The lightning of the wrath of sin;
She drinks her Saviour's cup of pain,
And, one with Jesus, thirsts again.

HOW SHALL I BUILD

By Wilfrid Scawen Blunt

How shall I build my temple to the Lord,
  Unworthy I, who am thus foul of heart?
How shall I worship who no traitor word
  Know but of love to play a suppliant's part?
  How shall I pray, whose soul is as a mart,
For thoughts unclean, whose tongue is as a sword
  Even for those it loves, to wound and smart?
Behold how little I can help Thee, Lord.

The Temple I would build should be all white,
  Each stone the record of a blameless day;
The souls that entered there should walk in light
  Clothed in high chastity and wisely gay.
Lord, here is darkness. Yet this heart unwise,
Bruised in Thy service, take in sacrifice.

SONG

By Wilfrid Scawen Blunt

O FLY not, Pleasure, pleasant-hearted Pleasure;
  Fold me thy wings, I prithee, yet and stay:
    For my heart no measure
    Knows, or other treasure
  To buy a garland for my love to-day.

And thou, too, Sorrow, tender-hearted Sorrow,
  Thou gray-eyed mourner, fly not yet away:
    For I fain would borrow
    Thy sad weeds to-morrow,
  To make a mourning for love's yesterday.

The voice of Pity, Time's divine dear Pity,
  Moved me to tears: I dared not say them nay,
    But passed forth from the city,
    Making thus my ditty
  Of fair love lost forever and a day.

THE DESOLATE CITY

By Wilfrid Scawen Blunt

DARK to me is the earth. Dark to me are the heavens.
  Where is she that I loved, the woman with eyes like stars?
Desolate are the streets. Desolate is the city.
  A city taken by storm, where none are left but the slain.

Sadly I rose at dawn, undid the latch of my shutters,
  Thinking to let in light, but I only let in love.
Birds in the boughs were awake; I listen'd to their chaunting;
  Each one sang to his love; only I was alone.

This, I said in my heart, is the hour of life and pleasure.
  Now each creature on earth has his joy, and lives in the sun,
Each in another's eyes finds light, the light of compassion,
  This is the moment of pity, this is the moment of love.
Speak, O desolate city! Speak, O silence in sadness!
  Where is she that loved in my strength, that spoke to my soul?
Where are those passionate eyes that appealed to my eyes in passion?
  Where is the mouth that kiss'd me, the breast that I laid to my own?

Speak, thou soul of my soul, for rage in my heart is kindled.
  Tell me, where didst thou flee in the day of destruction and fear?
See, my arms enfold thee, enfolding thus all heaven,
  See, my desire is fulfilled in thee, for it fills the earth.

Thus in my grief I lamented. Then turned I from the window,
  Turn'd to the stair, and the open door, and the empty street,

Crying aloud in my grief, for there was none to chide me,
  None to mock my weakness, none to behold my tears.

Groping I went, as blind. I sought her house, my beloved's.
  There I stopp'd at the silent door, and listen'd and tried the latch.
Love, I cried, dost thou slumber? This is no hour for slumber,
  This is the hour of love, and love I bring in my hand.

I knew the house with its windows barr'd, and its leafless fig-tree,
  Climbing round by the doorstep, the only one in the street;
I knew where my hope had climbed to its goal and there encircled,
  All those desolate walls once held, my beloved's heart.

There in my grief she consoled me. She loved when I loved not.
  She put her hand in my hand, and set her lips to my lips.
She told me all her pain and show'd me all her trouble.
  I, like a fool, scarce heard, hardly return'd her kiss.

Love, thy eyes were like torches. They changed as I beheld them.
  Love, thy lips were like gems, the seal thou settest on my life.

Love, if I loved not then, behold this hour thy vengeance;
　This is the fruit of thy love and thee, the unwise grown wise.

Weeping strangled my voice. I call'd out, but none answered;
　Blindly the windows gazed back at me, dumbly the door;
She whom I love, who loved me, look'd not on my yearning,
　Gave me no more her hands to kiss, show'd me no more her soul.

Therefore the earth is dark to me, the sunlight blackness,
　Therefore I go in tears and alone, by night and day;
Therefore I find my love in heaven, no light, no beauty,
　A heaven taken by storm, where none are left but the slain!

A CHRISTMAS SONG

By Teresa Brayton

O Lord, as You lay so soft and white,
　A Babe in a manger stall,
With the big star flashing across the night,
　Did you know and pity us all?
Did the wee hands, close as a rosebud curled,
　With the call of their mission ache,
To be out and saving a weary world
　For Your merciful Father's sake?

A CHRISTMAS SONG

Did You hear the cries of the groping blind,
  The woe of the leper's prayer,
The surging sorrow of all mankind,
  As You lay by Your Mother there?
Beyond the shepherds, low bending down,
  The long, long road did You see
That led from peaceful Bethlehem town
  To the summit of Calvary?

The world grown weary of wasting strife,
  Had called for the Christ to rise;
For sin had poisoned the springs of life
  And only the dead were wise.
But, wrapped in a dream of scornful pride,
  Too high were its eyes to see
A Child, foredoomed to be crucified,
  On a peasant Mother's knee.

But, while the heavens with glad acclaim
  Sang out the tale of Your birth,
A mystic echo of comfort came
  To the desolate souls of earth.
For the thrill of a slowly turning tide
  Was felt in that grey daybreak,
As if God, the Father, had sanctified
  All sorrow for One Man's sake.

O Child of the Promise! Lord of Love!
  O Master of all the earth!
While the angels are singing their songs above,
  We bring our gifts to Your birth.

Just the blind man's cry, and the lame man's pace,
   And the leper's pitiful call;
On these, over infinite fields of space,
   Look down, for You know them all.

LIKE ONE I KNOW

By Nancy Campbell

Little Christ was good, and lay
Sleeping, smiling in the hay;
Never made the cows round eyes
Open wider at His cries;
Never when the night was dim,
Startled guardian Seraphim,
Who above Him in the beams
Kept their watch round His white dreams;
Let the rustling brown mice creep
Undisturbed about His sleep.
Yet if it had not been so—
Had He been like one I know,
Fought with little fumbling hands,
Kicked inside His swaddling bands,
Puckered wilful crimsoning face—
Mary Mother, full of grace,
At that little naughty thing,
Still had been a-worshipping.

MEA CULPA

By Ethna Carbery

Be pitiful, my God!
  No hard-won gifts I bring—
But empty, pleading hands
  To Thee at evening.

Spring came, white-browed and young,
  I, too, was young with Spring.
There was a blue, blue heaven
  Above a skylark's wing.

Youth is the time for joy,
  I cried, it is not meet
To mount the heights of toil
  With child-soft feet.

When Summer walked the land
  In Passion's red arrayed,
Under green sweeping boughs
  My couch I made.

The noon-tide heat was sore,
  I slept the Summer through;
An angel waked me—"Thou
  Hast work to do."

I rose and saw the sheaves
  Upstanding in a row;
The reapers sang Thy praise
  While passing to and fro.

My hands were soft with ease,
  Long were the Autumn hours;
I left the ripened sheaves
  For poppy-flowers.

But lo! now Winter glooms,
  And gray is in my hair,
Whither has flown the world
  I found so fair?

My patient God, forgive!
  Praying Thy pardon sweet
I lay a lonely heart
  Before Thy feet.

IN TIR-NA'N-OG

By Ethna Carbery

In Tir-na'n-Og,
In Tir-na'n-Og,
Summer and spring go hand in hand, and in the radiant weather
Brown autumn leaves and winter snow come floating down together.

In Tir-na'n-Og,
In Tir-na'n-Og,
The sagans sway this way and that, the twisted fern uncloses,
The quicken-berry hides its red above the tender roses.

In Tir-na'n-Og,
In Tir-na'n-Og,

The blackbird lilts, the robin chirps, the linnet wearies never,
They pipe to dancing feet of *Sidhe* and thus shall pipe forever.

In Tir-na'n-Og,
In Tir-na'n-Og,

All in a drift of apple blooms my true love there is roaming,
He will not come although I pray from dawning until gloaming.

In Tir-na'n-Og,
In Tir-na'n-Og,

The *Sidhe* desired my Heart's Delight, they lured him from my keeping,
He stepped within a fairy ring while all the world was sleeping.

In Tir-na'n-Og,
In Tir-na'n-Og,

He hath forgotten hill and glen where misty shadows gather,
The bleating of the mountain sheep, the cabin of his father.

In Tir-na'n-Og,
In Tir-na'n-Og,

He wanders in a happy dream thro' scented golden hours,
He flutes, to woo a fairy love, knee deep in fairy flowers.

> *In Tir-na'n-Og,*
> *In Tir-na'n-Og,*

No memory hath he of my face, no sorrow for my sorrow,
My flax is spun, my wheel is hushed, and so I wait the morrow.

LADY DAY IN IRELAND

By P. J. Carroll, C.S.C.

Through the long August day, mantled blue with a sky of Our Lady,
   They are there at the well from the dawn till the sea birds go home;
And the trees bending down with broad leaves offer spots that are shady,
   Where the heart is at rest, sighing prayers till the shadows are come.

The brown beads and the crucifix pass in procession through fingers
   That are pale as the snow or are hardened from labor and pain.
In each *Ave* they whisper the deep Celtic tenderness lingers,
   Like a sweet phrase in song that is echoed and echoed again.

Marching down the white road with the sun in the noon of his splendor
   Are the children, with joy in the blue of their innocent eyes;

In their hearts is a song, breaking forth into words that are tender,
   Unto her with the gold of the stars and the blue of the skies.

In the still summer air there's a chorus of minstrelsy breaking,
   There are flashes of gold with a flutter and waving of wings:
Mary's birds are they, come with the dawn, all the green woods forsaking,
   Every heart in them breaking for love with the message it brings.

Through the calm August day, with Our Lady's blue sky far above them,
   And beyond the grey mountains where slumbers the Irish green sea,
There they speak to her, weep while they pray to her, beg her to love them,
   Till beyond the bright stars where their home and their treasure shall be.

ST. PATRICK'S TREASURE

By P. J. Carroll, C.S.C.

Called son by many lands,
   Thou art a father unto one.
Of all these mothers claiming thee,
By honored titles naming thee,
   We ask: Where is thy priceless birthright gone?

That blessed faith of thine,
  They mothering thee have sold.
But she, thy daughter dutiful,
Has kept thy treasure beautiful
  Through many sorrows in her heart of gold.

THE SPOUSE OF CHRIST

By D. A. Casey

He came to her from out eternal years,
A smile upon His lips, a tender smile
That, somehow, spoke of partings and of tears.

'Twas eventide, and silence brooded low
On earth and sky—the hour when haunting fears
Of mystery pursue us as we go.

Strange, mystic shadows filled the temple dim,
But on the Golden Door the ruby glow
Spoke orisons more sweet than vesper hymn.

No human accents voiced His gentle call,
No crashing thunderbolts did wait on Him,
As when of old He deigned to summon Saul.

But heart did speak to heart, an unseen chord
In Love's own scale did sweetly rise and fall;
Nor questioned she, but meekly answered "Lord!

To-night some household counts a vacant chair,
But far on high Christ portions the reward,
A hundred-fold for each poor human care.

CHRIST THE COMRADE

By Padraic Colum

Christ, by Thine own darkened hour
  Live within my heart and brain!
  Let my hands not slip the rein.

Ah, how long ago it is
Since a comrade rode with me!
  Now a moment let me see

Thyself, lonely in the dark,
Perfect, without wound or mark.

AN OLD WOMAN OF THE ROADS

By Padraic Colum

Oh, to have a little house,
  To own the hearth and stool and all—
The heaped-up sods upon the fire,
  The pile of turf against the wall!

To have a clock with weights and chains,
  And pendulum swinging up and down!
A dresser filled with shining delph,
  Speckled and white and blue and brown!

I could be busy all the day
  Clearing and sweeping hearth and floor,
And fixing on their shelf again
  My white and blue speckled store.

I could be quiet there at night
  Beside the fire and by myself,
Sure of a bed, and loth to leave
  The ticking clock and shining delph.

Och! but I'm weary of mist and dark,
  And roads where there's never a house or bush,
And tired I am of bog and road,
  And the crying wind and the lonesome hush.

And I am praying to God on high,
  And I am praying Him night and day,
For a little house—a house of my own—
  Out of the wind's and the rain's way.

THE HEAVIEST CROSS OF ALL

By Katherine Eleanor Conway

I've borne full many a sorrow, I've suffered many a loss—
But now, with a strange, new anguish, I carry this last dread cross;
For of this be sure, my dearest, whatever thy life befall,
The cross that our own hands fashion is the heaviest cross of all.

Heavy and hard I made it in the days of my fair strong youth,
Veiling mine eyes from the blessed light, and closing my heart to truth.

THE HEAVIEST CROSS OF ALL

Pity me, Lord, whose mercy passeth my wildest
    thought,
For I never dreamed of the bitter end of the work my
    hands had wrought!

In the sweet morn's flush and fragrance I wandered
    o'er dewy meadows,
And I hid from the fervid noontide glow in the cool
    green woodland shadows;
And I never recked, as I sang aloud in my wilful,
    selfish glee,
Of the mighty woe that was drawing nigh to darken
    the world for me.

But it came at last, my dearest—what need to tell
    thee how?
Mayst never know of the wild, wild woe that my heart
    is bearing now!
Over my summer's glory crept a damp and chilling
    shade,
And I staggered under the heavy cross that my sinful
    hands had made.

I go where the shadows deepen, and the end seems
    far off yet—
God keep thee safe from the sharing of this woeful
    late regret!
For of this be sure, my dearest, whatever thy life
    befall,
The crosses we make for ourselves, alas! are the
    heaviest ones of all.

SATURNINUS

By Katherine Eleanor Conway

He might have won the highest guerdon that heaven to earth can give,
For whoso falleth for justice—dying, he yet shall live.

He might have left us his memory to flame as a beacon light,
When clouds of the false world's raising shut the stars of heaven from sight.

He might have left us his name to ring in our triumph song
When we stand, as we'll stand at to-morrow's dawn, by the grave of a world-old wrong.

For he gave thee, O mother of valiant sons, thou fair, and sore oppressed,
The love of his youth and his manhood's choice—first-fruits of his life, and best.

Thine were throb of his heart and thought of his brain and toil of his strong right hand;
For thee he braved scorn and reviling, and loss of gold and land,

Threat and lure and false-hearted friend, and blight of a broken word—
Terrors of night and delay of light—prison and rack and sword.

For thee he bade death defiance—till the heavens opened wide,
And his face grew bright with reflex of light from the face of the Crucified.

And his crown was in sight and his palm in reach and his glory all but won,
And then—he failed—God help us! with the worst of dying done.

Only to die on the treacherous down by the hands of the tempters spread—
Nay, nay—make way for the strangers! we have no right in the dead.

But oh, for the beacon quenched, that we dreamed would kindle and flame!
And oh, for the standard smirched and shamed, and the name we dare not name!

Over the lonesome grave the shadows gather fast;
Only the mother, like God, forgives, and comforts her heart with the past.

DREAMING OF CITIES DEAD

By Eleanor Rogers Cox

Dreaming of cities dead,
Of bright Queens vanished,
Of kings whose names were but as seed wind-blown
E'en when white Patrick's voice shook Tara's throne,
My way along the great world-street I tread,
And keep the rites of Beauty lost, alone.

Cairns level with the dust—
Names dim with Time's dull rust—
Afar they sleep on many a wind-swept hill,
The beautiful, the strong of heart and will—
On whose pale dreams no sunrise joy shall burst,
No harper's song shall pierce with battle-thrill.

Long from their purpled heights,
Their reign of high delights,
The Queens have wended down Death's mildewed stair,
Leaving a scent of lilies on the air,
To gladden Earth through all her days and nights,
That once she cherished anything so fair.

DEATH OF CUCHULAIN

By Eleanor Rogers Cox

Silent are the singers in the purple halls of Emain,
  Silent all the harp-strings untouched of any hand,
Wan as twilight roses the radiant, royal women,
  Black unto the hearthstone the erstwhile flaming brand.

Inward far from ocean the storm's white birds are flying,
  Darting, like dim wraith flames across the falling night.
Winds like a *caoine* through the quicken groves are sighing,
  On no lip is laughter, in no heart delight.

For thitherwards witch-wafted athwart the sundering
    spaces,
  Lo, a word doom-freighted unto Conchubar has
    come,
Whispering of one who in far-off, hostile places
  Strikes a last defending blow for king and home.

And the King pacing lone in his place of High Decision,
  Gazing with rapt eyes on that far-flung battle-plain,
Through the red rains rising beholds with startled
    vision
  Sight such as man's eye shall not see again.

For one there is dying, of his foes at last outnumbered,
  One whose soul a sword was, shaped by God's own
    hand,
One who guarded Ulaidh when all her knighthood
    slumbered,
  Prone beneath the curse laid of old upon the land.

And dying so, alone, of all mortal aid forsaken,
  Dead his peerless war steeds, dead his charioteer,
Yet the high splendor of his spirit all unshaken,
  Shines morning-bright through the Death-mists
    drawing near.

And radiant round his brow yet the hero-flame is
    gleaming,
  And firm yet his footstep upon the reddened sod,
As with sword uplifted towards the day's last beaming,
  Forth goes the spirit of Cuchulain unto God.

Leaving to his land and the Celtic race forever
  That which shall not fail them throughout the fading years,
Heritage of faith unchanged, of fear-undimmed endeavor,
  And a quenchless laughter ringing down the edge of hostile spears.

GODS AND HEROES OF THE GAEL

By Eleanor Rogers Cox

Forth in shining phalanx marching from the shrouding mists of time,
  Bright the sunlight on their foreheads, bright upon their golden mail,
Lords of beauty, lords of valor, lords of Earth's unconquered prime,
  Come the gods, the kings, the heroes of the Gael.

Lugh, the splendor of whose shining lit the forest and the fen,
  He whose smile at first illuming all the shadow-haunted space
Of the vast, primeval ranges, death-engirdled, shunned of men,
  Over virgin seas to Erin led our race.

Mananaan, great lord of Ocean—he whose fair domain outspread
  Wheresoever tides foam-flowered to the moon's high mandate move,

Aengus, clothed in youth immortal, on immortal ardors fed,
  Who of old in golden Brugh reigned lord of Love.

And his name a knightly pennon on the ramparts of the world,
  And his fame a fire unfailing on Time's utmost purple height,
Erin's peerless gage of courage to the vaunting ages hurled—
  Sunward evermore Cuchulain holds his flight.

They are coming with the silver speech of Erin on their lips;
  The speech that once of all the mighty Celtic race made kin,
They are coming with the laughter that has known no age-eclipse,
  They are coming with the songs beloved of Finn.

Yea, with gifts regenerating to all men of women born—
  Flame of courage that shall fade not, flame of truth that shall not fail,
To the music of a thousand harps they're marching through the Morn,
  Deathless gods and kings and heroes of the Gael!

AT BENEDICTION

By Eleanor Rogers Cox

Joy, beauty, awe, supremest worship blending
　In one long breath of perfect ecstasy,
Song from our hearts to God's own Heart ascending
　The mortal merged in immortality.
There, veiled beneath that sacramental whiteness,
　The wonder that all wonders doth transcend,
The Word that kindled chaos into brightness,
　Our Lord, our God, our origin, our end.

Light, light, a sea of light, unshored, supernal,
　Is all about our finite being spread,
Deep, soundless waves of harmonies eternal
　Their balm celestial on our spirits shed.
O Source of Life! O Fount of waters living!
　O Love, to whom all powers of mind and soul,
We give, and find again within the giving,
　Of Thee renewed, made consecrate and whole.

PRIMROSE HILL

By Olive Custance

Wild heart in me that frets and grieves,
Imprisoned here against your will . . .
Sad heart that dreams of rainbow wings . . .
See! I have found some golden things!
The poplar trees on Primrose Hill

With all their shining play of leaves . . .
And London like a silver bride,
That will not put her veil aside!

Proud London like a painted Queen,
Whose crown is heavy on her head . . .
City of sorrow and desire,
Under a sky of opal fire,
Amber and amethyst and red . . .
And how divine the day has been!
For every dawn God builds again
This world of beauty and of pain. . .

Wild heart that hungers for delight,
Imprisoned here against your will;
Sad heart, so eager to be gay!
Loving earth's lovely things . . . the play
Of wind and leaves on Primrose Hill . . .
Or London dreaming of the night . . .
Adventurous heart, on beauty bent,
That only Heaven could quite content!

TWILIGHT

By Olive Custance

Spirit of Twilight, through your folded wings
I catch a glimpse of your averted face,
And rapturous on a sudden, my soul sings
"Is not this common earth a holy place?"

Spirit of Twilight, you are like a song
  That sleeps, and waits a singer,—like a hymn
That God finds lovely and keeps near Him long,
  Till it is choired by aureoled cherubim.

Spirit of Twilight, in the golden gloom
  Of dreamland dim I sought you, and I found
A woman sitting in a silent room
  Full of white flowers that moved and made no sound

These white flowers were the thoughts you bring to all
  And the room's name is Mystery where you sit,
Woman whom we call Twilight, when night's pall
  You lift across our Earth to cover it.

TO A THRUSH

By T. A. Daly

Sing clear, O! throstle,
    Thou golden-tongued apostle
  And little brown-frocked brother
    Of the loved Assisian!
Sing courage to the mother,
    Sing strength into the man,
For they, who in another May
    Trod Hope's scant wine from grapes of pain
Have tasted in thy song to-day
    The bitter-sweet red lees again.
To them in whose sad May-time thou
Sang'st comfort from thy maple bough,

TO A THRUSH

    To tinge the presaged dole with sweet,
O! prophet then, be prophet now
       And paraclete!

That fateful May! The pregnant vernal night
    Was throbbing with the first faint pangs of day,
The while with ordered urge toward life and light,
    Earth-atoms countless groped their destined way;
       And one full-winged to fret
       Its tender oubliette,
The warding mother-heart above it woke,
    Darkling she lay in doubt, then, sudden wise,
Whispered her husband's drowsy ear and broke
    The estranging seal of slumber from his eyes:
       "My hour is nigh: arise!"

Already, when, with arms for comfort linked,
    The lovers at an eastward window stood,
The rosy day, in cloudy swaddlings, blinked
    Through misty green new-fledged in Wister Wood.
       Breathless upon this birth
       The still-entranced earth
Seemed brooding, motionless in windless space.
    Then rose thy priestly chant, O! holy bird!
And heaven and earth were quickened with its grace;
    To tears two wedded souls were moved who heard,
       And one, unborn, was stirred!

O! Comforter, enough that from thy green
    Hid tabernacle in the wood's recess
To those care-haunted lovers thou, unseen,
    Should'st send thy flame-tipped song to cheer and bless.
       Enough for them to hear

And feel thy presence near;
And yet when he, regardful of her ease,
  Had led her back by brightening hall and stair
To her own chamber's quietude and peace,
  One maple-bowered window shook with rare,
  Sweet song—and thou wert there!

Hunter of souls! the loving chase so nigh
  Those spirits twain had never come before.
They saw the sacred flame within thine eye;
  To them the maple's depths quick glory wore,
    As though God's hand had lit
    His altar-fire in it,
And made a fane, of virgin verdure pleached,
  Wherefrom thou might'st in numbers musical
Expound the age-sweet words thy Francis preached
  To thee and thine, of God's benignant thrall
  That broodeth over all.

And they, athirst for comfort, sipped thy song,
  But drank not yet thy deeper homily.
Not yet, but when parturient pangs grew strong,
  And from its cell the young soul struggled free—
    A new joy, trailing grief,
    A little crumpled leaf,
Blighted before it burgeoned from the stem—
  Thou, as the fabled robin to the rood,
Wert minister of charity to them;
  And from the shadows of sad parenthood
  They heard and understood.

Makes God one soul a lure for snaring three?
  Ah! surely; so this nursling of the nest,

TO A THRUSH

This teen-touched joy, ere birth anoint of thee,
   Yet bears thy chrismal music in her breast.
      Five Mays have come and sped
      Above her sunny head,
And still the happy song abides in her.
   For though on maimed limbs the body creeps,
It doth a spirit house whose pinions stir
    Familiarly the far cerulean steeps
    Where God His mansion keeps.

      So come, O! throstle,
      Thou golden-tongued apostle
And little brown-frocked brother
   Of the loved Assisian!
Sing courage to the mother,
   Sing strength into the man,
That she who in another May
   Came out of heaven, trailing care,
May never know that sometimes gray
   Earth's roof is and its cupboards bare.
To them in whose sad May-time thou
Sang'st comfort and thy maple bough,
   To tinge the presaged dole with sweet,
O! prophet then, be prophet now
   And paraclete!

TO A PLAIN SWEETHEART

By T. A. Daly

I love thee, dear, for what thou art,
  Nor would I wish thee otherwise,
For when thy lashes lift apart
  I read, deep-mirrored in thine eyes,
The glory of a modest heart.

Wert thou as fair as thou art good,
  It were not given to any man,
With daring eyes of flesh and blood,
  To look thee in the face and scan
The splendor of thy womanhood.

TO A ROBIN

By T. A. Daly

I heard thee, joyous votary,
  Pour forth thy heart in one
Sweet simple strain of melody
  To greet the rising sun,
When he across the morning's verge his first faint
    flare had flung
And found the crimson of thy breast the whisp'ring
    leaves among,
      In thine own tree
      Which sheltered thee,
  Thy mate, thy nest, thy young.

I marked thee, sorrow's votary,
  When in the noon of day
Young vandals stormed, thy sacred tree
  And bore thine all away;
The notes of grief that rent thy breast touched kindred
    chords in mine,
For memories of other days, though slumbering still
    confine
      In mine own heart
      The bitter smart
    Of sorrow such as thine.

I hear thee now, sweet votary,
  Beside thy ruined nest,
Lift up thy flood of melody
  Against the crimsoned west,
Forgetful of all else in this, thy one sweet joyous strain.
I thank thee for this ecstasy of my remembered pain;
      Thou liftest up
      My sorrow's cup
    To sweeten it again.

THE POET

By T. A. Daly

The truest poet is not one
Whose golden fancies fuse and run
To moulded phrases, crusted o'er
With flashing gems of metaphor;
Whose art, responsive to his will,
Makes voluble the thoughts that fill

The cultured windings of his brain,
Yet takes no soundings of the pain,
The joy, the yearnings of the heart
Untrammeled by the bonds of art,
O! poet truer far than he
Is such a one as you may be,
When in the quiet night you keep
Mute vigil on the marge of sleep.

If then, with beating heart, you mark
God's nearer presence in the dark,
And musing on the wondrous ways
Of Him who numbers all your days,
Pay tribute to Him with your tears
For joys, for sorrows, hopes and fears
Which he has blessed and given to you,
You are the poet, great and true.
For there are songs within the heart
Whose perfect melody no art
Can teach the tongue of man to phrase
These are the songs His poets raise,
When in the night they keep
Mute vigil on the marge of sleep.

OCTOBER

By T. A. Daly

Come, forsake your city street!
Come to God's own fields and meet
    October.
Not the lean, unkempt and brown

Counterfeit that haunts the town,
Pointing, like a thing of gloom,
At dead summer in her tomb;
Reading in each fallen leaf
Nothing but regret and grief.
Come out, where, beneath the blue,
You may frolic with the true
    October.

Call his name and mark the sound,
Opulent and full and round:
    "October."
Come, and gather from his hand
Lavish largesse of the land;
Read in his prophetic eyes,
Clear as skies of paradise,
Not of summer days that died,
But of summer fructified!
Hear, O soul, his message sweet.
Come to God's own fields and meet
    October.

SORROW

By Aubrey De Vere

Count each affliction, whether light or grave,
  God's messenger sent down to thee; do thou
With courtesy receive him; rise and bow;
And, ere his shadow pass thy threshold, crave
Permission first His heavenly feet to lave;
  Then lay before Him all thou hast; allow

No cloud or passion to usurp thy brow,
Or mar thy hospitality; no wave
   Of mortal tumult to obliterate
   Thy soul's marmoreal calmness. Grief should be
Like joy, majestic, equable, sedate;
   Confirming, cleansing, raising, making free;
Strong to consume small troubles; to commend
Great thoughts, grave thoughts, thoughts lasting to the
      end.

HUMAN LIFE

By Aubrey De Vere

Sad is our youth, for it is ever going,
Crumbling away beneath our very feet;
Sad is our life, for onward it is flowing,
In current unperceived because so fleet;
Sad are our hopes, for they were sweet in sowing,
But tares, self-sown, have overtopped the wheat;
Sad are our joys, for they were sweet in blowing;
And still, O still, their dying breath is sweet;
And sweet is youth, although it hath bereft us
Of that which made our childhood sweeter still;
And sweeter our life's decline, for it hath left us
A nearer Good to cure an older Ill;
And sweet are all things, when we learn to prize them
Not for their sake, but His who grants them or denies
      them.

CARDINAL MANNING

By Aubrey De Vere

I learn'd his greatness first at Lavington:
The moon had early sought her bed of brine,
But we discours'd till now each starry sign
Had sunk: our theme was one and one alone:
"Two minds supreme," he said, "our earth has known;
One sang in science; one served God in song;
Aquinas—Dante." Slowly in me grew strong
A thought, "These two great minds in him are one;
'Lord, what shall this man do?'" Later at Rome
Beside the dust of Peter and of Paul
Eight hundred mitred sires of Christendom
In Council sat. I mark'd him 'mid them all;
I thought of that long night in years gone by
And cried, "At last my question meets reply."

SONG

By Aubrey De Vere

Seek not the tree of silkiest bark
    And balmiest bud,
To carve her name while yet 'tis dark
    Upon the wood!
The world is full of noble tasks
    And wreaths hard won:
Each work demands strong hearts, strong hands,
    Till day is done.

Sing not that violet-veined skin,
  That cheek's pale roses,
The lily of that form wherein
  Her soul reposes!
Forth to the fight, true man! true knight!
  The clash of arms
Shall more prevail than whisper'd tale,
  To win her charms.

The Warrior for the True, the Right,
  Fights in Love's name;
The love that lures thee from that flight
  Lures thee to shame:
That love which lifts the heart, yet leaves
  The spirit free,—
That love, or none, is fit for one
  Man-shap'd like thee.

THE SONS OF PATRICK

By James B. Dollard

Into the mists of the Pagan island
  Bearing God's message great Patrick came;
The Druid altars on plain and highland
  Fell at the sound of his mighty name!

Swift was the conquest—with hearts upswelling
  The Faith they took, and to God they swore:
That precious spark from their bosoms' dwelling,
  Man's guile or torture should snatch no more.

And ever since, while the wide world wonders
  This steadfast people their strength reveal,
As Time Earth's kingdoms and empires sunders,
  They stand by Patrick in ranks of steel!

The nations mock them, like Christ's tormentors;
  "Descend," they cry, "from your cross of shame;
Abjure the Faith—see the road that enters
  The groves of pleasure and wealth and fame!"

Like those that passed where the Cross rose dimly
  Their wise beards wagging—"What fools!" they say;
But the Sons of Patrick make answer grimly:
  "Our God we've chosen—the price we'll pay.

"Ever about us the foes' commotion,
  The anguish sweat on our brows ne'er dry;
Our martyr's bones strew the land and ocean,
  Lone deserts echo our exiles' cry.

"Unto our hearts is earth's pride forbidden,
  Unto our hands is its gold denied;
We do not question the Purpose hidden—
  Let Him who fashioned our souls decide!

"Yet though once more to us choice were given,
  And the long aeons were backward rolled,
We'd walk again before Earth and Heaven
  The blood-stained pathway we walked of old!"

SONG OF THE LITTLE VILLAGES

By James B. Dollard

The pleasant little villages that grace the Irish glynns
Down among the wheatfields—up amid the whins,
The little white-walled villages crowding close together,
Clinging to the Old Sod in spite of wind and weather:
  Ballytarsney, Ballymore, Ballyboden, Boyle,
  Ballingarry, Ballymagorry by the Banks of Foyle,
  Ballylaneen, Ballyporeen, Bansha, Ballysadare,
  Ballybrack, Ballinalack, Barna, Ballyclare.

The cozy little villages that shelter from the mist,
Where the great West Walls by ocean spray are kissed;
The happy little villages that cuddle in the sun
When blackberries ripen and the harvest work is done.
  Corrymeela, Croaghnakeela, Clogher, Cahirciveen,
  Cappaharoe, Carrigaloe, Cashel and Coosheen,
  Castlefinn, Carrigtohill, Crumlin, Clara, Clane,
  Carrigaholt, Carrigaline, Cloghjordan and Coolrain.

The dreamy little villages, where by the fires at night,
Old Sanachies with ghostly tale the boldest hearts affright;
The crooning of the wind-blast is the wailing Banshee's cry,
And when the silver hazels stir they say the fairies sigh,
  Kilfenora, Kilfinnane, Kinnity, Killylea,
  Kilmoganny, Kiltamagh, Kilronan and Kilrea,
  Killashandra, Kilmacow, Killiney, Killashee,
  Killenaule, Killmyshall, Killorglin and Killeagh.

Leave the little villages, o'er the black sea go,
Learn the stranger's welcome, learn the exile's woe,
Leave the little villages, but think not to forget,
Afar they'll rise before your eyes to rack your bosoms yet.
  Moneymore, Moneygall, Monivea and Moyne,
  Mullinahone, Mullinavatt, Mullagh and Mooncoin,
  Shanagolden, Shanballymore, Stranorlar and Slane,
  Toberaheena, Toomyvara, Tempo and Strabane.

On the Southern Llanos,—north where strange light gleams,
Many a yearning exile sees them in his dreams;
Dying voices murmur (passed all pain and care),
"Lo, the little villages, God has heard our prayer."
  Lisdoonvarna, Lissadil, Lisdargan, Lisnaskea,
  Portglenone, Portarlington, Portumna, Portmagee,
  Clondalkin and Clongowan, Cloondara and Clonae,
  God bless the little villages and guard them night and day!

THE SOUL OF KARNAGHAN BUIDHE

By James B. Dollard

It was the soul of Karnaghan Buidhe
  Left his lips with a groan.
Like arrowy lightning bolt released
  It sprang to the Judgment throne.

Spoke the Judge: "For as many years
  As the numbered drops of the sea
I grant you heaven—but thenceforth hell,
  Your bitter lot shall be."

Prayed the soul of Karnaghan Buidhe
    (*The trembling soul of Karnaghan Buidhe*)
"Dear Lord, who died on Calvary,
    Too brief that span of heaven for me."

Then spoke the Lord: "For as many years
    As numbered sands on the shore,
The joys of heaven I give—but thence
    You'll see my face no more."

Pleaded the soul of Karnaghan Buidhe
    (*The shuddering soul of Karnaghan Buidhe*)
"Blessed Lord who died on the shameful tree,
    Too brief that span of heaven for me."

Once more the Judge: "The blades of grass
    That earth-winds ever blew
A year of heaven I'll count for each
    Till hell shall yawn for you."

Prayed the soul of Karnaghan Buidhe
    (*The anguished soul of Karnaghan Buidhe*)
"Kind Lord, who died in agony,
    Too brief that spell of heaven for me.

But this I ask, O Christ—a year
    Of hell for each of these:
The blades of grass, the grains of sand,
    The drops that make the seas!
And after this, sweet Lord, with Thee
In heaven for all eternity!"

Spoke the Judge, and His smile of love
Gladdened the waiting choir above:
"Sin and sorrow forever past,
Heaven I grant you, first and last!"

THE ANGELIC CHORUS

By D. J. Donahoe

At midnight from the zenith burst a light
  More radiant and more beautiful than dawn,
  And the meek shepherds on the shadowy lawn
Gazed upward in mute wonder on the sight;
The stars sank back in pallor, and the skies
Trembled responsive to rich harmonies.

And lo! an angel spake, "Be not afraid!
  I bear glad tidings; for this happy morn
  A Saviour and a King to man is born;
He sleepeth in a manger lowly laid."
Then rolled along the heavens the glad refrain;
"Glory to God on high and peace to men!"

Soon from the skies the streaming light was gone,
  And Night and Silence rested on the hill;
  But the mute shepherds, looking upward still,
Could hear the heavenly echoes rolling on.
So evermore the listening world can hear
The Angelic Chorus ringing sweet and clear.

LADYE CHAPEL AT EDEN HALL

BY ELEANOR C. DONNELLY

CLOSE to the Sacred Heart, it nestles fair—
A marble poem; an aesthetic dream
Of sculptured beauty, fit to be the theme
Of angel fancies; a Madonna-prayer
Uttered in stone. Round columns light as air,
And fretted cornice, Sharon's Rose is wreathed—
The passion-flower, the thorn-girt lily rare,
The palm, the wheat, the grapes in vine-leaves sheathed
Tenderly bright, from mullioned windows glow
Our Lady's chaplet-mysteries. Behold,
Her maiden statue in that shrine of snow,
Looks upward to the skies of blue and gold;
Content that in the crypt, beneath her shining feet,
The holy ones repose in dreamless slumber sweet.

MARY IMMACULATE

BY ELEANOR C. DONNELLY

"PURE as the snow," we say. Ah! never flake
  Fell through the air
  One-tenth as fair
As Mary's soul was made for Christ's dear sake.
  Virgin Immaculate,
The whitest whiteness of the Alpine snows,
Beside thy stainless spirit, dusky grows.

"Pure as the stars." Ah! never lovely night
  Wore in its diadem
  So pure a gem
As that which fills the ages with its light.
  Virgin Immaculate,
The peerless splendors of thy soul by far
Outshine the glow of heaven's serenest star.

THE PILGRIM

By Eleanor Downing

Behind me lies the mistress of the East,
  Golden in evening, fairy dome on dome
  Poised and irised like the far-flung foam
  Lashed on the ribs of some forsaken coast.
  Wicked and lovely temptress, fruitless boast
Of all that man may build and little be,
Mart of the world's base passions, where thy feast
Of shame was spread, thy sin encompassed me,
  Where all desires and all dreams were rife
  With lust of flesh and eye and pride of life,
  Lo! I have reft thy carnal mastery—
  I have gone forth and shut the gates of thee.

Before me lies the desert and the night,
  White star and gold above a pathless waste,
  Blue shade and gray to where the world effaced
  Flings loose its shadows on the lap of God.
  Briars and dust upon my brow, unshod,
In pilgrim weeds athwart a vineless land,

My feet shall pass and mark the path aright,
For lo! Thy staff and rod are in my hand;
And with the light Thy city shall unfurl
Its golden oriflames and tents of pearl—
Dead Babylon, thy gilden clasp I flee;
Jerusalem, lift up thy gates to me!

ON THE FEAST OF THE ASSUMPTION

By Eleanor Downing

"Mary, uplifted to our sight
In cloudy vesture stainless-white,
Why are thine eyes like stars alight,
  Twin flames of charity?"
"Mine eyes are on His glorious face
That shone not on earth's darkened place,
But clothed and crowned me with grace—
  The God who fathered me!"

"Mary, against the sinless glow
Of angel pinions white as snow,
Why are thy fair lips parted so
  In ecstasy of love?"
"My lips are parted to His breath
Who breathed on me in Nazareth
And gave me life to live in death—
  My Spouse, the spotless Dove!"

"Mary, whose eager feet would spurn
The very clouds, whose pale hands yearn
Toward rifted Heaven that fires burn
  Where once was fixed the sword?"

"The fires I felt when His child head
Lay on this mother's heart that bled,
And when it lay there stark and dead—
My little Child, my Lord!"

MARY

By Eleanor Downing

A GARDEN like a chalice-cup,
  With bloom of almond white and pink,
  And starred hibiscus to the brink,
From which sweet waters bubble up.
A garden walled with ilex-trees
  And topped with blue, white clouds between
  Save where the glossed leaves' twinkling green
Is stirred by some soft-footed breeze
A place apart, a watered glade,
  Where sin and sorrow have not been,
  And earth's complaint grows hushed within
Its greening aisles of sacred shade.

The circling arms, the flower face,
  Such were they to the Child soft-pressed,
  Who drew all sweetness from the breast
Of her whom angels crowned with grace.

A night of storm and wailing stress,
  A coast that cradles to the shock
  Of waves that lap the pitted rock,
And winds that shriek their wrathfulness;
A night of all wild things unpent,

Strange voices and strange shapes that beat
To chill the heart and snare the feet.
And through the tempest, beacon-bent
To shelter from the driving damp
  Bespeaking warmth and sweet repose
  Within its sanctuary close,
The welcome of a red shrine-lamp.

So unto Him Who, weary, pressed
  Through the fierce storm of wrath and hate,
  Shone Mary's love, a chapel-gate
Where He might enter Him and rest.

A desert filled with shining sand,
  And still as death the skies that bend
  Where to horizon without end
The rounding distances expand.
A desert white with burning heat
  And parched silence without stir,
  And at its heart a voyager,
Where Death and daggered noonday meet;
And Thirst that grips him by the throat;
  When from the distance wreathing blue,
  No mirage, but a dream come true,
Crowned palm-tree and pale waters float.

To Christ upon the rood, when dim
  Fell on His brow the Shade accurst,
  So Mary slaked His burning thirst
With her white soul held up to Him.

EXTREME UNCTION

By Ernest Dowson

Upon the eyes, the lips, the feet,
  On all the passages of sense,
The atoning oil is spread with sweet
  Renewal of lost innocence.

The feet, that lately ran so fast
  To meet desire, are soothly sealed;
The eyes, that were so often cast
  On vanity, are touched and healed.

From troublous sights and sounds set free
  In such a twilight hour of breath,
Shall one retrace his life, or see,
  Through shadows, the true face of death?

Vials of mercy! Sacring oils!
  I know not where nor when I come,
Nor through what wanderings and toils,
  To crave of you Viaticum.

Yet, when the walls of flesh grow weak,
  In such an hour, it well may be,
Through mist and darkness, light will break,
  And each anointed sense will see.

BENEDICTIO DOMINI

By Ernest Dowson

Without, the sullen noises of the street!
 The voice of London, inarticulate,
Hoarse and blaspheming, surges in to meet
 The silent blessing of the Immaculate.

Dark is the church, and dim the worshippers,
 Hushed with bowed heads as though by some old spell,
While through the incense-laden air there stirs
 The admonition of a silver bell.

Dark is the church, save where the altar stands,
 Dressed like a bride, illustrious with light,
Where one old priest exalts with tremulous hands
 The one true solace of man's fallen plight.

Strange silence here: without, the sounding street
 Heralds the world's swift passage to the fire;
O Benediction, perfect and complete!
 When shall men cease to suffer and desire?

CARTHUSIANS

By Ernest Dowson

Through what long heaviness, assayed in what strange fire,
 Have these white monks been brought into the way of peace,
Despising the world's wisdom and the world's desire,
 Which from the body of this death bring no release?

CARTHUSIANS

Within their austere walls no voices penetrate;
  A sacred silence only, as of death, obtains;
Nothing finds entry here of loud or passionate;
  This quiet is the exceeding profit of their pain.

From many lands they came, in divers fiery ways;
  Each knew at last the vanity of earthly joys;
And one was crowned with thorns, and one was crowned with bays,
  And each was tired at last of the world's foolish noise.

It was not theirs with Dominic to preach God's holy wrath,
  They were too stern to bear sweet Francis' gentle sway;
Theirs was a higher calling and a steeper path,
  To dwell alone with Christ, to meditate and pray.

A cloistered company, they are companionless,
  None knoweth here the secret of his brother's heart:
They are but come together for more loneliness,
  Whose bond is solitude and silence all their part.

O beatific life! Who is there shall gainsay,
  Your great refusal's victory, your little loss,
Deserting vanity for the more perfect way,
  The sweetest service of the most dolorous Cross.

Ye shall prevail at last! Surely ye shall prevail!
  Your silence and your austerity shall win at last:
Desire and Mirth, the world's ephemeral lights shall fail,
  The sweet star of your queen is never overcast.

We fling up flowers and laugh, we laugh across the wine;
  With wine we dull our souls and careful strains of art;
Our cups are polished skulls round which the roses twine:
  None dares to look at Death who leers and lurks apart.

Move on, white company, whom that has not sufficed!
Our viols cease, our wine is death, our roses fail:
Pray for our heedlessness, O dwellers with the Christ!
Though the world fall apart, surely ye shall prevail.

MARIS STELLA

By Augusta Theodosia Drane

Mary, beautiful and bright
    "Velut Maris Stella,"
Brighter than the morning light,
    "Parens et Puella,"
I cry to thee, look down on me;
Ladye, pray thy Son for me,
    "Tam pia,"
That thy child may come to thee,
    "Maria."

Sad the earth was and forlorn,
    "Eva peccatrice,"
Until Christ our Lord was born
    "De te Genitrice":

Gabriel's "Ave" chased away
Darksome night, and brought the day.
   "Salutis";
Thou the Fount whence waters play
   "Virtutis."

Ladye, Flower of living thing,
   "Rosa sine spina";
Mother of Jesus, heaven's King,
   "Gratia divinia";
'Tis thou in all dost bear the prize,
Ladye, Queen of Paradise,
   "Electa,"

Maiden meek and Mother wise,
   "Effecta."
In care thou counsellest the best,
   "Felix fecundata";
To the weary thou are rest,
   "Mater honorata";
Plead in thy love to Him who gave
His precious Blood the world to save
   "In cruce,"
That we our home with Him may have
   "In luce."

Well knows he, that he is thy Son,
   "Ventre quem portasti";
All thou dost ask Him, then, is won,
   "Partum quem lactasti";
So pitiful He is and kind,
By Him the road to bliss we find
   "Superni";
He doth the gates of darkness bind
   "Inferni."

AN AUTUMN ROSE-TREE

By Michael Earls, S.J.

It seemed too late for roses
  When I walked abroad to-day,
October stood in silence,
  By the hedges all the way:
Yet did I hear a singing,
  And I saw a red rose-tree:—
In fields so gray with autumn
  How could song or roses be?

Oh, it was never maple
  Nor the dogwood's coat afire,
No sage with scarlet banners,
  Nor the poppy's vested choir:
The breeze that may be music
  When the summer lawns are fair
Will have no heart for singing
  In the autumn's mournful air.

As I went up the roadway,
  Under cold and lonely skies,
A song I heard, a rose-tree
  Waved to me in glad surprise:—
A red cloak and a ribbon,
  (Round the braided hair of jet)
And redder cheeks than roses
  Of a little Margaret.

Now God is good in autumn,
  He can name the birds that sing,

He loves the hearts of children
  More than flowery fields of spring:
And when the years of winter
  Gray with Margaret will be,
God will find her love still blossom
  Like a red rose-tree.

TO A CARMELITE POSTULANT

(San Francisco, May, 1910)

BY MICHAEL EARLS, S.J.

OH, the banks of May are fair,
  Charm of sound and sight,
Breath of heaven fills the air,
  To the world's delight.

Far more wondrous is a bower,
  Fairer than the May,
Love-of-God it wears in flower,
  Blooming night and day.

Love-of-God within the heart
  Multicolored grows,
Now a lily's counterpart,
  Now the blood-red rose.

Come the sun or chilling rain,
  Come the drought or dew,
Crocus health or violet pain,
  Love-of-God is true.

Hard may be the mountain-side,
  Soft the valley sod,
Yet will fragrance sure abide
  With the Love-of-God.

Where the grace of Heaven leads,
  There it makes a home,
Hills a hundred and the meads
  Will its pathway roam.

Carmel by the western sea
  Holds your blessed bower:
Love-of-God eternally
  Keep your heart a-flower.

A PURPOSE OF AMENDMENT

By Helen Parry Eden

He who mangold-patch doth hoe,
Sweating beneath a sturdy sun,
Clearing each weed-disguised row
Till day-light and the task be done,

Standeth to view his labour's scene—
Where now, within the hedge-row's girth
The little plant's untrammeled green
Stripes the brown fabric of the earth.

So when the absolution's said
Behind the grille, and I may go,
And all the flowers of sin are dead,
And all the stems of sin laid low,

And I am come to Mary's shrine
To lay my hopes within her hand—
Ah, in how fair and green a line
The seedling resolutions stand.

THE CONFESSIONAL

By Helen Parry Eden

My Sorrow diligent would sweep
That dingy room infest
With dust (thereby I mean my soul)
Because she hath a Guest
Who doth require that self-same room
Be garnished for His rest.

And Sorrow (who had washed His feet
Where He before had been)
Took the long broom of Memory
And swept the corners clean,
Till in the midst of the fair floor
The sum of dust was seen.

It lay there, settled by her tears,
That fell the while she swept—
Light fluffs of grey and earthly dregs;
And over these she wept,
For all were come since last her Guest
Within the room had slept.

And, for nor broom nor tears had power
To lift the clods of ill,
She called one servant of her Guest

Who came with right good will,
For, by his sweet Lord's bidding, he
Waiteth on Sorrow still;
So, seeing she had done her part
As far as in her lay
And had intent to keep the place
More cleanly from that day,
Did with his Master's dust-pan come
And take the dust away.

She thanked him, and Him who sent
Such succor, and she spread
Fair sheets of Thankfulness and Love
Upon her Master's bed,
Then on the new-scoured threshold stood
And listened for His tread.

AN ELEGY, FOR FATHER ANSELM, OF THE ORDER OF REFORMED CISTERCIANS, GUEST-MASTER AND PARISH PRIEST

"Et pastores erant in regione eadem vigilantes"

By Helen Parry Eden

You to whose soul a death propitious brings
Its Heaven, who attain a windless bourne
Of sanctity beyond all sufferings,
It is not ours to mourn;

For you, to whom the earth could nothing give,
Who knew no hint of our inspired pride,
You could not very well be said to live
Until the day you died.

AN ELEGY

'Tis upon us—father and kindly friend,
Holy and cheerful host—the unbidden guest
You welcomed and the souls you would amend,
The weight of sorrow rests.

From Sarum in the mesh of her five streams,
Her idle belfries and her glittering vanes,
We are clomb to where the cloud-race dusks and gleams
On turf of upland plains.

Southward the road through juniper and briar
Clambers the down, untrodden and unworn
Save where some flock pitted the chalky mire
With little feet at dawn.

Twice in a week the hooded carrier's lamp,
Flashing on wayside flints and grasses, spills
Its misty radiance where the dews lie damp
Among the untended hills;

Here lies the hamlet ringed with grassy mound
And brambled barrow where, superbly dead,
The dust of pagans turned to holy ground
Beneath your humble tread.

Here we descend at drooping dusk the side
Of the stony down beneath the planted ring
Of beeches where you showed with pastoral pride
The folded lambs in spring;

Here pull at eve the self-same bell that hastened
Your rough-shod feet behind the hollow door—
Yet never see you stand, the chain unfastened,
Your lantern on the floor.

AN ELEGY

Others will spread the board now you are gone
Here where you smiled and gave your guests to eat,
Learning your menial kingliness from One
Who washed His servant's feet;

Along the slumbering corridors betimes
Others will knock and other footsteps pass
Down the wet lane e'er the thin shivering chimes
Toll for the early mass.

Yet in the chapel's self no sorrows sing
In the strange priest's voice, nor any dolour grips
The heart because it is not you who bring
Your Master to its lips.

Here let us leave the things you would not have—
Vain grief and sorrow useless to be shown—
"God's gift and the Community's I gave
And nothing of my own,"

You would have said, self-deemed of no more worth
Then that green hands that guard a poppy's grace—
Blows the eternal flower and back to earth
Tumbles the withered case.

Nay, but Our Lord hath made renouncement vain,
Himself into those humble hands let fall,
Guerdon of willing poverty and pain,
The greatest gift of all;

To you and all who in that life austere
Mid fields remote your harsher labours ply
Singing His praise, girt round from year to year
With sheep-bells and the sky—

This, that to you is larger audience given
Where prayer and praise with sighing pinions shod
Piercing the starry ante-rooms of Heaven
Sway the designs of God:

And now yourself, standing where late hath stood
The echo of your voice, are prayer and praise—
O sweet reward and unsurpassing good
For that small gift of days.

Yourself, who now have heard such summoning
And seen such burning clarities alight
As broke the vigilant shepherds' drowsy ring
On the predestined night,

Who made such haste as theirs who rose and trod
To Bethlehem the dew-encumbered grass,
Trustful to see the showing forth of God
And the Word come to pass;

With how much more than home-spun Israelites'
Poor hungry glimpse of Godhead are you blest
Whom Mary shows for more than mortal nights
The Jewel on her breast.

Yet, as one kneeling churl might chance to think
Of the wan herd behind their wattled bars,
Moving unshepherded with bells that clink
And stir beneath the stars,

And, for the thought's space wishing he were back,
Pray to that Sum of Sweetness for his sheep—
"Take them, O Thou that dost supply our lack,
Into Thy hands to keep."

So you who in His presence move and live
Recall amid your glad celestial cares,
Your chosen office, to your children give
The charity of prayers.

SORROW

By Helen Parry Eden

Of Sorrow, 'tis as Saints have said—
That his ill-savoured lamp shall shed
A light to Heaven, when, blown about
By the world's vain and windy rout,
The candles of delight burn out.

Then usher Sorrow to thy board,
Give him such fare as may afford
Thy single habitation—best
To meet him half-way in his quest,
The importunate and sad-eyed guest.

Yet somewhat should he give who took
My hospitality, for look,
His is no random vagrancy;
Beneath his rags what hints there be
Of a celestial livery.

Sweet Sorrow, play a grateful part,
Break me the marble of my heart
And of its fragments pave a street
Where, to my bliss, myself may meet
One hastening with piercèd feet.

OUR LADY'S DEATH

By Father Edmund, C.P.

And didst thou die, dear Mother of our Life?
 Sin had no part in thee; then how should death?
 Methinks, if aught the great tradition saith
Could wake in loving hearts a moment's strife
(I said—my own with her new image rife),

 'Twere this. And yet 'tis certain, next to faith
 Thou didst lie down to render up thy breath:
'Though after the seventh sword, no meaner knife

Could pierce that bosom. No, nor did: no sting
 Of pain was there; but only joy. The love,
 So long thy life ecstatic, and restrained
From setting free thy soul, now gave it wing;
 Thy body, soon to reign with it above,
  Radiant and fragrant, as in trance, remained.

VIGIL OF THE IMMACULATE CONCEPTION

By Maurice Francis Egan

A sword of silver cuts the fields asunder—
 A silver sword to-night, a lake in June—
And plains of snow reflect, the maples under,
 The silver arrows of a wintry noon.

The trees are white with moonlight and with ice-pearls;
  The trees are white, like ghosts we see in dreams;
The air is still: there are no moaning wind-whirls;
  And one sees silence in the quivering beams.

December night, December night, how warming
  Is all thy coldness to the Christian soul:
Thy very peace at each true heart is storming
  In potent waves of love that surging roll.

December night, December night, how glowing
  Thy frozen rains upon our warm hearts lie:
Our God upon this vigil is bestowing
  A thousand graces from the silver sky.

O moon, O symbol of our Lady's whiteness;
  O snow, O symbol of our Lady's heart;
O night, chaste night, bejewelled with argent brightness
  How sweet, how bright, how loving, kind thou art.

O miracle: to-morrow and to-morrow,
  In tender reverence shall no praise abate;
For from all seasons shall we new jewels borrow
  To deck the Mother born Immaculate.

THE OLD VIOLIN

By Maurice Francis Egan

Though tuneless, stringless, it lies there in dust,
  Like some great thought on a forgotten page;
The soul of music cannot fade or rust,—
  The voice within it stronger grows with age;
Its strings and bow are only trifling things—
  A master-touch!—its sweet soul wakes and sings.

MAURICE DE GUERIN

By Maurice Francis Egan

The old wine filled him, and he saw, with eyes
  Anoint of Nature, fauns and dryads fair
  Unseen by others; to him maidenhair
And waxen lilacs, and those birds that rise
A-sudden from tall reeds at slight surprise,
  Brought charmed thoughts; and in earth everywhere
  He, like sad Jaques, found a music rare
As that of Syrinx to old Grecians wise.
A pagan heart, a Christian soul had he,
  He followed Christ, yet for dead Pan he sighed,
  Till earth and heaven met within his breast;
As if Theocritus in Sicily
  Had come upon the Figure crucified
  And lost his gods in deep, Christ-given rest.

HE MADE US FREE

By Maurice Francis Egan

As flame streams upward, so my longing thought
        Flies up with Thee,
Thou God and Saviour who hast truly wrought
Life out of death, and to us, loving, brought
A fresh, new world; and in Thy sweet chains caught,
        And made us free!

As hyacinths make way from out the dark,
      My soul awakes,
At thought of Thee, like sap beneath the bark;
As little violets in field and park
Rise to the trilling thrush and meadow-lark,
      New hope it takes.

As thou goest upward through the nameless **space**
      We call the sky,
Like jonquil perfume softly falls Thy grace;
It seems to touch and brighten every place;
Fresh flowers crown our wan and weary race,
      O Thou on high.

Hadst Thou not risen, there would be no more **joy**
      Upon earth's sod;
Life would still be with us a wound or toy,
A cloud without the sun,—O Babe, O Boy,
A Man of Mother pure, with no alloy,
      O risen God!

Thou, God and King, didst "mingle in the game,"
      (Cease, all fears; cease!)
For love of us,—not to give Virgil's fame
Or Croesus' wealth, not to make well the lame,
Or save the sinner from deserved shame,
      But for sweet Peace!

For peace, for joy,—not that the slave might lie
      In luxury,
Not that all woe from us should always fly,
Or golden crops with Syrian roses vie
In every field; but in Thy peace to die
      And rise.—be free!

THE GRANDEURS OF MARY

By Frederick William Faber, D.D.

What is this grandeur I see up in heaven,
  A splendour that looks like a splendour divine?
What creature so near the Creator is throned?
  O Mary, those marvellous glories are thine.

But who would have thought that a creature could live
  With the fires of the Godhead so awfully nigh?
Oh, who could have dreamed, mighty Mother of God,
  That ever God's power could have raised thee so
    high?

What name can we give to a queenship so grand?
  What thought can we think of a glory like this?
Saints and angels lie far in the distance, remote
  From the golden excess of thine unmated bliss.

Thy person, thy soul, thy most beautiful form,
  Thine office, thy name, thy most singular grace—
God hath made for them, Mother, a world by itself,
  A shrine all alone, a most worshipful place.

Mid the blaze of those fires, eternal, unmade,
  Thy Maker unspeakably makes thee his own;
The arms of the Three Uncreated, outstretched,
  Round the Word's mortal Mother in rapture are
    thrown.

Thy sinless conception, thy jubilant birth,
  Thy crib and thy cross, thine assumption and crown,
They have raised thee on high to the right hand of Him
  Whom the spells of thy love to thy bosom drew down.

I am blind with thy glory; in all God's wide world
  I find nothing like thee for glory and power:
I can hardly believe that thou grewest on earth,
  In the green fields of Juda, a scarce-noticed flower.

And is it not really eternal, divine?
  Is it human, created, a glorified heart,
So like God, and not God? Ah, Maker of men,
  We bless thee for being the God that thou art.

O Mary, what ravishing pageants I see,
  What wonders and works centre round thee in heaven,
What creations of grace fall like light from thy hands,
  What creator-like powers to thy prudence are given.

What vast jurisdiction, what numberless realms,
  What profusion of dread and unlimited power,
What holy supremacies, awful domains,
  The Word's mighty Mother enjoys for her dower.

What grand ministrations of pity and strength,
  What endless processions of beautiful light,
What incredible marvels of motherly love,
  What queenly resplendence of empire and right.

What sounds as of seas flowing all round thy throne,
  What flashings of fire from thy burning abode,
What thunders of glory, what tempests of power,
  What calms, like the calms in the Bosom of God.

Inexhaustible wonder; the treasures of God
  Seem to multiply under thy marvellous hand;
And the power of thy Son seems to gain and to grow,
  When He deigns to obey thy maternal command.

Ten thousand magnificent greatnesses blend
  Their vast oceans of light, at the foot of thy throne;
Ten thousand unspeakable majesties grace
  The royalty vested in Mary alone.

But look, what a wonder there is up in God:
  One love, like a special perfection, we see;
And the chief of thy grandeurs, great Mother, is there—
  In the love the Eternal Himself has for thee.

THE RIGHT MUST WIN

By Frederick William Faber, D.D.

Oh, it is hard to work for God,
  To rise and take His part
Upon this battlefield of earth,
  And not sometimes lose heart.

He hides Himself so wondrously,
  As though there were no God;
He is least seen when all the powers
  Of ill are most abroad.

THE RIGHT MUST WIN

Or He deserts us at the hour
  The fight is all but lost;
And seems to leave us to ourselves
  Just when we need Him most.

Ill masters good; good seems to change
  To ill with greatest ease;
And, worst of all, the good with good
  Is at cross-purposes.

Ah! God is other than we think;
  His ways are far above,
Far beyond reason's height, and reached
  Only by child-like love.

Workman of God! Oh, lose not heart,
  But learn what God is like;
And in the darkest battle-field
  Thou shalt know where to strike.

Thrice blessed is he to whom is given
  The instinct that can tell
That God is on the field when He
  Is most invisible.

Blessed too, is he who can divine
  Where real right doth lie,
And dares to take the side that seems
  Wrong to man's blindfold eye.

For right is right, since God is God;
  And right the day must win;
To doubt would be disloyalty,
  To falter would be sin.

MATER DOLOROSA

By John Fitzpatrick, O.M.I.

She stands, within the shadow, at the foot
  Of the high tree she planted: thirty-three
  Full years have sped, and such has grown to be
The stem that burgeoned forth from Jesse's root.
Spring swiftly passed and panted in pursuit
  The eager summer; now she stands to see
  The only fruit-time of her only tree:
And all the world is waiting for the Fruit.

Now is faith's sad fruition: this one hour
  Of gathered expectation wears the crown
    Of the long grief with which the years were rife;
As in her lap—a sudden autumn shower—
  The earthquake with his trembling hand shakes down
    The red, ripe Fruitage of the Tree of Life.

YULETIDE

By Alice Furlong

In a stable bare,
Lo, the great Ones are.
Strew the Ivy and the Myrtle
Round about the Virgin's kirtle!

Ass and oxen mild
Breathe soft upon the Child!
Blow the scent of bygone summer
On your breath to the New-comer!

Be ye well content
To be straitly pent
Backwards in the rocky chamber
From the angel's wings of amber!

Rapt the seraphs sit,
With godly faces lit
In a radiance shining solely
From the Christ-child, meek and holy.

High they chant and clear
Of the lovely cheer
Ring down the new evangels
Of the mystic, midnight angels.

Faring with good will
From the misty hill,
Every shepherd sacrificeth
To the prophet that ariseth.

Joseph, Mary's spouse,
Prince of David's House,
Bendeth low in adorations
To the Ruler of the Nations.

Who doth sweetly rest
On his Mother's breast,
Lord of the lightnings and the thunders!
Mary's heart keeps all these wonders.

OUR LADY OF THE ROSARY

By Francis A. Gaffney, O.P.

Lepanto marks the spot of victory,
  O'er crescent cruel and strong, by forces weak,
  Of hallowed cross; of which, "if sign you seek,"
'Tis not of man but a Divinity.
The white-robed Pius Fifth the Rosary
  Uplifted like the rod of Moses, meek;
  Whilst Ottomans on Christians wrath would wreak,
And, as of old, engulfed them in the sea.

O Lady of the Rosary to-day,
  Thy clients all beseech thee, hear their prayer,
    And beg the Christ Who raging storms did quell,
Bid warring nations cease their bloody fray;
  His power and thine honor, we declare,
    O Thou All-Fair, thou joy of Israel.

AT THE LEAP OF THE WATERS

By Edward F. Garesché, S.J.

How the swift river runs bright to its doom,
  Placid and shining and smooth-flowing by,
Blue with the gleam of the heavenly room,
  Smiling and calm with the smile of the sky!
Ah, but the plunge! and the shock and the roar,

The spray of vast waters that hurl to the deep,
The churn of its foam, as the measureless pour
   Of that wide-brimming torrent leaps sheer from the steep!
Look ye; it reaches small fingers of spray
   To clutch at the brink, as unwilling to go
Through the perilous air, and be fretted away
   In the tumult of vapor that boileth below.
List ye! the voice of the huge undertone
   That murmurs in pain from the cataract's breast,
Where the bruised, shattered waters perpetual moan
   And wander and toss in a weary unrest.
Feel ye the breath of the cool-spraying mist,
   Cloudy and gray from the depths of its pain;
Not as when sunbeams the waters have kissed,
   Rising in vapor to gather in rain,
But fiercely and madly flung forth on the air,
   A shroud for this river that leaps to its death,
A veil o'er the throes of the cataract there,
   And rolling and rent with its agonized breath!
Wild torrent! God put thee to thunder His name!
   With the roar of thy waters to call to the sky
Of His might, Who hath set thee forever the same,
   To topple in foam to the gulfs from on high.
Loud hymn of the lake-lands! from shore unto shore,
   Still clamor His praises Who called thee to be,
Till the ears of the nations are tuned to thy roar,
   And they hear the vast message He trusted to thee.

NIAGARA

By Edward F. Garesché, S.J.

God, in His ages past the dawn of days,
Writ one white line of praise,
Which now, in this great stress and hour of need,
I bend my soul to read.
I break the sullen bonds of wearying time,
And with one leap sublime,
Force my astounded soul go back and stand
In the primaeval land!

The tresses of the ancient flood are kissed
With virginal, white mist.
The same soft, thunderous sound
Thrills the wild woods around,
But oh the vast and mighty peace that broods
On these green solitudes,
Where the great land, with one tremendous tone,
Litanies to God, alone!

Tongue of the continent! Thou whose hymning shakes
The bosom of the lakes!
O sacrificial torrent, keen and bright,
Hurled from thy glorious height!
Thou sacerdotal presence, clothed in power,
At once the victim and the white-robed priest,
Whose praise throughout these ages hath not ceased,
Whose altar steams with incense every hour!
Lo, in all days, from thy white waters, rise
The savors of perpetual sacrifice!
I see pale prophecy of Christ's dear blood!—
The transubstantiation of thy flood!

NIAGARA

Oh the wild wonder of the vast emotion
Of the perturbed wave,
That cries and wanders like the fearful ocean,
Seeking, with none to save!
In their wide agony the rapids roam,
A world of waves, an universe of pain!
The vexed, tumultous clamor of their foam
Crying to God with agonized refrain,
Where the sad rocks their quivering summits hide
In the loud anguish of the refluent tide.

Yet, with a willingness that leaps to sorrow
Swift run the ragged surges to the height,
And from their pain is born a pure delight—
The fear to-day, the snowy peace to-morrow!—
Cleaving like darts their swift and silvery way
With sudden gleams, and barbs of glittering spray,
They hurry to the brink, and swift are lost
In that stupendous leap, that infinite holocaust!

Oh Christ-like glory of the praying water
That leaps forever to its mystic death!
And from the anguish of that sobbing slaughter
Lifts the clear glory of the torrent's breath,
Where like a paean of rapturous victory calls
The solemn jubilation of the falls!

O alabastrine priest—thy splendor spraying
More lasting than the immemorial hills!
O monument of waves, O undecaying
While God's right hand thy flowing chalice fills!
Under the transient world's astonished eyes
Thou offerest abiding sacrifice!

In the pale morning, when the rising sun
Flatters thy pouring flood with slanting beams,
Most reverent thy duteous waters run,
And hymn to God with all their thousand streams.
And in the blazing majesty of noon,
Still lifts thy wave its sacrificial tune,
And spills, like jewels of some eastern story,
Its bright, impetuous avalanche of glory!

And in the stilly spaces of the night,
While heaven wonders with its wakeful stars,
Thou prayest still, beneath the solemn light,
In booming tones that reach to heaven's bars,
Keeping thy vigils, while the angelic moon
Walks on thy perilous verge with glorious shoon,
Chanting from foam and spray without encease
Thy yearning immemorial prayer for peace!

COMMUNION

By Caroline Giltinan

Mother Mary, thee I see
Bringing Him, thy Babe, to me,
Thou dost say, with trusting smile:
"Hold Him, dear, a little while."
Mother Mary, pity me,
For He struggles to be free!
My heart, my arms—He finds defiled:
I am unworthy of thy Child.
Mary, Mother, charity!
Bring thy Baby back to me!

THE NIGHTINGALE

By Gerald Griffin

As the mute nightingale in closest groves
  Lies hid at noon, but when day's piercing eye
  Is locked in night, with full heart beating high
Poureth her plain-song o'er the light she loves;
So, Virgin Ever-pure and Ever-blest,
  Moon of religion, from whose radiant face
  Reflected streams the light of heavenly grace
On broken hearts, by contrite thoughts oppressed:
So, Mary, they who justly feel the weight
  Of Heaven's offended Majesty, implore
    Thy reconciling aid with suppliant knee:
Of sinful man, O sinless Advocate,
  To thee they turn, nor Him they less adore;
    'Tis still His light they love, less dreadful seen in thee.

TRYSTE NOEL

By Louise Imogen Guiney

The Ox he openeth wide the doore,
  And from the Snowe he calls her inne,
And he hath seen her smile therefore,
  Our Ladye without Sinne.
    Now soone from Sleep
    A Starre shall leap,
And soone arrive both King and Hinde:
    Amen, Amen:
But O the place co'd I but finde!

The Ox hath hushed his voyce and bent
   Trewe eyes of Pitty ore the Mow,
And on his lovelie Neck, forspent,
   The Blessed layes her Browe.
      Around her feet,
      Full Warme and Sweete,
His bowerie Breath doth meeklie dwell:
      Amen, Amen:
But sore am I with Vaine Travel!

The Ox is Host in Judah stall
   And Host of more than onlie one,
For close she gathereth withal
   Our Lorde her littel Sonne.
      Glad Hinde and King
      Their Gyfte may bring,
But wo'd to-night my Teares were there,
      Amen, Amen:
Between her Bosom and His hayre!

THE WILD RIDE

By Louise Imogen Guiney

I hear in my heart, I hear in its ominous pulses
All day, on the road, the hoofs of invisible horses,
All night, from their stalls, the importunate pawing and neighing.

Let cowards and laggards fall back! but alert to the saddle,
Weatherworn and abreast, go men of our galloping legion,

THE WILD RIDE

With a stirrup-cup each to the lily of women that loves
    him.

The trail is through dolor and dread, over crags and
    morasses;
There are shapes by the way, there are things that appal
    or entice us:
What odds? We are Knights of the Grail, we are vowed
    to the riding.

Thought's self is a vanishing wing, and joy is a cobweb,
And friendship a flower in the dust, and glory a sun-
    beam:
Not here is our prize, nor, alas! after these our pursuing.

A dipping of plumes, a tear, a shake of the bridle,
A passing salute to this world and her pitiful beauty:
We hurry with never a word in the track of our fathers.

I hear in my heart, I hear in its ominous pulses
All day, on the road, the hoofs of invisible horses,
All night, from their stalls, the importunate pawing and
    neighing.

We spur to a land of no name, outracing the stormwind;
We leap to the infinite dark like the sparks from the
    anvil.
Thou leadest, O God! All's well with Thy troopers that
    follow.

ODE FOR A MASTER MARINER ASHORE

By Louise Imogen Guiney

THERE in his room, whene'er the moon looks in,
And silvers now a shell, and now a fin,
And o'er his chart glides like an argosy,
Quiet and old sits he.
Danger! he hath grown homesick for thy smile.
Where hidest thou the while, heart's boast,
Strange face of beauty sought and lost,
Star-face that lured him out from boyhood's isle?
Blown clear from dull indoors, his dreams behold
Night-water smoke and sparkle as of old,
The taffrail lurch, the sheets triumphant toss
Their phosphor-flowers across.
Towards ocean's either rim the long-exiled
Wears on, till stunted cedars throw
A lace-like shadow over snow,
Or tropic fountains wash their agates wild.

Awhile, play up and down the briny spar
Odors of Surinam and Zanzibar,
Till blithely thence he ploughs, in visions new,
The Labradorian blue;
All homeless hurricanes about him break;
The purples of spent day he sees
From Samos to the Hebrides,
And drowned men dancing darkly in his wake.

Where the small deadly foam-caps, well descried,
Top, tier on tier, the hundred-mountained tide,

ODE FOR A MASTER MARINER ASHORE

Away, and far away, his pride is borne,
Riding the noisy morn,
Plunges, and preens her wings, and laughs to know
The helm and tightening halyards still
Follow the urging of his will,
And scoff at sullen earth a league below.

Mischance hath barred him from his heirdom high,
And shackled him with many an inland tie,
And of his only wisdom made a jibe
Amid an alien tribe:
No wave abroad but moans his fallen state,
The trade-wind ranges now, the trade-wind roars!
Why is it on a yellowing page he pores?
Ah, why this hawser fast to a garden gate?

Thou friend so long withdrawn, so deaf, so dim,
Familiar Danger, O forget not him!
Repeat of thine evangel yet the whole
Unto his subject soul,
Who suffers no such palsy of her drouth,
Nor hath so tamely worn her chain,
But she may know that voice again,
And shake the reefs with answer of her mouth.

O give him back, before his passion fail,
The singing cordage and the hollow sail,
And level with those aged eyes let be
The bright unsteady sea;
And move like any film from off his brain
The pasture wall, the boughs that run
Their evening arches to the sun,
The hamlet spire across the sown champaign;

And on the shut space and the trivial hour,
Turn the great floods! and to thy spousal bower,
With rapt arrest and solemn loitering,
Him whom thou lovedst bring:
That he, thy faithful one, with praising lip,
Not having, at the last, less grace
Of thee than had his roving race,
Sum up his strength to perish with a ship.

IN LEINSTER

By Louise Imogen Guiney

I try to knead and spin, but my life is low the while.
Oh, I long to be alone, and walk abroad a mile;
Yet if I walk alone, and think of naught at all,
Why from me that's young should the wild tears fall?

The shower-stricken earth, the earth-colored streams,
They breathe on me awake, and moan to me in dreams;
And yonder ivy fondling the broke castle-wall,
It pulls upon my heart till the wild tears fall.

The cabin-door looks down, a furze-lighted hill,
And far as Leighlin Cross the fields are green and still;
But once I hear the blackbird in Leighlin hedges call,
The foolishness is on me, and the wild tears fall!

AUNT MARY

A Christmas Chant

By Robert Stephen Hawker

Now, of all the trees by the king's highway,
    Which do you love the best?
O! the one that is green upon Christmas Day,
    The bush with the bleeding breast.
Now the holly with her drops of blood for me:
For that is our dear Aunt Mary's tree.

Its leaves are sweet with our Saviour's Name,
    'Tis a plant that loves the poor:
Summer and winter it shines the same
    Beside the cottage door.
O! the holly with her drops of blood for me:
For that is our kind Aunt Mary's tree.

'Tis a bush that the birds will never leave:
    They sing in it all day long;
But sweetest of all upon Christmas Eve
    Is to hear the robin's song.
'Tis the merriest sound upon earth or sea:
For it comes from our own Aunt Mary's tree.

So, of all that grows by the king's highway,
    I love that tree the best;
'Tis a bower for the birds upon Christmas Day
    The bush of the bleeding breast.
O! the holly with her drops of blood for me:
For that is our sweet Aunt Mary's tree.

KING ARTHUR'S WAES-HAEL

By Robert Stephen Hawker

Waes-hael for knight and dame;
  O merry be their dole;
Drink-hael! In Jesu's name
  We fill the tawny bowl;
But cover down the curving crest,
Mould of the Orient Lady's breast.

Waes-hael! yet lift no lid:
  Drain ye the reeds for wine.
Drink-hael! the milk was hid
  That soothed that Babe divine;
Hush'd, as this hollow channel flows,
He drew the balsam from the rose.

Waes-hael! thus glowed the breast
  Where a God yearned to cling;
Drink-hael! so Jesu pressed
  Life from its mystic spring;
Then hush and bend in reverend sign
And breathe the thrilling reeds for wine.

Waes-hael! in shadowy scene
  Lo! Christmas children we:
Drink-hael! behold we lean
  At a far Mother's knee;
To dream that thus her bosom smiled,
And learn the lip of Bethlehem's Child.

OLD NUNS

By James M. Hayes

Our Lady smiles on youthful nuns,
    She loves them well.
Our Lady's smile like sunshine floods
    Each convent cell,
But fondest falls Our Lady's smile
    Where old nuns dwell;

Old nuns whose hearts are young with love
    For Mary's Son,
Old nuns whose prayers for faltering souls
    Have victory won,
Old nuns whose lives are beautiful
    With service done.

Their love a loveless world has saved
    From God's dread rod,
The paths where Sorrow walks with Sin
    Their feet have trod,
Their knees have worn the flags that pave
    The house of God.

Our Lady smiles on youthful nuns,
    She loves them well;
Our Lady's smile like sunshine floods
    Each convent cell;
But fondest falls Our Lady's smile
    Where old nuns dwell.

THE MOTHER OF THE ROSE

By James M. Hayes

I kneel on Holy Thursday with the faithful worshipping
Where Christ is throned in splendor as the sacramental King.

I ever will remember it, that wondrous full-blown rose
Among the burning tapers on the altar of repose.

O blessed among roses all, to bloom in beauty there,
To give your heart unto your God and in His glory share.

. . . .

In quiet fields beyond the town, near where the river flows
There is a humble garden where a gentle rose-tree grows.

To-night Our Lord remembers on the altar of repose
This rose-tree in the fields afar, the mother of the rose.

THE TRANSFIGURATION

By James M. Hayes

He seeks the mountains where the olives grow,
   The Lord of Glory, veiled in humble guise;
His soul is shadowed with a coming woe,
   The grief of all the world is in His eyes:
His spirit struggles in the dark caress
Of anguish, pain and utter loneliness.

He always loved the mountain tops, for there
   Away from earth, He treads the mystic ways
And sees the vision of the Fairest Fair,
   As Heaven dawns upon His raptured gaze;
The loneliness, the pain, the grief depart;
Surpassing gladness fills His Sacred Heart.

That day He stood upon the olive hill,
   And Peter, James and John in wonder saw
The burning glories of the God-head fill
   His soul with grandeur, and in holy awe
They fell upon the ground and cried for grace,
Lest they should die beholding God's own Face

As minor chords that sob from strings of gold
   The Master speaks in accents sweet and sad
The vision past, the chosen three behold
   No one but Jesus and their souls are glad.
The awe, the splendor and the glory gone,
How sweet the face of Christ to look upon!

BELOVED, IT IS MORN

By Emily H. Hickey

Beloved, it is morn!
  A redder berry on the thorn,
  A deeper yellow on the corn,
For this good day new-born.
    Pray, Sweet, for me
    That I may be
    Faithful to God and thee.

Beloved, it is day!
  And lovers work, as children play,
  With heart and brain untired alway:
Dear love, look up and pray.
    Pray, Sweet, for me
    That I may be
    Faithful to God and thee.

Beloved, it is night!
  Thy heart and mine are full of light,
  Thy spirit shineth clear and white,
God keep thee in His sight!
    Pray, Sweet, for me
    That I may be
    Faithful to God and thee.

A SEA STORY

By Emily H. Hickey

Silence. A while ago
  Shrieks went up piercingly;
But now is the ship gone down;
  Good ship, well manned, was she.
There's a raft that's a chance of life for one,
  This day upon the sea.

A chance for one of two;
  Young, strong, are he and he,
Just in the manhood prime,
  The comelier, verily,
For the wrestle with wind and weather and wave,
  In the life upon the sea.

One of them has a wife
  And little children three;
Two that can toddle and lisp,
  And a suckling on the knee:
Naked they'll go, and hunger sore,
  If he be lost at sea.

One has a dream of home,
  A dream that well may be:
He never has breathed it yet;
  She never has known it, she.
But some one will be sick at heart
  If he be lost at sea.

"Wife and kids at home!—
    Wife, kids, nor home has he!—
Give us a chance, Bill!" Then,
    "All right, Jem!" Quietly
A man gives up his life for a man,
    This day upon the sea.

THE STARLIGHT NIGHT

By Gerard Hopkins, S.J.

Look at the stars! look, look up at the skies!
   O look at all the fire-folk sitting in the air!
   The bright boroughs, the quivering citadels there!
The dim woods quick with diamond wells; the elf-eyes!
The grey lawns cold where quaking gold-dew lies!
   Wind-beat white-beam; airy abeles all on flare!
   Flake-doves sent floating out at a farmyard scare!—
Ah well! it is a purchase and a prize.

Buy then! Bid then!—What?—Prayer, patience, alms,
      vows,—
Look, look! a May-mess, like on orchard boughs;
   Look! March-bloom, like on mealed-with-yellow
      sallows.—
These are indeed the barn: within-doors house
The shocks. This piece-bright paling hides the Spouse
   Christ, and the mother of Christ and all his hallows.

THE HABIT OF PERFECTION

By Gerard Hopkins, S.J.

Elected Silence, sing to me
And beat upon my whorled ear,
Pipe me to pastures still and be
The music that I care to hear.

Shape nothing, lips; be lovely-dumb:
It is the shut, the curfew sent
From there where all surrenders come
Which only make you eloquent.

Be shelled, eyes, with double dark
And find the uncreated light;
This ruck and reel which you remark
Coils, keeps, and teases simple sight.

Palate, the hutch of tasty lust,
Desire not to be rinsed with wine:
The can must be so sweet, the crust
So fresh that come in fasts divine!

Nostrils, your careless breath that spend
Upon the stir and keep of pride,
What relish shall the censers send
Along the sanctuary side!

O feel-of-primrose hands, O feet
That want the yield of plushy sward,
But you shall walk the golden street,
And you unhouse and house the Lord.

And, Poverty, be thou the bride
And now the marriage feast begun,
And lily-colored clothes provide
Your spouse not labored-at, nor spun.

SPRING

By Gerard Hopkins, S.J.

Nothing is so beautiful as spring—
  When weeds, in wheels, shoot long and lovely and lush:
    Thrush's eggs look little low heavens, and thrush
Through the echoing timber does so rinse and wring
The ear, it strikes like lightnings to hear him sing;
  The glassy pear-tree leaves and blooms, they brush
  The descending blue; that blue is all in a rush
With richness; the racing lambs too have fair their fling.

What is all this juice and all this joy?
  A strain of the earth's sweet being in the beginning
In Eden garden. Have, get, before it cloy,
  Before it cloud, Christ, lord, and sour with shining,
Innocent mind and Mayday in girl and boy,
  Most, O maid's child, thy choice and worthy the winning.

THE FRIAR OF GENOA

By Scharmel Iris

In Genoa a friar walked;
Of every sacred tale he talked;
Alone he dwelt, in prayer he knelt;
    "Ave Maria, Ave Maria!"
From dawn till dusk he sang.

His bruised and blistered feet were bare;
His head burned in the sunlight's glare.
On stones he slept, and worked and wept,
    "Ave Maria, Ave Maria!"
In every blow or pang.

Out of his dole he clothed the poor,
And every hardship did endure;
He blessed the meek and nursed the weak
    "Ave Maria, Ave Maria!"
With each succeeding day.

And begged for alms for those in need,
A kind word spoke with every deed,
With sinners dined and led the blind—
    "Ave Maria, Ave Maria!"
Until he passed away.

And is his work done? Ah, surprise!
Out of the tomb where low he lies
  A perfume blows, as of a rose:
    "Ave Maria, Ave Maria!"
It sings in shade or sun.

And he who breathes it, him it feeds,
And stirs his heart to noble deeds;
And one has said, "He is not dead—
    Ave Maria, Ave Maria!
His life has just begun!"

THE DARK ANGEL

By Lionel Johnson

Dark Angel, with thine aching lust
To rid the world of penitence:
Malicious Angel, who still dost
My soul such subtile violence!

Because of thee, no thought, no thing,
Abides for me undesecrate:
Dark Angel, ever on the wing,
Who never reachest me too late!

When music sounds, then changest thou
Its silvery to a sultry fire:
Nor will thine envious heart allow
Delight untortured by desire.

Through thee, the gracious Muses turn
To Furies, O mine Enemy!
And all the things of beauty burn
With flames of evil ecstasy.

Because of thee, the land of dreams
Becomes a gathering place of fears:
Until tormented slumber seems
One vehemence of useless tears.

When sunlight glows upon the flowers,
Or ripples down the dancing sea:
Thou, with thy troop of passionate powers,
Beleaguerest, bewilderest, me.

Within the breath of autumn woods,
Within the winter silences:
Thy venomous spirit stirs and broods,
O Master of impieties!

The ardour of red flame is thine,
And thine the steely soul of ice:
Thou poisonest the fair design
Of nature, with unfair device.

Apples of ashes, golden bright;
Waters of bitterness, how sweet!
O banquet of a foul delight,
Prepared by thee, dark Paraclete!

Thou art the whisper in the gloom,
The hinting tone, the haunting laugh:
Thou art the adorner of my tomb,
The minstrel of mine epitaph.

I fight thee, in the Holy Name!
Yet, what thou dost, is what God saith:
Tempter! should I escape thy flame,
Thou wilt have helped my soul from Death

The second Death, that never dies,
That cannot die, when time is dead:
Live Death, wherein the lost soul cries,
Eternally uncomforted.

Dark Angel, with thine aching lust!
Of two defeats, of two despairs:
Less dread, a change to drifting dust,
Than thine eternity of cares.

Do what thou wilt, thou shalt not so,
Dark Angel! triumph over me:
Lonely, unto the Lone I go;
Divine, to the Divinity.

TE MARTYRUM CANDIDATUS

By Lionel Johnson

Ah, see the fair chivalry come, the companions of Christ!
White Horsemen, who ride on white horses, the Knights
   of God!
They, for their Lord and their Lover who sacrificed
All, save the sweetness of treading, where He first trod!

These through the darkness of death, the dominion of
   night,
Swept, and they woke in white places at morning tide:
They saw with their eyes, and sang for joy of the sight,
They saw with their eyes the Eyes of the Crucified.

Now, whithersoever He goeth, with Him they go:
White Horsemen, who ride on white horses, oh fair to
   see!
They ride, where the Rivers of Paradise flash and flow,
White Horsemen, with Christ their Captain: forever
   He!

CHRISTMAS AND IRELAND

By Lionel Johnson

The golden stars give warmthless fire,
  As weary Mary goes through night:
Her feet are torn by stone and briar;
  She hath no rest, no strength, no light:
O Mary, weary in the snow,
    Remember Ireland's woe!

O Joseph, sad for Mary's sake!
  Look on our earthly Mother too:
Let not the heart of Ireland break
  With agony the ages through:
For Mary's love, love also thou
    Ireland, and save her now!

Harsh were the folk, and bitter stern,
  At Bethlehem, that night of nights.
For you no cheering hearth shall burn:
  We have no room here, you no rights.
O Mary and Joseph; hath not she,
    Ireland, been even as ye?

The ancient David's royal house
  Was thine, Saint Joseph! wherefore she,
Mary, thine Ever Virgin Spouse,
  To thine own city went with thee.
Behold! thy citizens disown
    The heir of David's throne!

Nay, more! The very King of Kings
  Was with you, coming to His own:
They thrust Him forth to lowliest things;
  The poor, meek beasts of toil alone
Stood by, when came to piteous birth
    The God of all the earth.

And she, our Mother Ireland, knows
  Insult, and infamies of wrong:
Her innocent children clad with woes,
  Her weakness trampled by the strong:
And still upon her Holy Land
    Her pitiless foemen stand.

From Manger unto Cross and Crown
  Went Christ: and Mother Mary passed
Through Seven Sorrows, and sat down
  Upon the Angel Throne at last.
Thence, Mary! to thine own Child pray,
    For Ireland's hope this day!

She wanders amid winter still,
  The dew of tears is on her face:
Her wounded heart takes yet its fill
  Of desolation and disgrace.
God still is God! And through God she
    Foreknows her joy to be.

The snows shall perish at the spring,
  The flowers pour fragrance round her feet:
Ah, Jesus! Mary! Joseph! bring
  This mercy from the Mercy Seat!
Send it, sweet King of Glory, born
    Humbly on Christmas Morn!

TO MY PATRONS

By Lionel Johnson

Thy spear rent Christ, when dead for me He lay:
  My sin rends Christ, though never one save He
Perfectly loves me, comforts me. Then pray,
  Longinus Saint! the Crucified, for me.

Hard is the holy war, and hard the way:
  At rest with ancient victors would I be.
O faith's first glory from our England! pray,
  St. Alban! to the Lord of Hosts, for me.

Fain would I watch with thee, till morning gray,
  Beneath the stars austere: so might I see
Sunrise, and light, and joy, at last. Then pray,
  John Baptist Saint! unto the Christ, for me.

Remembering God's coronation day;
  Thorns for His crown; His throne, a Cross: to thee
Heaven's kingdom dearer was than earth's. Then pray
  Saint Louis! to the King of kings, for me.

Thy love loved all things: thy love knew no stay,
  But drew the very wild beasts round thy knee.
O lover of the least and lowest! pray,
  Saint Francis! to the Son of Man, for me.

Bishop of souls in servitude astray,
  Who didst for holy service set them free:
Use still thy discipline of love, and pray,
  Saint Charles! unto the world's High Priest, for me.

OUR LADY OF THE SNOWS

(Upon reading the poem of that name in the
Underwoods of Mr. Stevenson)

By Lionel Johnson

Far from the world, far from delight,
Distinguishing not day from night;
Vowed to one sacrifice of all
The happy things, that men befall;
Pleading one sacrifice, before
Whom sun and sea and wind adore;
Far from earth's comfort, far away,
We cry to God, we cry and pray
For men, who have the common day.
Dance, merry world! and sing: but we,
Hearing, remember Calvary:
Get gold, and thrive you! but the sun
Once paled; and the centurion
Said: *This dead man was God's own Son.*
Think you, we shrink from common toil,
Works of the mart, works of the soil:
That, prisoners of strong despair,
We breathe this melancholy air;
Forgetting the dear calls of race,
And bonds of house, and ties of place;
That, cowards, from the field we turn,
And heavenward, in our weakness, yearn?
Unjust! unjust! while you despise
Our lonely years, our mournful cries:
You are the happier for our prayer;
The guerdon of our souls, you share.
Not in such feebleness of heart,
We play our solitary part;

OUR LADY OF THE SNOWS

Not fugitives of battle, we
Hide from the world, and let things be:
But rather, looking over earth,
Between the bounds of death and birth;
And sad at heart, for sorrow and sin,
We wondered, where might help begin.
And on our wonder came God's choice,
A sudden light, a clarion voice,
Clearing the dark, and sounding clear:
And we obeyed: behold us, here!
In prison bound, but with your chains:
Sufferers, but of alien pains.

Merry the world, and thrives apace,
Each in his customary place:
Sailors upon the carrying sea,
Shepherds upon the pasture lea,
And merchants of the town; and they,
Who march to death, the fighting way;
And there are lovers in the spring,
With those, who dance, and those, who sing
The commonwealth of every day,
Eastward and westward, far away,
Once the sun paled; once cried aloud
The Roman, from beneath the cloud:
This day the Son of God is dead!

Yet heed men, what the Roman said?
They heed not: we then heed for them,
The mindless of Jerusalem;
Careless, they live and die: but we
Care, in their stead, for Calvary.
O joyous men and women! strong,
To urge the wheel of life along,

With strenuous arm, and cheerful strain,
And wisdom of laborous brain:
We give our life, our heart, our breath,
That you may live to conquer death;
That, past your tomb, with souls in health,
Joy may be yours, and blessed wealth;
Through vigils of the painful night,
Our spirits with your tempters fight:
For you, for you, we live alone,
Where no joy comes, where cold winds moan:
Nor friends have we, nor have we foes;
Our Queen is of the lonely Snows.
Ah! and sometimes, our prayers between,
Come sudden thoughts of what hath been:
Dreams! And from dreams, once more we fall
To prayer: *God save, Christ keep, them all.*
And thou, who knowest not these things,
Hearken, what news our message brings!
Our toils, thy joy of life forgot:
Our lives of prayer forget thee not.

CADGWITH

By Lionel Johnson

My windows open to the autumn night,
In vain I watched for sleep to visit me:
How should sleep dull mine ears, and dim my sight,
Who saw the stars, and listened to the sea?

Ah, how the City of our God is fair!
If, without sea and starless though it be,
For joy of the majestic beauty there,
Men shall not miss the stars, nor mourn the sea.

A FRIEND

By Lionel Johnson

All, that he came to give,
He gave, and went again:
I have seen one man live,
I have seen one man reign,
With all the graces in his train.

As one of us, he wrought
Things of the common hour:
Whence was the charmed soul brought,
That gave each act such power;
The natural beauty of a flower?

Magnificence and grace,
Excellent courtesy:
A brightness on the face,
Airs of high memory:
Whence came all these, to such as he?

Like young Shakespearian kings,
He won the adoring throng:
And, as Apollo sings,
He triumphed with a song:
Triumphed, and sang, and passed along.

With a light word he took
The hearts of men in thrall:
And, with a golden look,
Welcomed them, at his call
Giving their love, their strength, their all

No man less proud than he,
Nor cared for homage less;
Only, he could not be
Far off from happiness:
Nature was bound to his success.

Weary, the cares, the jars
The lets, of every day:
But the heavens filled with stars,
Chanced he upon the way:
And where he stayed, all joy would stay.

Now, when sad night draws down,
When the austere stars burn:
Roaming the vast stars burn:
My thoughts and memories yearn
Toward him, who never will return.

Yet I have seen him live,
And owned my friend, a king:
And that he came to give,
He gave, and I, who sing
His praise, bring all I have to bring.

BY THE STATUE OF KING CHARLES AT CHARING CROSS

By Lionel Johnson

Sombre and rich, the skies;
   Great glooms and starry plains.
Gently the night wind sighs;
   Else a vast silence reigns.

BY THE STATUE OF KING CHARLES

The splendid silence clings
  Around me: and around
The saddest of all kings
  Crowned, and again discrowned.

Comely and calm, he rides
  Hard by his own Whitehall:
Only the night wind glides:
  No crowds, nor rebels, brawl.

Gone, too, his Court: and yet,
  The stars his courtiers are;
Stars in their stations set;
  And every wandering star.

Alone he rides, alone,
  The fair and fatal king:
Dark night is all his own,
  That strange and solemn thing.

Which are more full of fate:
  The stars; or those sad eyes?
Which are more still and great:
  Those brows; or the dark skies?

Although his whole heart yearn
  In passionate tragedy:
Never was face so stern
  With sweet austerity.

Vanquished in life, his death
  By beauty made amends:
The passing of his breath
  Won his defeated ends.

Brief life, and hapless? Nay:
  Through death, life grew sublime.
Speak after sentence? Yea:
  And to the end of time.

Armoured he rides, his head
  Bare to the stars of doom:
He triumphs now, the dead,
  Beholding London's gloom.

Our wearier spirit faints,
  Vexed in the world's employ:
His soul was of the saints;
  And art to him was joy.

King, tried in fires of woe!
  Men hunger for thy grace:
And through the night I go,
  Loving thy mournful face.

Yet, when the city sleeps;
  When all the cries are still:
The stars and heavenly deeps
  Work out a perfect will.

THE HOUSEWIFE'S PRAYER

By Blanche Mary Kelly

Lady, who with tender word
Didst keep the house of Christ the Lord,
Who didst set forth the bread and wine
Before the Living Wheat and Vine,
Reverently didst make the bed

Whereon was laid the holy Head
That such a cruel pillow prest
For our behoof, on Calvary's crest;
Be beside me while I go
About my labors to and fro.
Speed the wheel and speed the loom,
Guide the needle and the broom,
Make my bread rise sweet and light,
Make my cheese come foamy white,
Yellow may my butter be
As cowslips blowing on the lea.
Homely though my tasks and small,
Be beside me at them all.
Then when I shall stand to face
Jesu in the judgment place,
To me thy gracious help afford,
Who art the Handmaid of the Lord.

BROTHER JUNIPER

By Blanche Mary Kelly

As unto Francis Poverty,
So Folly was a bride to thee.
Not the jade that fashions quips
For the smiles of mocking lips,
And in the face of stony Death
Capers till she's out of breath,
But the maid that moves and sings
About divinely foolish things,
She that gives her substance all
For love, and laughs to find it small,

She that drew God's Son to be
A butt, a jest on Calvary,
And 'neath the leper's guise doth know
The King in his incognito.

The world is grown too wise, and we
Go our sad ways sensibly.
O, would that our lean souls might win
Some grace of thine, God's harlequin,
Whose days were lavished like fool's gold
Upon His pleasures manifold.
"Would God," cried Francis, on his knees,
"I had a forest of such trees!"

THE THRONE OF THE KING

By Francis Clement Kelley

The sun was setting, and its golden glow
Deepened the shadows on the village street,
And reverent touched the beauty of the head
Of Him who sat, in thought, beside the well
Of Nazareth. Two women came to fill
Their earthen jars; and sent their burdens down
To where the water lay; then drew them up.
But still the Boy, unmoved, gazed steadily
Upon the distant hills, that girded round
Jerusalem, the City of the Soul.

His eyes were deep as some unfathomed sea,
That tosses wreckage on its billowed crest;
But hides its treasures ever in the caves.

That men shall never touch, or touching die.
"How strange the Boy," one woman softly said
As back they went, their burdens on their heads.
"Yet He is Joseph's Son," the other spoke,
And Joseph is my neighbor, a just man;
But not more lettered than the other men,
Your own and mine. He is not priest nor scribe
That he could teach such wisdom to his Son.
And it doth sometimes seem the Boy is wise
Beyond His years, with knowledge overmuch."
"His mother, whom I know," her friend replied,
"As Mary, sweeps the shavings from the floor,
Cooks the poor fare for Joseph and her Son,
Cares for the water, and her jar brings here
As we do every day, who know not much
Beyond the things we hear from holy men.
Yet strange is Mary too; I know not where
To match the peace that's on her tranquil brow;
Though, through it all, I've seen the Shadow there
The dread of days to come, though all resigned.
So like His mother is this only Son
In beauty, in the peace that's on His face;
But sometimes, deeper still, the Shadow falls
Across His features. Look! behold it now.
For it doth speak the dread of awful things,
More awful than the ruin of a world!"

A-down the street there rang a clatter loud
Of horses dashing in a maddened run,
And sounds of wheels swift rolling on the pave.
The women shrank affrighted to the wall,
And cowered there in trembling, mortal fear.
In view the charging horses passed along

Straight to the well, no driver grasped the reins,
For he had fallen to the stony street.
Yet never moved the Boy, nor turned His eyes
From off the hills that held them so intent.
But from a doorway rushed a stranger lad
Who grasped the bit of one, and held him fast.
The others, panting, stopped so near the Boy
That, on His face He must have felt the heat
Which steaming rose from their perspiring flanks,
As now they stood, foam-flecked and trembling by.
The driver came and meekly murmured thanks,
Before he led his charges back again
To where his master waited for the steeds.
"He gave me naught but words, and I did save
The steeds. The chariot, too, would have been dashed
All broken on the stones, had I not come."
The lad was angered, but the Boy moved not,
Though from the distant hills His gaze was drawn.
"Dost thou not know," the lad said, wonderingly,
"How near was Death to thee a moment since?"

The Boy, now fully aroused, smiled at the lad
All kindly, as a loving father smiles
Upon his child that waked him unaware,
Whose sleep nor storm nor clatter could affect,
Yet at the touch of little baby hands
Opens wide his eyes, that twinkle joyfully.
"No nearer to grim Death," the Boy replied,
"Was I than thou, my friend, art near it now.
Thou seekest Joseph and hast wandered far
From distant Jaffa, where thy father died.
Thou'rt Fidus named. From Joseph thou wouldst learn
The craftsman's art, and how to handle tools

To work with wood, that thou thyself may'st be
Like him, a craftsman skilled in his own trade."
'A prophet Thou!" the lad in wonder cried.
'Come with me," made He answer. "I am known
As Joseph's Son; so I will speak for thee."

As evening fell on Nazareth's burning street
Each day these two would wander out alone;
And by the well, or in a quiet glade
Seated, would hold their talk, with none to hear.
Yet converse scarce it was; with ears intent,
Fidus did always listen, while the Boy
Poured out a tale of Kings and Prophets old;
Of marvels that they worked to testify
Unto a King whom yet the earth would see,
A King of all Judea and the world;
Whose glory, mounting even to the stars
Would dim with rich effulgence, their great light.
The Sun of Justice He, the Moon of night
That had for ages settled o'er the earth.
He told of wonders that the King would do
Before He mounted to His mighty throne.
He told of love surpassing every love
That earth had seen, and of His Kingdom wide;
Till all on fire Fidus hung'red to see
The King Himself, and worship at His throne.
"A Roman though I am," he oft would cry,
"Thy King I'd welcome and for Him I'd serve."
'Yet thou art craftsman and no soldier thou."
"A craftsman too can serve his loyal due."
'How wouldst thou serve?" the Boy inquiring spoke
"When Joseph bids me go, that I can learn no more.
This I can do—to build for Him His throne."

The Shadow swept across the boyish face—
The Shadow Fidus once had seen before;
And he was silent, for in awe he stood
When that mysterious shade shut off the light
That shone out from the radiant brow.
The Shadow was not fear, nor dread of death;
But dread of something worse than death could bring.
It was as if a lily, broken, bent,
But yet unsullied, now was stained with filth
By impious hand; more cruel far than death
The marring of the whiteness death had spared:
Or like a stream, that through its mountain bed
Had raced unfettered, toward the amber sea,
And o'er the rapids and the pebbles dashed
Clear, cold and placid when the mouth is reached;
Then, death unfeared before it, ready now
To give back to the ocean all it gave,
Into its pureness poured a stream so dark
That tainted all its life, when life was lost.
'Twas thus the Shadow seemed; but soon it passed,
And smiling boyhood turned a happy face
The while he said: "So thou wouldst build His throne?
But dost thou know the form that throne will take?"

" 'T will be a throne," Fidus replied, "so high
That all may see Him, while from it He reigns,
And know that He has come unto His own."

"Aye," quick the Boy made answer, "it shall be
Uplifted high that every man may see;
Not Jews alone but even ye of Rome;
And men from Britain too, on farthest shore
Of Rome's great Empire: they shall see and know

The King who reigns upon that living throne;
And in the Islands of unchartered seas
The King shall lifted be, that all may know;
And worlds still undiscovered shall bow down
To do Him homage, yet shall hate His name.
For homage goes with hate, and hate will be
The measure of the homage that shall swell
In pæans great around the royal throne."

Fidus looked wond'ring at the Boy Who spoke,
As if the right to build the throne were His
And He could give it to the friend who asked
This only boon, as pledge of love untold.

"And I would build it strong so it could go
O'er sea and land, and last for aye and aye."

"So thou wouldst build the throne?" again the Boy
Half musing spoke. Across His face once more
The Shadow fell; and, as he stood, His hands
He lifted up and out, as if in prayer.
Another Shadow fell upon the ground,
The arms and body strangely like a Cross.
Fidus was silent till the prayer was done.
The sun now set, and all the shadows passed.
They, arm in arm, ran fast to Joseph's house.
But, at the door they paused and, said the Boy:
"Thou must remember ever this thy day
When I the promise gave that I can keep,
For thou shalt build His throne!"

The years passed on,
And Fidus to the Roman hosts returned

Where, welcomed as a soldier's clever son,
He wrought in wood for all the legions there
In Jaffa, where his father had been killed.
For eighteen years he stayed beside the sea
And, working at the trade that Joseph taught,
He never once forgot the precious pledge
The Boy had made. But never saw nor heard
Aught of his friend. Then he was sent away
By Pilate's call, unto Jerusalem.

The evening of the day when he arrived
Great turmoil swept along the Jaffa road,
And near the Gate of Gardens, where the hill
Called Calvary lifted up its rocky head.
He heard the crowds discuss a Wonder-Man
The priests had taken, and was on His way
To judgment. "Out on such a King," cried one.
Himself He can not save from shameful death.
To-morrow's sun will see Him lifted up
Above the hill, and throw the Shadow of
A Cross upon you fools who thought Him King."

And on the faces dark of all around,
Fidus saw Hate he could not understand.
Then up a vision rose of Nazareth
When evening fell; a Boy of beauty rare,
With a strange Shadow on His lovely face,
Standing with arms outstretched in prayer,
The glory of the setting sun upon His head.
But long and grim the shadow of a Cross
Before Him as He stood. Then to his mind
Came swift the stories of the mighty King,
And then the promise: "Thou shalt build His throne."

Alas! the long and wav'ring years had swept
The dreams of youth away; but still remained
The love, that hungered now to feel the hand
Within his own of Mary's Son. The day
Rose brightly in the East. At Pilate's door
He met by chance a captain he had known
In Jaffa, who bade him attentive wait
Within the hall, amongst the soldiers there.
But soon a tumult rose without the doors;
The Wonder-Man was coming to be judged.
Then, as the cries increased, his friend came in.
"Make thou a Cross," he said, "We have but two
And, if I judge aright, three shall be sent
Beyond the wall this day to Calvary."

No more of shouting Fidus heard, for he
Alone made ready a great Cross of wood;
And, that his craftsman skill should be confessed,
He made it well, both strong and workmanlike.
" 'Tis fit," he said, "to serve a King," and smiled
At his grim jest; then went he on his way.

Out in the streets the crowd was surging on
Along the way that leads to Calvary's hill.
And o'er it Fidus saw his Cross; and then,
Sometimes, a thorn-crowned head with waving hair
Blood-clotted now, and stained a deeper hue;
And Hate seemed in the air vibrating round.
When sudden, like a bell that sweetly rings
Above a storm, and seems a messenger
Of Peace and Love, there woke upon his soul
From out the sleeping past, some prophet words:
"For homage goes with hate, and hate shall be

The measure of the homage that shall swell
In pæans great around the royal throne."

The surging crowd hid from his eyes the things
He did not care to see, but faint he heard
The hammer strokes, that seemed to drive the nails
Deep in his heart. Then turned he to a man
Who silent stood beside him, and he said:
"A stranger I, from Jaffa, yesternight
I came. This man? What evil hath He done?"
"I know not any wrong that He hath done,"

Came answer fast. "I only know the good
That He had wrought. Behold my eyes that see!
Once they were dark. He passed me by one day
And loud I cried: 'O Son of David, mercy show
That I may see.' He touched me and I saw."
Another silent man near Fidus stood,
To him he spoke, "And friend, what knowest thou?"
"I know that now I live though I was dead;
For I had gone into the ending tomb
All spiced for rest and bound with linen bands;
And He did come, and He did call me forth.
I heard His voice that sounded far away,
As if I stood within a valley deep,
And some one, from the mountain crest,
Kept calling me. Then clearer was the Voice;
As if on wings, I soared aloft to Him,
Who had the Power to bid me come or stay.
Again my heart did beat and vital blood
Surged through my wid'ning veins. I lived again."

Then Fidus quick recalled a wondrous thing:
He saw the Boy in Joseph's little shop,

A sick lamb refuged in His tender arms.
He gently stroked the lamb and then the pain
Was gone from out its piteous pleading eyes.
And, lo, the man felt hot tears on his cheeks.

The Cross was raised, and faint the outline stood
'Twixt Fidus and the lurid, murky sky
That threatened from afar a terror dark.
Then swift it came, for all of darkness dread
That air could hold, fell down upon the earth.
The stumbling crowd in panic slunk away;
But Fidus groped through darkness to the Cross.

He heard a moan of sorrow. Well he knew
The voice of Mary, she of Joseph's house.
His heart stood still; the Vision came again:
That evening fair—the Boy—the distant hills—
The Shadow of the Cross upon the earth
As He stood silent all absorbed in prayer—
The promise that himself should build a throne.
"Aye," so the Boy had said, "for it shall be
Raised up on high that every man may see,
Not Jews alone, but even ye of Rome;
And men from Britain too, on farthest shore
Of Rome's great Empire: they shall see and know
The King Who reigns upon that living throne;
And, in the Islands of uncharted seas
The King shall lifted be that all may know;
And worlds still undiscovered shall bow down
To do Him homage, yet shall hate His name.
For homage goes with hate, and hate will be
The measure of the homage that shall swell
In pæans great around His royal throne."

A lightning flash! The rocks asunder rent,
The tombs burst open and the dead arose.
One moment Fidus saw the Crucified
Ere darkness fell again around the Cross.
But in that moment a new vision rose;
He saw the hill rise high, and higher still,
Till over all the mountains of the world
It towering stood; and nations, worshipping
Gazed on a mighty throne that bore a King!
Blood red the jewels in His crown of thorns,
With ermine pain that wrapped Him all about,
Deep in His hands the orb and sceptre nails,
Quite gone the Shadow of the primal sin
And, on His brow, fulfilled the ancient pledge
Of Earth's Redemption.

THE CHILD'S WISH GRANTED

By George Parsons Lathrop

Do you remember, my sweet, absent son,
How in the soft June days forever done
You loved the heavens so warm and clear and high;
And, when I lifted you, soft came your cry,—
"Put me 'way up,—'way up in the blue sky"?

I laughed and said I could not,—set you down
Your gray eyes wonder-filled beneath that crown
Of bright hair gladdening me as your raced by,
Another Father now, more strong than I,
Has borne you voiceless to your dear blue sky.

CHARITY

By George Parsons Lathrop

Unarmed she goeth, yet her hands
Strike deeper awe than steel-caparisoned bands,
No fatal hurt of foe she fears,—
Veiled, as with mail, in mist of gentle tears.

'Gainst her thou canst not bar the door;
Like air she enters; where none dared before.
Even to the rich she can forgive
Their regal selfishness,—and let them live!

A SONG BEFORE GRIEF

By Rose Hawthorne Lathrop

Sorrow, my friend,
When shall you come again?
The wind is slow, and the bent willows send
Their silvery motions wearily down the plain.
The bird is dead
That sang this morning through the summer rain!

Sorrow, my friend,
I owe my soul to you.
And if my life with any glory end
Of tenderness for others, and the words are true,
Said, honoring, when I'm dead,—
Sorrow, to you, the mellow praise, the funeral wreath
   are due.

And yet, my friend,
When love and joy are strong,
Your terrible visage from my sight I rend
With glances to blue heaven. Hovering along,
By mine your shadow led,
"Away!" I shriek, "nor dare to work my new-sprung mercies wrong!"

Still, you are near:
Who can your care withstand?
When deep eternity shall look most clear,
Sending bright waves to kiss the trembling land,
My joy shall disappear,—
A flaming torch thrown to the golden sea by your pale hand.

THE CLOCK'S SONG

By Rose Hawthorne Lathrop

Eileen of four,
Eileen of smiles;
Eileen of five,
Eileen of tears;
Eileen of ten, of fifteen years,
Eileen of youth
And woman's wiles;
Eileen of twenty,
In love's land,
Eileen all tender
In her bliss,
Untouched by sorrow's treacherous kiss,

And the sly weapons in life's hand,—
Eileen aroused to share all fate,
Eileen a wife,
Pale, beautiful,
Eileen most grave and dutiful,
Mourning her dreams in queenly state.
Eileen! Eileen! . . .

IRELAND

By Edmund Leamy (Senior)

I loved a love—a royal love—
  In the golden long ago;
And she was fair as fair could be.
The foam upon the broken sea,
The sheen of sun, or moon, or star,
The sparkle from the diamond spar,
Not half so rare and radiant are
  As my own love—my royal love—
    In the golden long ago.

And she had stately palace halls—
  In the golden long ago;
And warriors, men of stainless swords,
Were seated at her festive boards,
Fierce champions of her lightest words,
While hymned the bard the chieftain's praise,
And sang their deed of battle days.
  To cheer my love, my royal love,
    In the golden long ago.

She wore a stately diadem—
  In the golden long ago;
Wrought by a cunning craftsman's hand,
And fashioned from a battle brand,
Full fit for the queen of a soldier land;
Her sceptre was a sabre keen,
Her robe a robe of radiant green,
  My queenly love, my royal love,
    In the golden long ago.

Alas for my love, my royal love,
  Of the golden long ago!
For gone are all her warrior bands,
And rusted are her battle brands,
And broken her sabre bright and keen,
And torn her robe of radiant green,
A slave where she was a stainless queen,
  My own love, my royal love,
    Of the golden long ago.

But there is hope for my royal love
  Of the golden long ago;
Beyond the broad and shining sea
Gathers a stubborn chivalry,
That yet will come to make her free,
And hedge her round with gleaming spears,
And crown her queen of all the years,
  My own love, my royal love,
    Of the golden long ago.

MUSIC MAGIC

By Edmund Leamy

Perhaps there is no magic in this dull old world of ours;
Perhaps there are no Fairy Tales to gladden heart-break hours;
Perhaps there is no beauty, and perhaps all things are wrong,
But still there is the wonder of a little, old-time song!

A squeaking and battered old organ, rattling a moss-covered tune,
Stood in the street of the city, there, in the heat of the noon;
Banging of roses and sunshine, thrilling of lands far away,
Whispering songs of my childhood,—sorrowful, simple and gay;
I was a child for a moment, filled with a child's petty fears,
Dreaming, and dreaming, and dreaming, never a thought of the tears.
Then as the music softened, singing of love and of life,
Brought it back thought of the old days, far from the toil and the strife,
Glimmer of gold in the star-light, shimmer of silk by the sea;
Words that were whispered, half-spoken, dreams that were never to be.

Sweet intermingled with sadness, what is as dear as the past?
Is there a day in the future that is as fair as the last?

Music, oh, music the master, there in the heat of the noon,
A squeaking and battered old organ, rattling a moss-covered tune,
Carried me back in my dreaming, far, to the long, long ago;
Feeling, 'way down in my heart-chords, hope I thought never could glow;
Brought to me, who was a failure, beaten and crossed in the fight,
Help in the hour of the darkness—pointed the way to the light.

Perhaps there is no magic in this dull, old world of ours;
Perhaps there are no Fairy Tales to gladden heart-break hours;
Perhaps there is no beauty and perhaps all things are wrong;
But still there is the wonder of a little, old-time song!

GETHSEMANE
By Edmund Leamy

BREATHES there a man who claimeth not
   One lonely spot,
     His own Gethsemane,
  Whither with his inmost pain
  He fain
    Would weary plod,
  Find the surcease that is known
  In wind a-moan
    And sobbing sea,
  Cry his sorrow hid of men,
  And then—
    Touch hands with God.

MY LIPS WOULD SING —

By Edmund Leamy

My lips would sing a song for you, a soulful little song
    for you,
  A plaintive little song for you, upon a summer's day;
But for the very life of me, the merry, merry life of me,
  The laughter-loving life of me, I cannot but be gay.

For oh, the sun is shining, Dear, and who could be re-
    pining, Dear,
  And who would be unhappy, Dear, when all the world
    is young?
So I will hum a melody, a mirthful little melody,
  A joyous little melody that never yet was sung.

And you shall hear of Fairyland, of Kings and Queens
    of Fairyland,
  Of men and maids of Fairyland, and Love shall be the
    theme,
And straight before your brimming eyes, a golden glint
    of Paradise
  Shall steal, My Dear, to still your sighs, and give you
    back your dream.

And you will taste of happiness, a tiny bit of happiness,
  A wistful bit of happiness, upon a summer's day;
And just a little smile from you, a sunny little smile
    from you,
  A trembly little smile from you shall be a poet's pay!

MY SHIP

By Edmund Leamy

My ship is an old ship and her sails are grey and torn,
And in the dim and misty night she seems a thing forlorn;
Her battered sides are beetle black, her decks are scarred and old,
And heavy rise the musty scents from out her crumbling hold.

The young ships in the tide-way with a sneering smile sail by,
And fair they flash their white sails against a sun-drenched sky,
And fleet they run before the clouds that usher in a blow,
But could a storm coerce my ship whene'er she wished to go!

My ship is an old ship and her sails are torn and grey,
And she's not white and beautiful, nor fragile such as they,
But she has sailed o'er every sea to every land a-gleam,
And on her decks make merry now the wraiths of youthful dream!

VISIONS

By Edmund Leamy

I never watch the sun set a-down the Western skies
But that within it's wonderness I see my mother's eyes;
I never hear the West wind sob softly in the trees

*But that there comes her broken call far o'er the distant
    seas;*
And never shine the dim stars but that my heart would go
Away and back to olden lands and dreams of long ago.

A rover of the wide world, when yet my heart was young
The sea came whispering to me in well-beloved tongue,
And oh! the promises she held of golden lands a-gleam
That clung about my boy-heart and filled mine eyes with
    dream,
And Wanderlust came luring me till 'neath the stars I
    swore
That I would be a wanderer for ever, ever more.

A-rover of the wide world, I've seen the Northern lights
A-flashing countless colours in the knife-cold wintry
    nights;
I've watched the Southern Cross ablaze o'er smiling,
    sunny lands,
And seen the lazy sea caress palm-sheltered, silvery
    sands;
Still wild unrest is scouring me, the Wanderlust of yore,
And I must be a wanderer for ever, ever more.

And yet, I see the sun set a-down the Western skies
*And glimpse within the wonderness my mother's pleading
    eyes;*
And yet I hear the West wind sob softly in the trees,
*That vainly cloaks her broken call far o'er the distant
    seas;*
*And still when shine the dim stars my wander heart
    would go*
Away and back to her side, and dreams of long ago.

IRELAND, MOTHER OF PRIESTS

By Shane Leslie

The fishwife sits by the side
Of her childing bed,
Her fire is deserted and sad,
Her beads are long said;
Her tears ebb and flow with the sea,
Her grief on the years,
But little she looks to the tide,
And little she hears:
For children in springtime play round
Her sorrowing heart,
To win them their feeding she loves
To hunger apart;
Her children in summer she counts
Awhile for her own;
But winter is ever the same,
The loved ones are flown.
Far over the sea they are gone,
Far out of her ken
They travel the furthest of seas
As fishers of men.
Yet never a word to her sons
To keep them at home,
And never a motherly cry
Goes over the foam;
She sits with her head in her hands,
Her eyes on the flame,
And thinks of the others that played,
Yet left her the same.

With vesture she wove on the loom
Four-coloured to be,
And lanterns she trimmed with her hair
To light them to sea.
Oh, far have the living ones gone,
And further the dead,
For spirits come never to watch
The fisherwife's bed;
And sonless she sits at the hearth,
And peers in the flame,
She knows that their fishing must come
As ever it came—
A fishing that never set home,
But seaways it led,
For God who has taken her sons
Has buried her dead.

THE HUNTERS

By Ruth Temple Lindsay

"The Devil, as a roaring lion, goeth about seeking whom
    he may devour."

The Lion, he prowleth far and near,
  Nor swerves for pain or rue;
He heedeth nought of sloth nor fear,
  He prowleth—prowleth through
The silent glade and the weary street,
  In the empty dark and the full noon heat;
And a little Lamb with aching feet—
  He prowleth too.

THE HUNTERS

The Lion croucheth alert, apart—
  With patience doth he woo;
He waiteth long by this shuttered heart,
  And the Lamb—He waiteth too.
Up the lurid passes of dreams that kill,
  Through the twisting maze of the great Untrue,
The Lion followeth the fainting will—
  And the Lamb—He followeth too.

From the tickets dim of the hidden way
  Where the debts of Hell accrue,
The Lion leapeth upon his prey:
  But the Lamb—He leapeth too.
Ah! loose the leash of the sins that damn,
  Mark Devil and God as goals,
In the panting love of a famished Lamb,
  Gone mad with the need of souls.

The Lion, he strayeth near and far;
  What heights hath he left untrod?
He crawleth nigh to the purest star,
  On the trail of the saints of God.
And throughout the darkness of things unclean,
  In the depths where the sin-ghouls brood,
There prowleth ever with yearning mien—
  A lamb as white as Blood!

IN CHERRY LANE

By Rev. William Livingston

In Cherry Lane the blossoms blow
  In wreaths of white around the trees,
And spread their petals wide, as though
  They longed for nectar-seeking bees.

O'erhead, the arching boughs that spring
  From pillar trunks look down and smile
On lowly currant shrubs that cling
  Around their feet along the aisle.

In Cherry Lane the sunbeams steal
  Through many a leaf and branch above,
And tender shoots come forth to feel
  The touches of a wondrous love.

And life grows warmer with the hours,
  Unmoved, unchilled by human pang,
Till from the stems now robed in flowers
  The great red drops in clusters hang.

Ah, Mother mine! white blossoms came
  And filled my soul with thoughts of thee,
Who art to those that love thy name
  What honeyed buds are to the bee.

Thou art the floweret white and fair,
  A virgin from thy stainless birth,
The fruitful stem designed to bear
  A Saviour to our sinful earth.

And when the cherries, ripe and red,
  Come forth upon the breast of June,
They'll tell me of a heart that bled,
  By men forgotten all too soon.

Ah, precious drops! through future days
  Preserve my soul from spot or stain,
With tender thoughts of love and praise
  That once were mine in Cherry Lane.

SURRENDER

By S. M. M.

If thou art merely conscious clay—ah, well,
  Tire not such stuff with futile, tread-mill climb
  Which lifts to leave thee level with the slime;
Nor think that death can break thy earth-born spell;
Clay hath no heel Achillean, vulnerable.
  Be animate till some deliberate time
  Shall choke and crunch thee to potential grime,
For thou art fit for neither heaven nor hell.

But He Who made thee cousin to the clod
  First plunged thee in the Spirit Which is He,
Whence thou hast risen, divinely armed and shod
  To scale the ramparts of eternity.
Already stricken with the shafts of God,
  Thou fallest prisoner to the Deity.

HYMN FOR PENTECOST

By James Clarence Mangan

Pure Spirit of the always-faithful God,
Kindler of Heaven's true light within the soul!
From the lorn land our sainted fathers trod,
Ascends to Thee our cry of hope and dole.
Thee, Thee we praise;
To Thee we raise
Our choral hymn in these awakening days:
O send us down anew that fire
Which of old lived in David's and Isaiah's lyre.

Centuries had rolled, and earth lay tombed in sleep,
The nightmare-sleep of nations beneath kings;
And far abroad o'er liberty's great deep
Death's angel waved his black and stilling wings.
Then struck Thine hour!
Thou, in Thy power,
But breathedst, and the free stood up, a tower;
And tyranny's thrones and strongholds fell,
And men made jubilee for an abolished hell.

And she, our mother-home, the famed, the fair,
The golden house of light and intellect,
Must she still groan in her intense despair?
Shall she lie prone while Europe stands erect?
Forfend this, Thou
To whom we vow
Souls even our giant wrongs shall never bow:
Thou wilt not leave our green flag furled,
Nor bear that we abide the byword of the world

Like the last lamp that burned in Tullia's tomb
Through ages, vainly, with unwaning ray;
Our star of hope lights but a path of gloom
Whose false track leads us round and round alway.
But Thou canst open
A gate from hope
To victory! Thou canst nerve our arms to cope
With looming storm and danger still,
And lend a thunder-voice to the land's lightning will.
Descend, then, Spirit of the Eternal King!
To Thee, to Him, to His avenging Son,
The Triune of God, in boundless trust we cling;
His help once ours, our nationhood is won.
We watch the time
Till that sublime
Event shall thrill the free of every clime.
Speed, mighty Spirit! speed its march,
And thus complete for earth mankind's triumphal arch.

DARK ROSALEEN

By James Clarence Mangan

O my dark Rosaleen,
  Do not sigh, do not weep!
The priests are on the ocean green,
  They march along the deep.
There's wine from the royal Pope
  Upon the ocean green,
And Spanish ale shall give you hope,
  My dark Rosaleen!
  My own Rosaleen!

Shall glad your heart, shall give you hope
Shall give you health, and help, and hope,
  My dark Rosaleen!

Over hills and through dales
  Have I roamed for your sake;
All yesterday I sailed the sails
  On river and on lake.
The Erne, at its highest flood,
  I dashed across unseen,
For there was lightning in my blood,
  My dark Rosaleen!
  My own Rosaleen!
Oh! there was lightning in my blood,
Red lightning through my blood,
  My dark Rosaleen!

All day long, in unrest,
  To and fro do I move,
The very soul within my breast
  Is wasted for you, love!
The heart in my bosom faints
  To think of you, my Queen,
My life of life, my saint of saints,
  My dark Rosaleen!
  My own Rosaleen!
To hear your sweet and sad complaints,
My life, my love, my saint of saints,
  My dark Rosaleen!

Woe and pain, pain and woe,
  Are my lot, night and noon,
To see your bright face clouded so,

Like to the mournful moon.
But yet will I rear your throne
  Again in golden sheen;
'Tis you shall reign, shall reign alone,
  My dark Rosaleen!
  My own Rosaleen!
'Tis you shall have the golden throne,
'Tis you shall reign, and reign alone,
  My dark Rosaleen!

Over dews, over sands,
  Will I fly for your weal:
Your holy, delicate white hands
  Shall girdle me with steel.
At home in your emerald bowers,
  From morning's dawn till e'en,
You'll pray for me, my flower of flowers,
  My dark Rosaleen!
  My own Rosaleen!
You'll think of me through daylight's hours,
My virgin flower, my flower of flowers,
  My dark Rosaleen!

I could scale the blue air,
  I could plough the high hills,
Oh, I could kneel all night in prayer,
  To heal your many ills!
And one beamy smile from you
  Would float like light between
My toils and me, my own, my true,
  My dark Rosaleen!
  My own Rosaleen!
Would give me life and soul anew,

A second life, a soul anew,
  My dark Rosaleen!

Oh! the Erne shall run red
  With redundance of blood,
The earth shall rock beneath our tread,
  And flames wrap hill and wood,
And gun-peal and slogan-cry
  Wake many a glen serene,
Ere you shall fade, ere you shall die,
  My dark Rosaleen!
  My own Rosaleen!
The Judgment Hour must first be nigh,
Ere you shall fade, ere you can die,
  My dark Rosaleen!

WHAT IS WHITE?

By Thomas MacDonagh

What is white?
  The soul of the sage, faith-lit,
The trust of Age,
  The infant's untaught wit.
What more white?
  The face of Truth made known,
The Voice of Youth
  Singing before her throne.

WISHES FOR MY SON
Born on St. Cecilia's Day, 1912

BY THOMAS MACDONAGH

Now, my son, is life for you—
And I wish you joy of it,—
Joy of power in all you do,
Deeper passion, better wit
Than I had who had enough,
Quicker life and length thereof,
More of every gift but love.

Love I have beyond all men,
Love that now you share with me—
What have I to wish you then
But that you be good and free,
And that God to you may give
Grace in stronger days to live?

For I wish you more than I
Ever knew of glorious deed,
Though no rapture passed me by
That an eager heart could heed,
Though I followed heights and sought
Things the sequel never brought.

Wild and perilous holy things
Flaming with a martyr's blood,
And the joy that laughs and sings
Where a foe must be withstood,
Joy of headlong happy chance
Leading on the battle dance.

But I found no enemy,
No man in a world of wrong,
That Christ's word of Charity
Did not render clean and strong—
Who was I to judge my kind,
Blindest groper of the blind?

God to you may give the sight
And the clear undoubting strength
Wars to knit for single right,
Freedom's war to knit at length,
And to win, through wrath and strife
To the sequel of my life.

But for you, so small and young,
Born on Saint Cecilia's Day,
I in more harmonious song
Now for nearer joys should pray—
Simple joys: the natural growth
Of your childhood and your youth,
Courage, innocence and truth:

These for you, so small and young,
In your hand and heart and tongue.

RESIGNATION

By Seumas MacManus

Be still, sad soul, be still,
Bend you to Heaven's high will.
When the toilsome race is run,
And the summit strove for won—
When secrets are unsealed,

RESIGNATION

All hidden things revealed,
All mysteries made known,
The good we doubted shown,
Vexed questionings at rest,
I'll say, "Well, God knew best."

. . . . . .

Me thought you went full soon,
In the rapture of the noon,
In the glory of the sun,
Your noble work begun—
In your grasp the magic wand
That would raise a stricken land—
A while you fain would stay;
But the call brooked no delay:
You sighed, and bowed your head,
And they put you with the dead.

Our God is kind, and He
Will blunt the shaft to me;
Will stay the dripping woe
Ere the chalice overflow;
May let me end the race
With the high sun on my face,
And the hot blood bounding free,
Through the beating veins of me.
At most but some sad hours
And He'll call me when Night lowers.

Oh, at the Trysting Gate,
With radiant face you'll wait!
With arms in love outspread
To take a weary head,
And clasp it to your breast

Where always it found rest.
You'll speak no word for joy,
But, crooning o'er your boy,
Draw him into the Light,
Where nevermore comes Night.

IN DARK HOUR

By Seumas MacManus

I turn my steps where the Lonely Road
   Winds far as the eye can see,
And I bend my back for the burden sore
   That God has reached down to me.

I have said farewell to the sun-kissed plains,
   To joy I gave good-bye;
Now the bleak wide wastes of the world are mine
   And the winds that wail in the sky.

No bright flower blooms, no sweet bird calls,
   Nor hermit ever abode,
Not a green thing lifts one lowly leaf,
   O God, on the Lonely Road!

The thick dank mists come stealing down,
   And press me on every side.
With never a voice to cheer me on,
   And never a hand to guide.

I shall cry in my need for a Voice and Hand,
   And the solace of love-wet eyes—
And an icy clutch will close on my heart,
   When Echo, the mocker, replies.

I know my good soul will fail me not,
  When Forms from the Dark round me creep,
And whisper 'twere sweet to journey no more,
  But lay down the burden and sleep.

(Look onward and up, O Heart of my Heart,
  Where the road strikes the skies afar!
To cheer you, and guide, thro' your darkest hour,
  Behold yon beckoning Star!)

I set my face to the grey wild wastes,
  I bend my back to the load—
Dear God be kind with the heart-sick child
  Who steps on the Lonely Road.

A SONG OF COLOURS

By Theodore Maynard

Gold for the crown of Mary,
  Blue for the sea and sky,
Green for the woods and the meadows
  Where small white daisies lie,
And red for the colour of Christ's blood
  When He came to the cross to die.

These things the high God gave us
  And left in the world He made—
Gold for the hilt's enrichment,
  And blue for the sword's good blade,
And red for the roses a youth may set
  On the white brows of a maid.

Green for the cool, sweet gardens
　Which stretch about the house,
And the delicate new frondage
　The winds of spring arouse,
And red for the wine which a man may drink
　With his fellows in carouse.

Blue and green for the comfort
　Of tired hearts and eyes,
And red for that sudden hour which comes
　With danger and great surprise,
And white for the honour of God's throne
　When the dead shall all arise.

Gold for the cope and chalice,
　For kingly pomp and pride,
And red for the feathers men wear in their caps
　When they win a war or a bride,
And red for the robe which they dressed God in
　On the bitter day He died

THE WORLD'S MISER

By Theodore Maynard

I

A MISER with an eager face
Sees that each roseleaf is in place.

He keeps beneath strong bolts and bars
The piercing beauty of the stars.

The colours of the dying day
He hoards as treasure—well He may!—

And saves with care (lest they be lost)
The dainty diagrams of frost.

He counts the hairs of every head,
And grieves to see a sparrow dead.

II

Among the yellow primroses
He holds His Summer palaces,

And sets the grass about them all
To guard them as His spearmen small.

He fixes on each wayside stone
A mark to show it as His own,

And knows when raindrops fall through air
Whether each single one be there,

That gathered into ponds and brooks.
They may become His picture books,

To show in every spot and place
The living glory of His face.

CECIDIT, CECIDIT BABYLON MAGNA!

By Theodore Maynard

The aimless business of your feet,
  Your swinging wheels and piston rods,
The smoke of every sullen street
  Have passed away with all your Gods.

For in a meadow far from these
   A hodman treads across the loam,
Bearing his solid sanctities
   To that strange altar called his home.

I watch the tall, sagacious trees
   Turn as the monks do, every one;
The saplings, ardent novices,
   Turning with them towards the sun,

That Monstrance held in God's strong hands,
   Burnished in amber and in red;
God, His Own priest, in blessing stands;
   The earth, adoring, bows her head.

The idols of your market place,
   Your high debates, where are they now?
Your lawyers' clamour fades apace—
   A bird is singing on the bough!

Three fragile, sacramental things
   Endure, though all your pomps shall pass—
A butterfly's immortal wings,
   A daisy and a blade of grass.

A SONG OF LAUGHTER

By Theodore Maynard

The stars with their laughter are shaken;
   The long waves laugh at sea;
And the little Imp of Laughter
   Laughs in the soul of me.

I know the guffaw of a tempest,
  The mirth of a blossom and bud—
But I laugh when I think of how Cuchulain laughed
  At the crows with their bills in his blood.

The mother laughs low at her baby,
  The bridegroom with joy in his bride—
And I think that Christ laughed when they Took Him
    with staves
  On the night before He died.

APOCALYPSE

*"And I saw a new heaven and a new earth: for the first heaven
and the first earth are passed away."*—Apoc. xxi. L

By Theodore Maynard

Shall summer wood where we have laughed our fill;
  Shall all your grass so good to walk upon;
Each field that we have loved, each little hill,
  Be burnt like paper—as hath said Saint John?

Then not alone they die! For God hath told
  How all His plains of mingled fire and glass,
His walls of hyacinth, His streets of gold,
  His aureoles of jewelled light shall pass,

That He may make us nobler things that these,
  And in her royal robes of blazing red
Adorn His bride. Yea, with what mysteries
  And might and mirth shall she be diamonded.

And what new secrets shall our God disclose;
  Or set what suns of burnished brass to flare;
Or what empurpled bloom to oust the rose;
  Or what strange grass to glow like angels' hair!

What pinnacles of silvery tracery,
  What dizzy, rampired towers shall God devise
Of topaz, beryl and chalcedony
  To make Heaven pleasant to His children's eyes!

And in what cataclysms of flame and foam
  Shall the first Heaven sink—as red as sin—
When God hath cast aside His ancient home
  As far too mean to house His children in.

ST. BRIGID

By Denis A. McCarthy

Brigid, the daughter of Duffy, she wasn't like other
    young things,
Dreaming of lads for her lovers, and twirling her brace-
    lets and rings;
Combing and coiling and curling her hair that was black
    as the sloes,
Painting her lips and her cheeks that were ruddy and
    fresh as the rose.
Ah, 'twasn't Brigid would waste all her days in such
    follies as these—
Christ was the Lover she worshipped for hour after hour
    on her knees;
Christ and His Church and His poor,—and 'twas many
    a mile that she trod

Serving the loathsomest lepers that ever were stricken by God.

Brigid, the daughter of Duffy, she sold all her jewels and gems,
Sold all her finely-spun robes that were braided with gold to the hems;
Kept to her back but one garment, one dress that was faded and old,
Gave all her goods to the poor who were famished with hunger and cold.
Ah, 'twasn't Brigid would fling at the poor the hard word like a stone—
Christ the Redeemer she saw in each wretch that was ragged and lone;
Every wandering beggar who asked for a bite or a bed
Knocked at her heart like the Man who had nowhere to shelter His head.

Brigid, the daughter of Duffy, she angered her father at last.
"Where are your dresses, my daughter? Crom Cruach! You wear them out fast!
Where are the chains that I bought you all wrought in red gold from the mine?
Where the bright brooches of silver that once on your bosom would shine?"
Ah, but 'twas he was the man that was proud of his name and his race,
Proud of their prowess in battle and proud of their deeds in the chase!
Knew not the Christ, the pale God Whom the priests from afar had brought in,

Held to the old Gaelic gods that were known to Cuchullin
  and Finn.

Brigid, the daughter of Duffy, made answer, "O father,"
  said she,
"What is the richest of raiment, and what are bright
  jewels to me?
Lepers of Christ must I care for, the hungry of Christ
  must I feed;
How can I walk in rich robes when His people and mine
  are in need?"
Ah, but 'twas she didn't fear for herself when he
  blustered and swore,
Meekly she bowed when he ordered his chariot brought
  to the door;
Meekly obeyed when he bade her get in at the point of
  his sword,
Knowing whatever her fate she'd be safe with her Lover
  and Lord.

Brigid, the daughter of Duffy, was brought to the court
  of the King,
(Monarch of Leinster, MacEnda, whose praises the poets
  would sing).
"Hither, O monarch," said Duffy, "I've come with a
  maiden to sell;
Buy her and bind her to bondage—she's needing such
  discipline well!"
Ah, but 'twas wise was the King. From the maid to the
  chieftain he turned;
Mildness he saw in her face, in the other 'twas anger
  that burned;
"This is no bondmaid, I'll swear it, O chief, but a girl
  of your own.

Why sells the father the flesh of his flesh and the bone
 of his bone?"

Brigid, the daughter of Duffy, was mute while her father
 replied—
"Monarch, this maid has no place as the child of a
 chieftain of pride.
Beggars and wretches whose wounds would the soul of
 a soldier affright,
Sure, 'tis on these she is wasting my substance from
 morning till night!"
Ah, but 'twas bitter was Duffy; he spoke like a man that
 was vext.
Musing, the monarch was silent; he pondered the question perplexed.
"Maiden," said he, "if 'tis true, as I've just from your
 father heard tell,
Might it not be, as my bondmaid, you'd waste all my
 substance as well?"

Brigid, the daughter of Duffy, made answer. "O monarch," she said,
"Had I the wealth from your coffers, and had I the
 crown from your head—
Yea, if the plentiful yield of the broad breasts of Erin
 were mine,
All would I give to the people of Christ who in poverty
 pine."
Ah, but 'twas then that the King felt the heart in his
 bosom upleap,
"I am not worthy," he cried, "such a maiden in bondage
 to keep!

Here's a king's sword for her ransom, and here's a king's word to decree
Never to other than Christ and His poor let her servitude be!"

ROSA MYSTICA

By Denis A. McCarthy

O Mystic Rose, in God's fair garden growing,
O Mystic Rose, in Heaven's high courtyard blowing—
Make sweet, make sweet the pathway I am going,
    O Mystic Rose!
The darkling, deathward way that I am going,
    O Mystic Rose!

O Rose, more white than snow-wreath in December!
O Rose, more red than sunset's dying ember,
My sins forget, my penitence remember,
    O Mystic Rose!
Though all should fail, I pray that thou remember,
    O Mystic Rose!

O Mystic Rose, the moments fly with fleetness;
To judgment I, with all my incompleteness—
But thou, make intercession by thy sweetness,
    O Mystic Rose!
Be near to soothe and save me by the sweetness,
    O Mystic Rose!

THE POOR MAN'S DAILY BREAD

By Denis A. McCarthy

Not only there where jewelled vestments blaze,
  And princely prelates bow before Thy shrine,
Where myriads line the swept and garnished ways
  Through which is borne Thy Majesty Divine—
O Jesus of the ever loving heart,
  Not only there Thou art!

But where the lowliest church its cross uplifts
  Above the city's sordidness and sin;
Where all unheeded human wreckage drifts
  And drowns amid the foulness and the din—
There, too, anear the very gates of hell,
O Saviour, dost Thou dwell!

Oh, meet it is that round Thy altar thrones,
  Thy highest priests should ministering throng
With silken robe, with gold and precious stones,
  With solemn chant and loud triumphant song:
What beauty that the world could give would be
Too beautiful for Thee?

And yet to those that work with grimy hands
  And sweaty brows in ditches and in drains,
Thou comest with a love that understands
  Their labor ill-requited, and their pains.
Who knows so well as Thou what they endure,
  O Father of the poor?

And so, deep-hid in many a city street,
  Or far where lonely workers break the soil,
Are shrines where Thou, the Merciful, dost meet,
  In love's embrace, the weary ones that toil.
For them Thy hospitable board is spread,
  With Thee, Thy very Self, their Daily Bread!

TO ASK OUR LADY'S PATRONAGE FOR A BOOK ON COLUMBUS: A FRAGMENT

By Thomas D'Arcy McGee

Star of the Sea, to whom, age after age,
  The maiden kneels whose lover sails the sea;
Star, that the drowning death-pang can assuage,
  And shape the soul's course to eternity;
Mother of God, to Egypt's realm exiled,
  Mother of God, in Bethlehem's crib confined,
Thee do I ask to aid my anxious mind,
  And make this book find favour with thy Child.

Of one who lived and laboured in thy ray,
  I would rehearse the striving and success;
Through the dense past I ne'er shall find my way,
  Unless thou helpest, hold Comfortress;
A world of doubt and darkness to evade;
  An ocean all unknown to Christian kind;
Another world by nature's self arrayed,
  O'er the wide waste of waves, I seek to find.

A GENERAL COMMUNION

By Alice Meynell

I saw the throng, so deeply separate,
    Fed at one only board—
The devout people, moved, intent, elate,
    And the devoted Lord.

Oh struck apart! not side from human side,
    But soul from human soul,
As each asunder absorbed the multiplied,
    The ever unparted whole.

I saw this people as a field of flowers,
    Each grown at such a price
The sum of unimaginable powers
    Did no more than suffice.

A thousand single central daisies they,
    A thousand of the one;
For each the entire monopoly of day;
    For each, the whole of the devoted sun.

THE SHEPHERDESS

By Alice Meynell

She walks—the lady of my delight—
    A shepherdess of sheep.
Her flocks are thoughts. She keeps them white;
    She guards them from the steep;
She feeds them on the fragrant height,
    And folds them in for sleep.

She roams maternal hills and bright,
  Dark valleys safe and deep.
Into that tender breast at night
  The chastest stars may peep.
She walks—the lady of my delight—
  A shepherdess of sheep.

She holds her little thoughts in sight,
  Though gay they run and leap.
She is so circumspect and right;
  She has her soul to keep.
She walks—the lady of my delight—
  A shepherdess of sheep.

CHRIST IN THE UNIVERSE

By Alice Meynell

With this ambiguous earth
His dealings have been told us. These abide:
The signal to a maid, the human birth,
The lesson, and the young Man crucified.

But not a star of all
The innumberable host of stars has heard
How He administered this terrestrial ball.
Our race have kept their Lord's entrusted Word.

Of His earth-visiting feet
None knows the secret, cherished, perilous,
The terrible, shamefast, frightened, whispered, sweet,
Heart-shattering secret of His way with us.

No planet knows that this
Our wayside planet, carrying land and wave,
Love and life multiplied, and pain and bliss,
Bears, as chief treasure, one forsaken grave,

Nor, in our little day,
May his devices with the heavens be guessed,
His pilgrimage to tread the Milky Way
Or His bestowals there be manifest.

But in the eternities,
Doubtless we shall compare together, hear
A million alien Gospels, in what guise
He trod the Pleiades, the Lyre, the Bear.

O, be prepared, my soul!
To read the inconceivable, to scan
The million forms of God those stars enroll
When, in our turn, we show to them a Man.

"I AM THE WAY"

By Alice Meynell

Thou art the Way.
Hadst Thou been nothing but the goal,
    I cannot say
If Thou hadst ever met my soul.

    I cannot see—
I, child of process—if there lies
    An end for me,
Full of repose, full of replies.

I'll not reproach
The road that winds, my feet that err.
Access, approach
Art Thou, Time, Way, and Wayfarer.

VIA, ET VERITAS, ET VITA

By Alice Meynell

"You never attained to Him." "If to attain
Be to abide, then that may be."
"Endless the way, followed with how much pain!"
"The way was He."

UNTO US A SON IS GIVEN

By Alice Meynell

Given, not lent,
And not withdrawn—once sent,
This Infant of mankind, this One,
Is still the little welcome Son.

New every year,
New born and newly dear,
He comes with tidings and a song,
The ages long, the ages long;

Even as the cold
Keen winter grows not old,
As childhood is so fresh, foreseen,
And spring in the familiar green.

Sudden as sweet
Come the expected feet.
All joy is young, and new all art,
And He, too, Whom we have by heart.

TO A DAISY

By Alice Meynell

Slight as thou art, thou art enough to hide
  Like all created things, secrets from me,
  And stand a barrier to eternity.
And I, how can I praise thee well and wide

From where I dwell—upon the hither side?
  Thou little veil for so great mystery,
  When shall I penetrate all things and thee,
And then look back? For this I must abide.

Till thou shalt grow and fold and be unfurled
Literally between me and the world.
  Then I shall drink from in beneath a spring.

And from a poet's side shall read his book.
O daisy mine, what will it be to look
  From God's side even of such a simple thing?

THE NEWER VAINGLORY

By Alice Meynell

Two men went up to pray; and one gave thanks,
    Not with himself aloud,
With proclamation, calling on the ranks
    Of an attentive crowd.

"Thank God, I clap not my own humble breast,
    But other ruffians' backs,
Imputing crime—such is my tolerant haste—
    To any man that lacks.

"For I am tolerant, generous, keep no rules,
    And the age honors me.
Thank God, I am not as these rigid fools,
    Even as this Pharisee."

THE FOLDED FLOCK

By Wilfrid Meynell

I saw the shepherd fold the sheep,
With all the little lambs that leap.

O Shepherd Lord, so I would be
Folded with all my family.

Or go they early, come they late,
Their mother and I must count them eight.

And how, for us, were any heaven
If we, sore-stricken, saw but seven?

Kind Shepherd, as of old Thou'lt run
And fold at need a straggling one.

CONVENT ECHOES

By Helen Louise Moriarty

Clear on the air, their pulsing cadence pealing,
   I hear a sweet refrain,
While o'er my thoughts a gentle mist is stealing,
   And mem'ries come again,

Of quiet halls where dusk is slow descending,
   Where peace has spread her wings.
Soft music in the distance only lending
   More charms where twilight clings.

Anon appear the black robed nuns, their faces
   Serene in sweet repose;
Across their brows the world has left no traces
   Of earthly dreams or woes.

Now loud on air the organ music swelling,
   They reach the chapel door—
The sweet faint incense stealing upward, telling
   'Tis Benediction's hour.

Now low-bowed heads, and hearts to Him ascending
   On incense laden air.
Ah surely Heaven must smile with ear attending
   The nun's low whispered prayer.

Fond memory lingers on those dim old hallways—
  Lingers and drops a tear,
And kind affection drapes the picture always
  Through each succeeding year.

ENGLAND

By John Henry Newman

Tyre of the West, and glorying in the name
  More than in Faith's pure fame!
O trust not crafty fort nor rock renown'd
  Earn'd upon hostile ground;
Wielding Trade's master-keys, at thy proud will
To lock or loose its waters, England! trust not still.

Dread thine own power! Since haughty Babel's prime,
  High towers have been man's crime.
Since her hoar age, when the huge moat lay bare,
  Strongholds have been man's snare.
Thy nest is in the crags; ah, refuge frail!
Mad counsels in its hour, or traitors, will prevail.

He who scann'd Sodom for His righteous men
  Still spares thee for thy ten;
But, should vain tongues the Bride of Heaven defy,
  He will not pass thee by;
For, as earth's kings welcome their spotless guests,
So gives He them by turn, to suffer or be blest.

THE PILLAR OF THE CLOUD

By John Henry Newman

Lead, Kindly Light, amid the encircling gloom,
    Lead Thou me on!
The night is dark, and I am far from home—
    Lead Thou me on!
Keep Thou my feet; I do not ask to see
The distant scene,—one step enough for me.

I was not ever thus, nor pray'd that Thou
    Shouldst lead me on.
I lov'd to choose and see my path; but now
    Lead Thou me on!
I lov'd the garish day, and, spite of fears,
Pride rul'd my will: remember not past years.

So long Thy power hath bless'd me, sure it still
    Will lead me on,
O'er moor and fen, o'er crag and torrent, till
    The night is gone;
And with the morn those angel faces smile
Which I have lov'd long since, and lost awhile.

THE GREEK FATHERS

By John Henry Newman

Let heathen sing thy heathen praise,
Fall'n Greece! the thought of holier days
    In my sad heart abides;
For sons of thine in Truth's first hour

Were tongues and weapons of His power,
Born of the Spirit's fiery shower,
   Our fathers and our guides.

All thine is Clement's varied page;
And Dionysius, ruler sage,
   In days of doubt and pain;
And Origen with eagle eye;
And saintly Basil's purpose high
To smite imperial heresy,
   And cleanse the Altar's stain.

From thee the glorious preacher came,
With soul of zeal and lips of flame,
   A court's stern martyr-guest;
And thine, O inexhaustive race!
Was Nazianzen's heaven-taught grace;
And royal-hearted Athanase,
   With Paul's own mantel blessed.

RELICS OF SAINTS

By John Henry Newman

"He is not the God of the dead, but of the living; for all live unto Him."

"The Fathers are in dust, yet live to God:"
  So says the Truth; as if the motionless clay
Still held the seeds of life beneath the sod,
  Smouldering and straggling till the judgment day.

And hence we learn with reverence to esteem
   Of these frail houses, though the grave confines;
Sophist may urge his cunning tests, and deem
   That they are earth;—but they are heavenly shrines.

THE SIGN OF THE CROSS

By John Henry Newman

Whene'er across this sinful flesh of mine
   I draw the Holy Sign,
All good thoughts stir within me, and renew
   Their slumbering strength divine;
Till there springs up a courage high and true
   To suffer and to do.

And who shall say, but hateful spirits around,
   For their brief hour unbound,
Shudder to see, and wail their overthrow?
   While on far heathen ground
Some lonely Saint hails the fresh odour, though
   Its source he cannot know?

THE SON OF GOD

By Charles L. O'Donnell, C.S.C.

The fount of Mary's joy
   Revealed now lies,
For, lo, has not the Boy
   His Father's eyes?

TO ST. JOSEPH

By Charles L. O'Donnell, C.S.C.

St. Joseph, when the day was done
  And all your work put by,
You saw the stars come one by one
  Out in the violet sky.

You did not know the stars by name,
  But there sat at your knee
One who had made the light and flame
  And all things bright that be.

You heard with Him birds in the tree
  Twitter "Good-night" o'erhead,—
The Maker of the world must see
  His little ones to bed.

Then when the darkness settled round,
  To Him your prayers were said;
No wonder that your sleep was ground
  The angels loved to tread.

THE DEAD MUSICIAN

In memory of Brother Basil,
Organist for half a century at Notre Dame

By Charles L. O'Donnell, C.S.C.

He was the player and the played upon,
He was the actor and the acted on,
Artist, and yet himself a substance wrought;
God played on him as he upon the keys,
Moving his soul to mightiest melodies
Of lowly serving, hid austerities,
And holy thought that our high dream out-tops,—
He was an organ where God kept the stops.
        Naught, naught
Of all he gave us came so wondrous clear
As that he sounded to the Master's ear.

Wedded he was to the immortal Three,
Poverty, Obedience and Chastity,
And in a fourth he found them all expressed,
For him all gathered were in Music's breast,
        And in God's house
He took her for his spouse,—
High union that the world's eye never scans
        Nor world's way knows.
Not any penny of applauding hands
He caught, nor would have caught,
        Not any thought
        Save to obey
Obedience that bade him play,
        And for his bride

THE DEAD MUSICIAN

  To have none else beside,
That both might keep unflecked their virgin snows.

Yet by our God's great law
Such marriage issue saw,
As they who cast away may keep,
        Who sow not reap.
        In Chastity entombed
        His manhood bloomed,
        And children not of earth
        Had spotless birth.
With might unmortal was he strong
        That he begot
        Of what was not,
Within the barren womb of silence, song.
        Yea, many sons he had
      To make his sole heart glad—
Romping the boundless meadows of the air,
Skipping the cloudy hills, and climbing bold
The heavens' nightly stairs of starry gold.
        Nay, winning heaven's door
        To mingle evermore
With deathless troops of angel harmony.
        He filled the house of God
        With servants at his nod,
A music-host of moving pagentry.
Lo, this priest, and that an acolyte:
        Ah, such we name aright
        Creative art,
To body forth love slumbering at the heart . . .
        Fools, they who pity him,
        Imagine dim

THE DEAD MUSICIAN

Days that the world's glare brightens not.
        Until the seraphim
   Shake from their flashing hair
   Lightnings, and weave serpents there,
        His days we reckon fair. . . .

        Yet more he had than this;
        Lord of the liberative kiss,
        To own and yet refrain,
        To hold his hand in reign.
   High continence of his high power,
   That turns from virtue's very flower,
        In loss of that elected pain
        A greater prize to gain.
   As one who long had put wine by
        Would now himself deny
        Water, and thirsting die.
So, sometimes he was idle at the keys,
Pale fingers on the aged ivories;
        Then, like a prisoned bird,
        Music was seen, not heard,
Then were his quivering hands most strong
With blood of the repressed song,—
   A fruitful barrenness. Oh, where
        Out of angelic air,
   This side the heavens' spheres
   Such sight to start and hinder tears.
Who knows, perhaps while silence throbbed
He heard the De Profundis sobbed
   By his own organ at his bier to-day,—
   It is the saints' anticipative way,
   He knew both hand and ear were clay.
        That was one thought

Never is music wrought,
For silence only could that truth convey.
Widowed of him, his organ now is still,
His music-children fled, their echoing feet yet fill
The blue, far reaches of the vaulted nave,
The heart that sired them, pulseless in the grave.
Only the song he made is hushed, his soul,
Responsive to God's touch, in His control
Elsewhere shall tune the termless ecstasy
  Of one who all his life kept here
        An alien ear,
Homesick for harpings of eternity.

GIOTTO'S CAMPANILE

By Thomas O'Hagan

O PULSING heart with voice attuned
  To all the soul builds high,
Framing in notes of love divine
  A drama of the sky,
Across the Arno's flowing tide
  The notes chime on the air,
Deep as the mysteries of God
  And tender as a prayer.

Here, where the Poet of Sorrows dwelt,
  Whose altar Love had built,
And framed his morn in dreams so pure
  That knew not stain nor guilt:
O *Vita Nuova!* Earthly Love
  Then changed to love Divine;

Transfigured at the wedding-feast,
   Earth's grapes are heavenly wine.

Where cowled monk with soul of fire
   Struck vice athwart the face,
With God's anointed sword of truth
   That flashed with beams of grace.
O bitter days of war and strife!
   Heaven's ardor was too great;
The Empire of the earth held sway
   And sealed with saddest fate.

Methinks I hear from thy strong lips,
   O century-dowered bell!
The story of the Whites and Blacks,
   As banners rose or fell;
Methinks I hear an epic voice,
   Full of God's love and power,
With accent of an Exile sad
   Speaking from out thy tower!

NAME OF MARY

By John Boyle O'Reilly

Dear, honored name, beloved for human ties,
   But loved and honored first that One was given
In living proof, to erring mortal eyes,
   That our poor flesh is near akin to heaven.

Sweet word of dual meaning: one of grace,
   And born of our kind Advocate above;
And one, by mercy linked to that dear face
   That blessed my childhood with its mother-love,

And taught me first the simple prayer: "To thee
    Poor banished sons of Eve, we send our cries."
Through mist of years, those words recall to me
    A childish face upturned to loving eyes.

And yet, to some the name of Mary bears
    No special meaning and no gracious power;
In that dear word they seek for hidden snares,
    As wasps find poison in the sweetest flower.

But faithful hearts can see, o'er doubts and fears
    The Virgin-link that binds the Lord to earth;
Which, to the upturned trusting face, appears
    Greater than angel, though of human birth.

The sweet-faced moon reflects, on cheerless night,
    The rays of hidden sun that rise to-morrow;
So, unseen God still lets his promised light,
    Through holy Mary, shine upon our sorrow.

A CHRISTMAS CAROL

By Mary A. O'Reilly

Night in the far Judean land,
    The pregnant air is still,
The sky one blue unclouded band,
    Seems drooping o'er each hill.
The hills then toward each other bend,
Some mighty secret to portend.
    Gloria in excelsis Deo.

A CHRISTMAS CAROL

The sheep in near-by pastures browse,
  Some bleat as if in pain;
The youthful shepherds watch and drowse,
  Then drowse and watch again;
When lo! a light from Heaven appears
Which makes them huddle in their fears.
  Gloria in excelsis Deo.

God's glory shone around them there,
  And then an angel cried—
"Fear not, for I good tidings bear
  To you, and all beside.
For unto you is born this day
A Savior, Christ the Lord." We pray—
  Gloria in excelsis Deo.

Then swinging from the skies there came
  Groups of the heavenly host,
Praising the Lord in sweet acclaim—
  The burden of their toast—
"Glory to God on High," again—
His "Peace on earth, good will to men."
  Gloria in excelsis Deo.

Within a stable sweet with hay,
  And warm with breath of kine,
The Baby and His Mother lay,
  O, mystery divine!
The bed of straw a cloud appears,
We hear the music of the spheres.
  Gloria in excelsis Deo.

Dear maiden mother, let us now,
  While to your breast He clings,
In humble adoration bow
  With shepherds and with kings,
And at His feet our off'ring be
Praise, love, faith, hope and charity.
  Gloria in excelsis Deo.

ROMA MATER SEMPAETERNA

By Shaemas O'Sheel

The blue skies bend and are about her furled,
  A maiden mantle; and with lilies bright
  The sun daywhiles doth crown her, and at night
With stars her garment's border is empearled.
Not a king's favorite, perfumed and curled,
    Is half so fair; no queen of martial might
  So potent as the Mother of the Light,
The Mary of the Cities of the World!

Eternal Mother, at whose breasts of white
  The infant Church was suckled and made strong
    With the sweet milk of heavenly Truth and Love
  O thou that art all nations set above,
Strengthen us still because the way is long,
Mary of Cities, Mother of the Light!

MARY'S BABY

By Shaemas O'Sheel

Joseph, mild and noble, bent above the straw:
A pale girl, a frail girl, suffering, he saw;
"O my Love, my Mary, my bride, I pity thee!"
"Nay, Dear," said Mary, "All is well with me!"
  "Baby, my Baby, O my Babe," she sang.
  Suddenly the golden night all with music rang.

Angels leading shepherds, shepherds leading sheep:
The silence of worship broke the mother's sleep.
All the meek and lowly of the world were there;
Smiling she showed them that her Child was fair.
  "Baby, my Baby," kissing Him she said.
  Suddenly a flaming star through the heavens sped.

Three old men and weary knelt them side by side,
The world's wealth forswearing, majesty and pride;
Worldly might and wisdom before the Babe bent low:
Weeping, maid Mary said "I love Him so!"
  "Baby, my Baby," and the Baby slept.
  Suddenly on Calvary all the olives wept.

THEY WENT FORTH TO BATTLE

By Shaemas O'Sheel

They went forth to battle, but they always fell;
  Their eyes were fixed above the sullen shields;
Nobly they fought and bravely, but not well,
And sank heart-wounded by a subtle spell.

They knew not fear that to the foeman yields,
They were not weak, as one who vainly wields
A futile weapon, yet the sad scrolls tell
How on the hard-fought field they always fell.

It was a secret music that they heard,
  A sad sweet plea for pity and for peace;
And that which pierced the heart was but a word,
Though the white breast was red-lipped where the sword
  Pressed a fierce cruel kiss, to put surcease
  On its hot thirst, but drank a hot increase.
Ah, then by some strange troubling doubt were stirred,
And died for hearing what no foeman heard.

They went forth to battle but they always fell;
  Their might was not the might of lifted spears;
Over the battle-clamor came a spell
Of troubling music, and they fought not well.
  Their wreaths are willows and their tribute, tears;
  Their names are old sad stories in men's ears;
Yet they will scatter the red hordes of Hell,
Who went to battle forth and always fell.

HE WHOM A DREAM HATH POSSESSED

By Shaemas O'Sheel

He whom a dream hath possessed knoweth no more of
    doubting,
  For mist and the blowing of winds and the mouthing of
    words he scorns;
Not the sinuous speech of schools he hears, but a knightly
    shouting,

And never comes darkness down, yet he greeteth a
   million morns.

He whom a dream hath possessed knoweth no more of
      roaming;
   All roads and the flowing of waves and the speediest
      flight he knows,
But wherever his feet are set, his soul is forever homing,
   And going he comes, and coming he heareth a call and
      goes.

He whom a dream hath possessed knoweth no more of
      sorrow,
   At death and the dropping of leaves and the fading of
      suns he smiles,
For a dream remembers no past and scorns the desire of
      a morrow,
   And a dream in a sea of doom sets surely the ultimate
      isles.

He whom a dream hath possessed treads the impalpable
      marches,
   From the dust of the day's long road he leaps to a
      laughing star,
And the ruin of worlds that fall he views from eternal
      arches,
   And rides God's battle-field in a flashing and golden
      car.

MARIA IMMACULATA

By Condé Benoist Pallen

I

How may I sing, unworthy I,
Our Lady's glorious sanctity?
She whose celestial shoon
Rest on the horned moon
In Heaven's highest galaxy;
She whom the poet sang of old
In that rare vision told
In soft Tuscan speech of gold,
The spotless spouse and mother-maid
The goodliest sapphire in Heaven's floor inlaid
Around whom wheels the circling flame
Of the rapt seraph breathing Mary's name,
While choir to choir replies
In growing harmonies
Through all the glowing spheres of Paradise,
Till universal Heaven's glad estate
Rings jubilation to their queen immaculate.

II

Ah me! Unworthy I to sing
The stainless mother of my King,
My King and Lord,
The Incarnate Word,
Heaven itself comprest
Within her virgin breast!
How may my faltering rhyme
Sing of Eternity in time,

Omnipotence in human frailty exprest,
Our earthly garden fragrant with celestial thyme.
What Muse, though great Urania guide her flight,
May dare the sacrosanct and awful height
Of that mysterious sublime
Within the secret counsels of the Infinite!
Omniscence there supreme and sole
Clasps the beginning and the whole
Of Love beyond created sight,
Uncreate and quintessential light!
Before the splendor of that ray
Cherub and seraph fall away
Dazzled and broken by excess
Of everpowering blessedness,
Yet panting for the fulness of the bliss
That breathes consuming fire from Love's unkenned abyss.
Not through that fiery sphere my way,
But here where shines the veiléd day,
The flames of mystery insteeped
In this our mortal clay;
For in her maiden breast asleep
Lies all the Love of Heaven's deep,
The holy circle of her zone
Incarnate Love's terrestrial throne.

III

The great archangel veils his face
Before her: "Hail, full of grace!"
And Heaven is clasped of earth;
While all the wheeling spheres with all their choirs
Around her wheel seraphic fires.
Eden rises to its second birth;

Again the prime estate
Of man is renovate,
And all the elder worth renewed in her immaculate;
Virgin and spouse of Him
Who breathes the virtue of the Seraphim,
Virgin and mother of the Eternal Son,
Daughter, Virgin, Spouse in one!
The spotless mate of spotless Dove,
The one great miracle of God's love,
From all eternity the chosen bride,
Save only her none, none
Exempt from sin's dominion;
Save only her of Adam's race
Or heavenly line, none full of grace;
On her alone, on her alone
The torrent of His love poured down
The deep abundance of its flood
Into the pure channels of her maidenhood,
The fleckless mirror of her grace
Reflecting all the beauty of His Face.

IV

She looks with human eyes
Into the eyes of Paradise;
Upon her virgin breast the Babe Divine
Gazes again into her eyne;
O vanity of words to tell
The wonder of that spell,
The ravishment of bliss
Upwelling from the deep abyss
Of Love incarnate gazing in the eyes
Of his terrestrial paradise!
See Heaven within her arms.

Gathered against all harms,
Innocence by innocence addrest,
Virgin love by virgin love carest,
The sinless mother and the sinless Son
For Heaven and earth to gaze upon!
Her living image on her knee,
O the depths of her maternity!
Her God, her Infant at her breast,
O Love beyond all utterance exprest,
The Eternal Word in virgin flesh made manifest!

V

Ye sons of Adam rejoice
With exultant voice!
Shake off your chains! Arise!
The ancient dragon has no power
O'er Jesse's virgin flower,
And stricken 'neath a maiden's sandal lies.
Nor may his venomed breath so much
As her garment's outer margin touch;
And sin's torrential flood,
That whelmed all Adam's flesh and blood,
Its loathsome stream turns back
Before her footsteps' radiant track.

VI

Rejoice, children of men!
Behold again
Your flesh rejuvenate
In her immaculate!
Rejoice with exceeding joy,
For in her free from sin's alloy
Your renovated race

In plentitude of grace
Dare look again unshamed upon its Maker's Face!
Chosen to bear the Eternal Word,
In her your more than dignity restored;
In her the more than golden worth
Of Eden's prime when Heaven was linked with earth
Unstained by Adam's guilty forfeiture,
In her your long corrupted flesh made pure;
For of her, flesh of flesh and bone of bone,
Eternal Love builds up His stainless throne!

VII

Rejoice and be glad this day!
In jubilation lay
Your tribute at her feet,
Spotless and most meet,
The mystic rose of Jesse's root,
To bear the heavenly fruit;
Wisdom's seat and Heaven's gate,
Our surest advocate,
Mother of God immaculate!
Be glad, O Adam's clay,
Be glad this happy day.
And with accordant voice acclaim
Our spotless Lady's stainless fame;
Be ye exceeding glad and sing
The mother of our King.
And though unworthy be my strain,
She is too tender not to deign
To lend a gracious ear
To this her children's humble prayer:
Mother of Mercy, hear!
Mother whose face is likest His,

Who our Redeemer is,
Grant us one day to share
Thy happiness in gazing on His Face,
Who found thee without spot and full of grace!

THE RAISING OF THE FLAG

By Condé Benoist Pallen

Lift up the banner of our love
To the kiss of the winds above,
The banner of the world's fair hope,
Set with stars from the azure cope,
When liberty was young,
And yet unsung
Clarioned her voice among
The trodden peoples, and stirred
The pulses with her word,
Till the swift flood red
From the quick heart sped,
Flushing valour's cheek with flame
At sounding of her august sacred name!

Lift up the banner of the stars,
The standard of the double bars,
Red with the holy tide
Of heroes' blood, who died
At the feet of liberty,
Shouting her battle-cry
Triumphantly
As they fell like sickled corn
In that first resplendent morn

THE RAISING OF THE FLAG

Of freedom, glad to die
In the dawn of her clear eye!

Lift up the flag of starry blue
Caught from the crystal hue
Of central heaven's glowing dome,
Where the great winds largely roam
In unrestrainéd liberty;
Caught from the cerulean sea
Of midmost ocean tossing free,
Flecked with the racing foam
Of rushing waters, as they leap
Unbridled from the laughing deep
In the gulfs of liberty!

Lift up the banner red
With the blood of heroes shed
In victory!
Lift up the banner blue
As heaven, and as true
In constancy!
Lift up the banner white
As sea foam in the light
Of liberty;
The banner of the triple hue,
The banner of the red and white and blue,
Bright ensign of the free!

Lift up the banner of the days to come,
When cease the trumpet and the rolling drum;
When peace in the nest of love
Unfolds the wings of the dove,
Brooding o'er the days to-be,

THE RAISING OF THE FLAG

Peace born of freedom's might,
Peace sprung from the power of right,
The peace of liberty!

Lift up the flag of high surprise
To greet the gladdened eyes
Of peoples far and near,
The glorious harbinger
Of earth's wide liberties,
Streaming pure and clear
In freedom's lofty atmosphere!

Lift up our hearts to Him who made to shine
In Heaven's arch the glorious sign
Of mercy's heavenly birth
To all the peoples of the earth,
The pledge of peace divine!
And let our glorious banner, too,
The banner of the rainbow's hue,
In heaven's wide expanse unfurled,
Be for a promise to the world
Of peace to all mankind;
Banner of peace and light,
Banner of red and blue and white,
Red as the crimson blood
Of Christ's wide brotherhood,
Blue with the unchanging hope
Of heaven's steadfast sun,
White as the radiant sun
The whole earth shining on!

THE BABE OF BETHLEHEM

By Condé Benoist Pallen

O CRUEL manger, how bleak, how bleak!
  For the limbs of the Babe, my God;
Soft little limbs on the cold, cold straw;
  Weep, O eyes, for thy God!

Bitter ye winds in the frosty night
  Upon the Babe, my God,
Piercing the torn and broken thatch;
  Lament, O heart, for thy God!

Bare is the floor, how bare, how bare
  For the Babe's sweet mother, my God;
Only a stable for mother and Babe;
  How cruel thy world, my God!

Cast out, cast out, by his brother men
  Unknown the Babe, my God;
The ox and the ass alone are there;
  Soften, O heart, for thy God!

Dear little arms and sweet little hands,
  That stretch for thy mother, my God;
Soft baby eyes to the mother's eyes;
  Melt, O heart, for thy God!

Waxen touches on mother's heart,
  Fingers of the Babe, my God;
Dear baby lips to her virgin breast,
  The virgin mother of God.

The shepherds have come from the hills to adore
  The Babe in the manger, my God;
Mary and Joseph welcome them there;
  Worship, O soul, thy God!

But I alone may not come near
  The Babe in the manger, my God;
Weep for thy sins, O heart, and plead
  With Mary the mother of God.

May I not come, oh, just to the door,
  To see the Babe, my God;
There will I stop and kneel and adore,
  And weep for my sins, O God!

But Mary smiles, and rising up,
  In her arms the Babe, my God,
She comes to the door and bends her down,
  With the Babe in her arms, my God!

Her sinless arms in my sinful arms
  Place the Babe, my God;
"He has come to take thy sins away;"
  Break, O heart, for thy God!

THE TOYS

By Coventry Patmore

My little son, who look'd from thoughtful eyes
And mov'd and spoke in quiet grown-up wise,
Having my law the seventh time disobey'd,
I struck him, and dismiss'd
With hard words and unkiss'd.

THE TOYS

His Mother, who was patient, being dead.
Then fearing lest his grief should hinder him sleep
I visited his bed,
But found him slumbering deep,
With darken'd eyelids, and their lashes yet
From his late sobbing wet.
And I, with moan,
Kissing away his tears, left others of my own;
For, on a table drawn beside his head,
He had put, within his reach,
A box of counters and a red-vein'd stone,
A piece of glass abraded by the beach,
And six or seven shells,
A bottle with bluebells
And two French copper coins, ranged there with careful art,
To comfort his sad heart.
So when that night I pray'd
To God, I wept, and said:
Ah, when at last we lie with trancéd breath,
Not vexing Thee in death,
And Thou rememberest of what toys
We made our joys,
How weakly understood
Thy great commanded good,
Then, fatherly not less
Than I whom Thou hast moulded from the clay,
Thou'lt leave Thy wrath, and say,
"I will be sorry for their childishness."

"IF I WERE DEAD"

By Coventry Patmore

"IF I were dead, you'd some time say, Poor Child!"
The dear lips quiver'd as they spake,
And the tears break
From eyes, which, not to grieve me, brightly smiled.
Poor Child, poor Child!
I seem to hear your laugh, your talk, your song.
It is not true that Love will do no wrong.
Poor Child!
And did you think, when you so cried and smiled,
How I, in lonely nights, should lie awake,
And of those words your full avengers make?
Poor Child, poor Child!
And now, unless it be
That sweet amends thrice told are come to thee,
O God, have Thou *no* mercy upon me!
Poor Child!

DEPARTURE

By Coventry Patmore

IT was not like your great and gracious ways!
Do you, that have nought other to lament,
Never, my Love, repent
Of how, that July afternoon,
You went,
With sudden, unintelligible phrase,
And frightened eye,
Upon your journey of so many days

DEPARTURE

Without a single kiss, or a good-bye?
I knew, indeed, that you were parting soon;
And so we sate, within the low sun's rays,
You whispering to me, for your voice was weak,
Your harrowing praise.
Well, it was well
To hear you such things speak,
And I could tell
What made your eyes a growing gloom of love,
As a warm South-wind sombres a March grove.
And it was like your great and gracious ways
To turn your talk on daily things, my Dear,
Lifting the luminous, pathetic lash
To let the laughter flash,
Whilst I drew near,
Because you spoke so low that I could scarcely hear.
But all at once to leave me at the last,
More at the wonder than the loss aghast,
With huddled, unintelligible phrase,
And frighten'd eye,
And go your journey of all days
With not one kiss, or a good-bye,
And the only loveless look the look with which you passed;
'Twas all unlike your great and gracious ways.

REGINA CŒLI

By Coventry Patmore

Say, did his sisters wonder what could Joseph see
In a mild, silent little Maid like thee?
And was it awful, in that narrow house,
With God for Babe and Spouse?
Nay, like thy simple, female sort, each one
Apt to find Him in Husband and in Son,
Nothing to thee came strange in this.
Thy wonder was but wondrous bliss:
Wondrous, for, though
True Virgin lives not but does know,
(Howbeit none ever yet confess'd,)
That God lies really in her breast,
Of thine He made His special nest!
And so
All mothers worship little feet,
And kiss the very ground they've trod;
But, ah, thy little Baby sweet
Who was indeed thy God!

IDEAL

P. H. Pearse
(Translated from the Irish by Thomas MacDonogh)

Naked I saw thee,
 O beauty of beauty!
And I blinded my eyes
 For fear I should flinch.

I heard thy music,
   O sweetness of sweetness!
And I shut my ears
   For fear I should fail.

I kissed thy lips,
   O sweetness of sweetness!
And I hardened my heart
   For fear of my ruin.

I blinded my eyes,
   And my ears I shut,
I hardened my heart
   And my love I quenched.

I turned my back
   On the dream I had shaped,
And to this road before me
   My face I turned.

I set my face
   To the road here before me,
To the work that I see,
   To the death that I shall meet.

MUSIC

By Charles Phillips

There is a hunger in my heart to-night,
   A longing in my soul, to hear
The voice of heaven o'er the noise of earth
   That doth assail mine ear.

For we are exiled children of the skies,
   Lone and lost wanderers from home . . .
The stars come out like lamps in windows lit
   Far, far from where we roam;

Like candles lit to show the long late way,
   Dear kindly beacons sure and bright;
But O, the heavy journeying, and O
   The silence of the night!—

The dark and vasty silences that lie
   Between the going and the goal!
Will not God reach a friendly hand to lift
   And land my weary soul?

Will not God speak a friendly word to me
   Above the tumult and the din
Of earthly things—one little word to hush
   The voice of care and sin? . . .

He speaks! He answers my poor faltering prayer!
   He opens heaven's lattice wide;
He bids me bathe my brow in heavenly airs
   Like to a flowing tide!

He calls; He gives unto my famished soul,
   Unto my eager heart, its meed:
He breathes upon me with the breath of song,
   And O, my soul is freed,

And I am lifted up and up, and held
   A little while—a child, to see
The beauties of my Father's house, which shall
   No more be shut from me!

I SEE HIS BLOOD UPON THE ROSE

By Joseph Mary Plunkett

I SEE His blood upon the rose
   And in the stars the glory of His eyes,
His Body gleams amid eternal snows,
   His tears fall from the skies.

I see His face in every flower;
   The thunder and the singing of the birds
Are but His voice—and carven by His power
   Rocks are His written words.

All pathways by His feet are worn,
   His strong heart stirs the ever-beating sea,
His crown of thorns is twined with every thorn,
   His cross is every tree.

THE STARS SANG IN GOD'S GARDEN

By Joseph Mary Plunkett

THE stars sang in God's garden;
The stars are the birds of God;
The night-time is God's harvest,
Its fruits are the words of God.

God ploughed His fields at morning,
God sowed His seed at noon,
God reaped and gathered in His corn
With the rising of the moon.

The sun rose up at midnight,
The sun rose red as blood,
It showed the Reaper, the dead Christ,
Upon His cross of wood.

For many live that one may die,
And one must die that many live—
The stars are silent in the sky
Lest my poor songs be fugitive.

"IS IT NOTHING TO YOU?"

By May Probyn

We were playing on the green together,
  My sweetheart and I—
Oh, so heedless in the gay June weather,
  When the word went forth that we must die.
Oh, so merrily the balls of amber
  And of ivory tossed we to the sky,
While the word went forth in the King's chamber,
  That we both must die.

Oh, so idly, straying through the pleasaunce,
  Plucked we here and there
Fruit and bud, while in the royal presence
  The King's son was casting from his hair
Glory of the wreathen gold that crowned it,
  And, ungirding all his garment fair,
Flinging by the jewelled clasp that bound it,
  With his feet made bare.

Down the myrtled stairway of the palace,
  Ashes on his head,
Came he, through the rose and citron alleys,
  In the rough sark of sackcloth habited,
And in a hempen halter—oh! we jested,
  Lightly, and we laughed as he was led
To the torture, while the bloom we breasted
  Where the grapes grew red.

Oh, so sweet the birds, when he was dying,
  Piped to her and me—
Is no room this glad June day for sighing—
  He is dead, and she and I go free!
When the sun shall set on all our pleasure
  We will mourn him—What, so you decree
We are heartless?—Nay, but in what measure
  Do you more than we?

THE BEES OF MYDDLETON MANOR
17th Century

By May Probyn

Buzzing, buzzing, buzzing, my golden-belted bees:
My little son was seven years old—the mint-flower
    touched his knees;
  Yellow were his curly locks;
  Yellow were his stocking-clocks;
His plaything of a sword had a diamond in its hilt;
  Where the garden beds lay sunny,
  And the bees were making honey,
"For God and the king—to arms! to arms!" the day long
    would he lilt.

THE BEES OF MYDDLETON MANOR

Smock'd in lace and flowered brocade, my pretty son of seven
Wept sore because the kitten died, and left the charge uneven.
  "I head one battalion, mother—
  Kitty," sobbed he, "led the other!
  And when we reach'd the bee-hive bench
  We used to halt and storm the trench:
  If we could plant our standard here,
  With all the bees a-buzzing near,
  And fly the colors safe from sting,
  The town was taken for the king!"
Flirting flitting over the thyme, by bees with yellow band—
My little son of seven came close, and clipp'd me by the hand;
  A wreath of mourning cloth was wound
  His small left arm and sword-hilt round,
And on the thatch of every hive a whisp of black was bound.
"Sweet mother, we must tell the bees, or they will swarm away:
Ye little bees!" he called, "draw nigh, and hark to what I say,
And make us golden honey still for our white wheaten bread,
  Though never more
  We rush on war
  With Kitty at our head:
    Who'll give the toast
    When swords are cross'd,
  Now Kitty lieth dead?"

Buzzing, buzzing, buzzing, my bees of yellow girth!
My son of seven changed his mood, and clasp'd me in
his mirth.
"Sweet mother, when I grow a man and fall on battle-
field,"
He cried, and down in the daisied grass upon one knee
he kneel'd,
"I charge thee, come and tell the bees how I for the
king lie dead;
And thou shalt never lack fine honey for thy wheaten
bread!"

. . . .

Flitting, flitting, flitting, my busy bees, alas!
No footsteps of my soldier son came clinking through
the grass.
  Thrice he kiss'd me for farewell;
  And far on the stone his shadow fell;
He buckled spurs and sword-belt on, as the sun began
to stoop,
Set foot in stirrup, and sprang to horse, and rode to
join his troop.
  To the west he rode, where the winds were at play,
  And Monmouth's army mustering lay;
  Where Bridgewater flew her banner high,
  And gave up her keys, when the Duke came by;
  And the maids of Taunton paid him court
  With colors their own white hands had wrought;
  And red as a field, where blood doth run,
  Sedgemoor blazed in the setting sun.

Broider'd sash and clasp of gold, my soldier son, alas!
The mint was all in flower, and the clover in the grass:
    "With every bed

In bloom," I said,
"What further lack the bees,
That they buzz so loud,
Like a restless cloud,
Among the orchard trees?"
No voice in the air, from Sedgemoor field,
Moan'd out how Grey and the horse had reel'd;
Met me no ghost, with haunting eyes,
That westward pointed 'mid its sighs,
And pull'd apart a bloody vest,
And show'd the sword-gash in his breast.

Empty hives, and flitting bees, and sunny morning hours;
I snipp'd the blossom'd lavender, and the pinks, and the gillyflowers;
No petal trembled in my hold—
I saw not the dead stretched stark and cold
On the trampled turf at the shepherd's door,
In the cloak and the doublet Monmouth wore,
With Monmouth's scarf and headgear on,
And the eyes, not clos'd, of my soldier son;
I knew not how, ere the cocks did crow, the fight was fought in the dark,
With naught for guide but the enemy's guns, when the flint flash'd out a spark,
Till, routed at first sound of fire, the cavalry broke and fled,
And the hoofs struck dumb, where they spurn'd the slain, and the meadow stream ran red;
I saw not the handful of horsemen spur through the dusk, and out of sight,
My soldier son at the Duke's left hand, and Grey that rode on his right.

Buzzing, buzzing, buzzing, my honey-making bees,
They left the musk, and the marigolds and the scented
 faint sweet peas;
They gather'd in a darkening cloud, and sway'd, and
 rose to fly;
A blackness on the summer blue, they swept across the
 sky.
Gaunt and ghastly with gaping wounds—(my soldier
 son, alas!)
Footsore and faint, the messenger came halting through
 the grass.
The wind went by and shook the leaves—the mint-stalk
 shed its flower—
And I miss'd the murmuring round the hives, and my
 boding heart beat slower.

  His soul we cheer'd with meat and wine;
  With woman's craft and balsam fine
  We bathed his hurts, and bound them soft,
  While west the wind played through the croft,
  And the low sun dyed the pinks blood red,
  And, straying near the mint-flower shed,
  A wild bee wantoned o'er the bed.

He told how my son, at the shepherd's door, kept watch
 in Monmouth's clothes,
While Monmouth donned the shepherd's frock, in hope
 to cheat his foes.
  A couple of troopers spied him stand,
  And bade him yield to the king's command:
  "Surrender, thou rebel as good as dead,
  A price is set on thy traitor head!"
  My soldier son, with secret smile,
  Held both at bay for a little while,

THE BEES OF MYDDLETON MANOR

Dealt them such death blow as he fell,
Neither was left the tale to tell;
With dying eyes that asked no grace,
They stared on him for a minute's space,
And felt that it was not Monmouth's face.
Crimsoned through was Monmouth's cloak, when the soldier dropped at their side—
"Those knaves will carry no word," he said, and he smiled in his pain, and died.
"Two days," told the messenger, "did we lie
Hid in the fields of peas and rye,
Hid in the ditch of brake and sedge,
With the enemy's scouts down every hedge,
Till Grey was seized, and Monmouth seized, that under the fern did crouch,
Starved and haggard, and all unshaved, with a few raw peas in his pouch."

. . . .

No music soundeth in my ears, but a passing bell that tolls
For gallant lords with head on block—sweet Heaven receive their souls!
And a mound, unnamed, in Sedgemoor grass,
That laps my soldier son, alas!
The bloom is shed—
The bees are fled—
Middleton luck it's done and dead.

A LEGEND

By Adelaide Anne Procter

I

The Monk was preaching: strong his earnest word,
  From the abundance of his heart he spoke,
And the flame spread,—in every soul that heard
  Sorrow and love and good resolve awoke:—
The poor lay Brother, ignorant and old,
  Thanked God that he had heard such words of gold

II

"Still let the glory, Lord, be thine alone,"—
  So prayed the Monk, his heart absorbed in praise:
"Thine be the glory: if my hands have sown
  The harvest ripened in Thy mercy's rays,
It was Thy blessing, Lord, that made my word
  Bring light and love to every soul that heard.

III

"O Lord, I thank Thee that my feeble strength
  Has been so blest; that sinful hearts and cold
Were melted at my pleading,—knew at length
  How sweet Thy service and how safe Thy fold:
While souls that loved Thee saw before them rise
  Still holier heights of loving sacrifice."

IV

So prayed the Monk: when suddenly he heard
  An Angel speaking thus: "Know, O my Son,
The words had all been vain. but hearts were stirred.

And saints were edified, and sinners won,
By his, the poor lay Brother's humble aid
Who sat upon the pulpit stair and prayed."

THE SACRED HEART

By Adelaide Anne Procter

What wouldst thou have, O soul,
  Thou weary soul?
Lo! I have sought for rest
On the Earth's heaving breast,
  From pole to pole.
Sleep—I have been with her,
  But she gave dreams;
Death—nay, the rest he gives
  Rest only seems.
Fair nature knows it not—
  The grass is growing;
The blue air knows it not—
  The winds are blowing:
Not in the changing sky,
  The stormy sea,
Yet somewhere in God's wide world
  Rest there must be.
Within thy Saviour's Heart
  Place all thy care,
And learn, O weary soul,
  Thy Rest is there.

What wouldst thou, trembling soul?
  Strength for the strife,—

Strength for this fiery war
  That we call Life.
Fears gather thickly round;
  Shadowy foes,
Like unto armed men,
  Around me close.
What am I, frail and poor,
  When griefs arise?
No help from the weak earth,
  Or the cold skies.
Lo! I can find no guards,
  No weapons borrow;
Shrinking, alone I stand,
  With mighty sorrow.
Courage, thou trembling soul,
  Grief thou must bear,
Yet thou canst find a strength
  Will match despair;
Within thy Saviour's Heart—
  Seek for it there.

What wouldst thou have, sad soul
  Oppressed with grief?—
Comfort: I seek in vain,
  Nor find relief.
Nature, all pitiless,
  Smiles on my pain;
I ask my fellow-men,
  They give disdain.
I asked the babbling streams,
  But they flowed on;
I asked the wise and good,
  But they gave none.

THE SACRED HEART

Though I have asked the stars,
  Coldly they shine.
They are too bright to know
  Grief such as mine.
I asked for comfort still,
  And I found tears,
And I have sought in vain
  Long, weary years.
Listen, thou mournful soul,
   Thy pain shall cease;
Deep in His sacred Heart
  Dwells joy and peace.

Yes, in that Heart divine
  The Angels bright
Find, through eternal years,
  Still new delight.
From thence his constancy
  The martyr drew,
And there the virgin band
  Their refuge knew.
There, racked by pain without,
  And dread within,
How many souls have found
  Heaven's bliss begin.
Then leave thy vain attempts
  To seek for peace;
The world can never give
  One soul release;
But in thy Saviour's Heart
  Securely dwell,
No pain can harm thee, hid
  In that sweet cell.

Then fly, O coward soul,
  Delay no more:
What words can speak the joy
  For thee in store?
What smiles of earth can tell
  Of peace like thine?
Silence and tears are best
  For things divine.

THE ANNUNCIATION

By Adelaide Anne Procter

How pure, and frail, and white
  The snowdrops shine!
Gather a garland bright
  For Mary's shrine.

For, born of winter snows,
  These fragile flowers
Are gifts to our fair Queen
  From Spring's first hours.

For on this blessèd day
  She knelt at prayer;
When, lo! before her shone
  An Angel fair.

"Hail, Mary!" thus he cried,
  With reverent fear:
She, with sweet wondering eyes,
  Marvelled to hear.

THE ANNUNCIATION

Be still, ye clouds of Heaven!
  Be silent, Earth!
And hear an Angel tell
  Of Jesus' birth,

While she, whom Gabriel hails
  As full of grace,
Listens with humble faith
  In her sweet face.

Be stilll,—Pride, War, and Pomp,
  Vain Hopes, vain Fears,
For now an Angel speaks,
  And Mary hears.

"Hail, Mary!" lo, it rings
  Through ages on;
"Hail Mary!" it shall sound,
  Till Time is done

"Hail, Mary!" infant lips
  Lisp it to-day;
"Hail, Mary!" with faint smile
  The dying say.

"Hail, Mary!" many a heart
  Broken with grief,
In that angelic prayer
  Has found relief.

And many a half-lost soul,
  When turned at bay,
With those triumphant words
  Has won the day.

"Hail, Mary, Queen of Heaven!
　　Let us repeat,
And place our snowdrop wreath
　　Here at her feet.

OUR DAILY BREAD

By Adelaide Anne Procter

Give us our daily Bread,
　　O God, the bread of strength!
For we have learnt to know
　　How weak we are at length.
As children we are weak,
　　As children must be fed;—
Give us Thy Grace, O Lord,
　　To be our daily Bread.

Give us our daily Bread:—
　　The bitter bread of grief.
We sought earth's poisoned feasts
　　For pleasure and relief;
We sought her deadly fruits,
　　But now, O God, instead,
We ask thy healing grief
　　To be our daily Bread.

Give us our daily Bread
　　To cheer our fainting soul;
The feast of comfort, Lord,
　　And peace, to make us whole:

For we are sick of tears,
    The useless tears we shed;—
Now give us comfort, Lord,
    To be our daily Bread.

Give us our daily Bread,
    The Bread of Angels, Lord,
For us, so many times,
    Broken, betrayed, adored:
His Body and His Blood;—
    The feast that Jesus spread:
Give Him—our life, our all—
    To be our daily Bread!

MY MARYLAND

By James Ryder Randall

The despot's heel is on thy shore,
    Maryland!
His torch is at thy temple door,
    Maryland!
Avenge the patriotic gore
That flecked the streets of Baltimore,
And be the battle-queen of yore,
    Maryland, my Maryland!

Hark to an exiled son's appeal,
    Maryland!
My Mother State, to thee I kneel,
    Maryland!
For life and death, for woe and weal,

Thy peerless chivalry reveal,
And gird thy beauteous limbs with steel,
    Maryland, my Maryland!

Thou wilt not cower in the dust,
    Maryland!
Thy beaming sword shall never rust,
    Maryland!
Remember Carroll's sacred trust,
Remember Howard's warlike thrust,
And all thy slumberers with the just,
    Maryland, my Maryland!

Come! 'tis the red dawn of the day,
    Maryland!
Come with thy panoplied array,
    Maryland!
With Ringgold's spirit for the fray,
With Watson's blood at Monterey,
With fearless Lowe and dashing May,
    Maryland, my Maryland!

Dear Mother, burst the tyrant's chain,
    Maryland!
Virginia should not call in vain,
    Maryland!
She meets her sisters on the plain,—
"*Sic semper!*" 't is the proud refrain
That baffles minions back amain,
    Maryland!
Arise in majesty again,
    Maryland, my Maryland!

MY MARYLAND

Come! for thy shield is bright and strong,
    Maryland!
Come! for thy dalliance does thee wrong,
    Maryland!
Come to thine own heroic throng
Stalking with Liberty along,
And chant thy dauntless slogan-song,
    Maryland, my Maryland!

I see the blush upon thy cheek,
    Maryland!
For thou wast ever bravely meek,
    Maryland!
But lo! there surges forth a shriek,
From hill to hill, from creek to creek,
Potomac calls to Chesapeake,
    Maryland, my Maryland!

Thou wilt not yield the Vandal toll,
    Maryland!
Thou wilt not crook to his control,
    Maryland!
Better the fire upon thee roll,
Better the shot, the blade, the bowl,
Than crucifixion of the soul,
    Maryland, my Maryland!

I hear the distant thunder hum,
    Maryland!
The Old Line's bugle, fife and drum,
    Maryland!
She is not dead, nor deaf, nor dumb;
Huzza! she spurns the Northern scum!
She breathes! She burns! She'll come! She'll come!
    Maryland, my Maryland!

MAGDALEN

By James Ryder Randall

The Hebrew girl, with flaming brow,
  The banner-blush of shame,
Sinks at the sinless Saviour's Knees
  And dares to breathe His name.
From the full fountain of her eyes
  The lava-globes are roll'd—
They wash His feet; she spurns them off
  With her ringlet-scarf of gold.

The Meek One feels the eloquence
  Of agonizing prayer,
The burning tears, the suppliant face,
  The penitential hair;
And when, to crown her brimming woe,
  The ointment box is riven—
"Rise, daughter, rise! Much hast thou **loved**,
  Be all thy sins forgiven!"

Dear God! The prayer of good and pure,
  The canticles of light,
Enrobe Thy throne with gorgeous skies,
  As incense in Thy sight;
May the shivered vase of Magdalen
  Soothe many an outcast's smart,
Teaching what fragrant pleas may spring
  From out a *broken heart!*

WHY THE ROBIN'S BREAST WAS RED

By James Ryder Randall

The Saviour, bowed beneath His Cross, climbed up the dreary hill,
And from the agonizing wreath ran many a crimson rill;
The cruel Roman thrust Him on with unrelenting hand,
Till, staggering slowly 'mid the crowd, He fell upon the sand.

A little bird that warbled near, that memorable day,
Flitted around and strove to wrench one single thorn away;
The cruel spike impaled his breast,—and thus 'tis sweetly said,
The robin has his silver vest incarnadined with red.

Ah, Jesu! Jesu! Son of man! my dolor and my sighs
Reveal the lesson taught by this winged Ishmael of the skies.
I, in the palace of delight or cavern of despair,
Have plucked no thorns from Thy dear brow, but planted thousands there!

LE REPOS EN EGYPTE: THE SPHINX

By Agnes Repplier

All day I watch the stretch of burning sand;
   All night I brood beneath the golden stars;
Amid the silence of a desolate land,
   No touch of bitterness my reverie mars.

Built by the proudest of a kingly line,
  Over my head the centuries fly fast;
The secrets of the mighty dead are mine;
  I hold the key of a forgotten past.
Yet, ever hushed into a rapturous dream,
  I see again that night. A halo mild
Shone from the liquid moon. Beneath her beam
  Traveled a tired young Mother and the Child.
Within mine arms she slumbered, and alone
  I watched the Infant. At my feet her guide
Lay stretched o'er-wearied. On my breast of stone
  Rested the Crucified.

ANDROMEDA

By James Jeffrey Roche

They chained her fair young body to the cold and cruel stone;
The beast begot of sea and slime had marked her for his own;
The callous world beheld the wrong, and left her there alone.
Base caitiffs who belied her, false kinsmen who denied her,
        Ye left her there alone!

My Beautiful, they left thee in thy peril and thy pain;
The night that hath no morrow was brooding on the main:
But, lo! a light is breaking of hope for thee again;
'T is Perseus's sword a-flaming, thy dawn of day proclaiming
        Across the western main.
O Ireland! O my country! he comes to break thy chain!

NATURE THE FALSE GODDESS

By James Jeffrey Roche

The vilest work of vilest man,
   The cup that drugs, the sword that slays,
The purchased kiss of courtesan,
   The lying tongue of blame or praise,

The cobra's fang, the tiger's tongue,
   The python's murderous embrace—
The wrath of any living thing
   A man may fear but bravely face.

But thou, cold Mother, knowest naught
   Of love, of hate, or joy, or woe;
Thy bounties come to man unsought,
   Thy curses fall on friend and foe.

Thou bearest balm upon thy breath,
   Or sowest poison in the air;
And if man reapeth life or death,
   Thou dost not know, thou dost not care.

Thou art God's instrument of fate,
   Obedient, mighty, soulless, blind,
No demon to propitiate,
   No deity in love enshrined.

Let him who turns from God away
   To Bel or Moloch bend the knee;
Defile his soul to wood or clay,
   Or thrill with Voodoo's ecstasy.

Seek any fetich undivine,
  Be any superstition's thrall,
From Heaven or Hell will come a sign;
  But thou alone art deaf to all.

THREE DOVES

By James Jeffrey Roche

Seaward, at morn, my doves flew free;
At eve they circled back to me.
The first was Faith; the second, Hope;
The third, the whitest, Charity.

Above the plunging surges play
Dream-like they hovered, day by day.
At last they turned, and bore to me
Green signs of peace thro' nightfall gray,

No shore forlorn, no loveliest land
Their gentle eye had left unscanned,
'Mid hues of twilight-heliotrope
Or daybreak fires by heaven-breath fanned.

Quick visions of celestial grace,—
Hither they waft, from earth's broad space,
Kind thoughts for all humanity,
They shine with radiance from God's face.

Ah, since my heart they choose for home,
Why loose them,—forth again to roam?
Yet look; they rise with loftier scope
They wheel in flight toward Heaven's pure dome

Fly, messengers that find no rest
Save in such toil as makes man blest!
Your home is God's immensity;
We hold you but at His behest.

THE WAY OF THE WORLD

By James Jeffrey Roche

The hands of the King are soft and fair
   They never knew labor's strain
The hands of the Robber redly wear
   The bloody brand of Cain.
But the hands of the Man are hard and scarred
   With the scars of toil and pain.

The slaves of Pilate have washed his hands
   As white as a kings might be.
Barrabas with wrists unfettered stands
   For the world has made him free.
But Thy palms toil-worn by nails are torn,
   O Christ, on Calvary.

AVE MARIA

By John Jerome Rooney

Lady, thy soldier I would be,
   This day I choose thy shield,
And go, thrice-armored for the fight,
   Forth to the world's wide field.

There I shall meet the dark allies,
  The Flesh, the Fiend, the World,
And fiercely shall their darts of fire
  Upon my heart be hurled.

But I will raise my buckler strong
  Betwixt me and the foe,
And, with the spirit's flaming sword,
  Shall give them blow for blow.

Lady, thy sailor I would be,
  This day I sign my name
To sail the high seas of the earth
  For glory of thy fame.

The tempest may besiege my bark,
  The pirate lie in wait:
The perils of the monstrous deep
  May tempt o'erwhelming fate:

Yet, wheresoe'er my ship may steer
  Upon the waters wide,
Thy name shall be my compass sure,
  Thy star my midnight guide.

Thy poet, Lady, I would be
  To sing thy peerless praise;
Thy loyal bard, I'd bring to thee
  Heart-music from all lays.

Soft melody, outpoured in June
  By God's dear feathered throng,
Would mingle with the organ's roll
  To glorify my song;

And Dante's voice and Petrarch's strain
　　And Milton's matchless line
Would lend to my poor minstrel note
　　A harmony divine.

Lady, I choose to be thy son;
　　For Mother thee I choose;
O, for thy sweet and holy Child,
　　Do not my claim refuse!

Alone and motherless am I:
　　Tho' strong, I long for rest—
The thunder of the world's applause
　　Is not a mother's breast.

Ave Maria! Shield us all.
　　Thy sons we choose to be.
Mother of grace, we raise our hearts,
　　Our hearts, our love to thee!

REVELATION

"And I saw a new heaven and a new earth: for the first heaven and the first earth were passed away."—Revelation XXI:1

By John Jerome Rooney

The Lord God said to His angel: "Let the old things pass away.
They have heaped the earth with slaughter their sin obscures the day.
Roll up the night on a curtain: let the stars fade one by one:

Out of the face of the heavens my anger shall blot the sun.
For the man I made and breathed on, filled with my breath of breath,
Hath sown the seas with hatred, his skies are dark with death.
The babe is slain at the bosom, the babe who beholds my face;
A welter of woe he leaves it,—the dream of my love and grace.

"Love was the dower I gave him, love the light of his days,
Love the core of his being, love, and the upward gaze.
Hate is the meat he feeds on, hate is his daily bread:
His drink is the blood of his brother, whom Cain hath stricken dead.
I said to the man in the Garden: 'Where is thy brother, Cain?'
'Am I my brother's keeper?' now comes the answer again."
The Lord God said to His angel: "This Thing is accursed and a lie:
It hath sinned from the Law I gave it, and surely it shall die."

"The Beasts of the field are patient, the birds rejoice in song,—
But what is this Thing of blood-lust, and where does it belong?
Lo, I shall establish a judgment: Let the old things pass away:

They have heaped the fields with slaughter: their sin
defiles the day.
They have laid on the weak sore burdens, on the just,
their whips and ban:
For a handful of crimsoned silver they have kissed the
Son of Man.
Roll back the scroll of the heavens; from out of the
womb of birth
Come forth new heavens untainted; come forth, renewed, the Earth!"

MARQUETTE ON THE SHORES OF THE MISSISSIPPI

On seeing the original manuscript map of the Mississippi River
by its discoverer, Father Marquette

By John Jerome Rooney

Here, in the midnight of the solemn wood,
   He heard a roar as of a mighty wind,—
   The onward rush of waters unconfined
Trampling in legions thro' the solitude.
Then lo! before him swept the conquering flood,
   Free as the freedom of the truth-strong mind
   Which hills of Doubt could neither hide nor bind,
Which, all in vain, the valley mounds withstood!

With glowing eye he saw the prancing tide
   With yellow mane rush onward thro' the night
   Into the vastness he had never trod:
Nor dreamt of conquest of that kingdom wide
   As down the flood his spirit took its flight
     Seeking the long-lost children of his God!

THE EMPIRE BUILDER

(On the death of a Catholic gentleman)

BY JOHN JEROME ROONEY

I

This is the song of the Empire Builder,
  Who out of the ends of the earth,
Thro' travail of war and of carnage
  Brings strange, new realms to birth.

This is the boast of the Empire Builder:
  Give heed to the deeds of his hands
And scorn thou not the glory he hath
  In his gold and his wasted lands.

He hath counted his neighbors' cattle
  With the cold, gray eye of greed:
He hath marked for his own the fields of wheat
  Where he never had sown the seed:

The vine-clad cot by the hillside,
  Where the farmer's children play,—
"This shall fit in my plan," he said;
  "What use for such as they?"

And so, in the dusk of evening,
  He brought his arméd men,
And where had shone the clustering grapes
  There stretched a waste again.

Homeless, the children wandered
  Thro' the fields their father won:

THE EMPIRE BUILDER

No more shall they feel his clasp and kiss—
   Aye, never beneath the sun.

Vex, vex not the Empire Builder,
   Nor babble of Mercy's shield;
Hath he not his vaster issue—
   The linking of field to field?

Hath he not noted the boundary
   That lies 'twixt "mine and thine"?
Hath he not said, " 'Twere better for thee
   If thine henceforth be mine"?

And so doth the Empire Builder,
   From out of the ends of the earth,
Thro' travail of war and of carnage
   Bring strange, new realms to birth—

Realms builded on broken hearthstones,
   The triumph of Rapine's hour—
That one may boast in the halls of Fame
   And sit in the seats of Power!

II

This is the song of the Empire Builder,
   Who built not of wasted lands,
But who builded a kingdom of golden deeds
   And of things not made by hands!

The fields of the spirit were his to roam,
   The paths where the love-flowers grew:
He felt the breath of the spirits' spring
   In every wind that blew:

It came not laden with dying groans
  And homeless orphans' cries:
It blew from the mountains of the Lord
  And the fields of Paradise.

This is the boast of the Empire Builder
  Who built not of mouldering clay:
That the kingdom He built, not made by hands,
  Shall never pass away!

The mind cannot measure its boundaries,
  All Space is its outer gate:
It is broader than ever a man conceived
  And more durable than Fate.

This is the Empire our brother built,
  In His little hour of Earth,
Thro' the spirit's travail of righteous deeds
  And the spirit's glad rebirth.

He had silenced the boast of the Empire Builder,
  With his gold and wasted lands,
By his deathless kingdom of golden deeds
  And of things not made by hands.

This is the kingdom our brother built:
  It is good: it hath sufficed;—
For who can measure the glory he keeps
  With our Elder Brother, Christ?

THE MEN BEHIND THE GUNS

By John Jerome Rooney

A cheer and salute for the Admiral, and here's to the Captain bold,
And never forget the Commodore's debt when the deeds of might are told!
They stand to the deck through the battle's wreck when the great shells roar and screech—
And never they fear when the foe is near to practice what they preach:
But off with your hat and three times three for Columbia's true-blue sons,
The men below who batter the foe—the men behind the guns!

Oh, light and merry of heart are they when they swing into port once more,
When, with more than enough of the "green-backed stuff," they start for their leave-o'-shore;
And you'd think, perhaps, that the blue-bloused chaps who loll along the street
Are a tender bit, with salt on it, for some fierce "mustache" to eat—
Some warrior bold, with straps of gold, who dazzles and fairly stuns
The modest worth of the sailor boys—the lads who serve the guns.

But say not a word till the shot is heard that tells the fight is on,
Till the long, deep roar grows more and more from the ships of "Yank" and "Don,"

Till over the deep the tempests sweep of fire and bursting shell,
And the very air is a mad Despair in the throes of a living hell;
Then down, deep down, in the mighty ship, unseen by the midday suns,
You'll find the chaps who are giving the raps—the men behind the guns!

Oh, well they know the cyclones blow that they loose from their cloud of death,
And they know is heard the thunder-word their fierce ten-incher saith!
The steel decks rock with the lightning shock, and shake with the great recoil,
And the sea grows red with the blood of the dead and reaches for his spoil—
But not till the foe has gone below or turns his prow and runs
Shall the voice of peace bring sweet release to the men behind the guns!

A THOUGHT FROM CARDINAL NEWMAN*
By Matthew Russell, S. J.

The world shines bright for inexperienced eyes,
  And death seems distant to the gay and strong,
  And in the youthful heart proud fancies throng,

---

*In the last of his "Discourses to Mixed Congregations," Dr. Newman calls the Blessed Virgin the Mother of Emanuel, and says: "It is the boast of the Catholic religion that it has the gift of making the young heart chaste; and why is this, but that it gives us Jesus for our food and Mary for our nursing Mother?"

And only present good can nature prize.
How then shall youth o'er these low vapours rise,
  And climb the upward path so steep and long?
  And how, amid earth's sights and sounds of wrong,
Walk with pure heart and face raised to the skies?

By gazing on the Infinitely Good,
  Whose love must quell, or hallow every other—
By living in the shadow of the Rood,
  For He that hangs there is our Elder Brother,
Who dying gave to us Himself as food,
  And His own Mother as our nursing Mother.

THE CONQUERED BANNER

By Abram J. Ryan

Furl that Banner, for 'tis weary;
Round its staff 'tis drooping dreary:
  Furl it, fold it,—it is best;
For there's not a man to wave it,
And there's not a sword to save it,
And there's not one left to lave it
In the blood which heroes gave it,
And its foes now scorn and brave it:
  Furl it, hide it,—let it rest!

Take that Banner down! 'tis tattered;
Broken is its staff and shattered;
And the valiant hosts are scattered,
  Over whom it floated high.
Oh, 'tis hard for us to fold it,
Hard to think there's none to hold it,
  Now must furl it with a sigh!

THE CONQUERED BANNER

Furl that Banner!—furl it sadly!
Once ten thousands hailed it gladly,
And ten thousands wildly, madly,
　Swore it should forever wave;
Swore that foeman's sword should never
Hearts like theirs entwined dissever
Till that flag should float forever
　O'er their freedom or their grave!

Furl it! for the hands that grasped it,
And the hearts that fondly clasped it,
　Cold and dead are lying low;
And that Banner—it is trailing
While around it sounds the wailing
　Of its people in their woe.

For, though conquered, they adore it,—
Love the cold, dead hands that bore it,
Weep for those who fell before it,
Pardon those who trailed and tore it;
And oh, wildly they deplore it.
　Now to furl and fold it so!

Furl that Banner! True, 'tis gory,
Yet 'tis wreathed around with glory,
And 'twill live in song and story
　Though its folds are in the dust!
For its fame on brightest pages,
Penned by poets and by sages,
Shall go sounding down the ages—
　Furl its folds though now we must.

Furl that Banner, softly, slowly!
Treat it gently—it is holy,
　For it droops above the dead.
Touch it not—unfold it never;
Let it droop there, furled forever,—
　For its people's hopes are fled!

A CHILD'S WISH

By Abram J. Ryan

I wish I were the little key
　That locks Love's Captive in,
And lets Him out to go and free
　A sinful heart from sin.

I wish I were the little bell
　That tinkles for the Host,
When God comes down each day to dwell
　With hearts He loves the most.

I wish I were the chalice fair,
　That holds the Blood of Love,
When every gleam lights holy prayer
　Upon its way above.

I wish I were the little flower
　So near the Host's sweet face,
Or like the light that half an hour
　Burns on the shrine of grace.

I wish I were the altar where,
  As on His mother's breast,
Christ nestles, like a child, fore'er
  In Eucharistic rest.

But, oh, my God, I wish the most
  That my poor heart may be
A home all holy for each Host
  That comes in love to me.

THE SWORD OF ROBERT LEE

By Abram J. Ryan

Forth from its scabbard, pure and bright
  Flashed the sword of Lee!
Far in the front of the deadly fight,
High o'er the brave in the cause of Right,
Its stainless sheen, like a beacon bright,
  Led us to Victory.

Out of its scabbard, where, full long,
  It slumbered peacefully,
Roused from its rest by the battle's song,
Shielding the feeble, smiting the strong,
Guarding the right, avenging the wrong,
  Gleamed the sword of Lee.

Forth from its scabbard, high in air
  Beneath Virginia's sky—
And they who saw it gleaming there,
And knew who bore it, knelt to swear
That where that sword led they would dare
  To follow—and to die.

Out of its scabbard! Never hand
  Waved sword from stain as free,
Nor purer sword led braver band,
Nor braver bled for a brighter land,
Nor brighter land had a cause so grand,
  Nor cause a chief like Lee!

Forth from its scabbard! How we prayed
  That sword might victor be;
And when our triumph was delayed,
And many a heart grew sore afraid,
We still hoped on while gleamed the blade
  Of noble Robert Lee.

Forth from its scabbard all in vain
  Bright flashed the sword of Lee;
'Tis shrouded now in its sheath again,
It sleeps the sleep of our noble slain,
Defeated, yet without a stain,
  Proudly and peacefully.

SONG OF THE MYSTIC

By Abram J Ryan

I walk down the Valley of Silence—
  Down the dim voiceless Valley—alone!
And I hear not the fall of a footstep
  Around me, save God's and my own;
And the hush of my heart is as holy
  As hovers where angels have flown!

SONG OF THE MYSTIC

Long ago was I weary of voices
  Whose magic my heart could not win;
Long ago was I weary of noises
  That fretted my soul with their din;
Long ago was I weary of places
  Where I met but the human—and sin.

I walked through the world with the worldly
  I craved what the world never gave;
And I said: "In the world, each Ideal
  That shines like a star on life's wave,
Is wrecked on the shores of the Real,
  And sleeps like a dream in a grave."

And still did I pine for the Perfect,
  And still found the false with the true;
I sought 'mid the human for heaven,
  And caught a mere glimpse of its blue;
And I wept when the clouds of the mortal
  Veiled even that glimpse from my view.

And I toiled on, heart-tired of the Human;
  And I moaned 'mid the mazes of men;
Till I knelt, long ago, at an altar
  And heard a voice call me. Since then
I walk down the Valley of Silence
  That lies far beyond human ken.

Do you ask what I found in the Valley?
  'Tis my trysting-place with the Divine;
And I fell at the feet of the Holy,
  And above me a voice said: "Be mine!"
And there rose from the depths of my spirit
  An echo—"My heart shall be thine."

SONG OF THE MYSTIC

Do you ask how I live in the Valley?
   I weep—and I dream—and I pray.
But my tears are as sweet as the dewdrops
   That fall on the roses in May;
And my prayers, like a perfume from censers,
   Ascendeth to God, night and day.

In the hush of the Valley of Silence,
   I dream all the songs that I sing;
And the music floats down the dim Valley,
   Till each finds a word for a wing,
That to men, like the Dove of the Deluge,
   A message of Peace they may bring.

But far on the deep there are billows
   That never shall break on the beach;
And I have heard songs in the Silence
   That never shall float into speech;
And I have had dreams in the Valley
   Too lofty for language to reach.

And I have seen Thoughts in the Valley—
   Ah, me! how my spirit was stirred!
And they wear holy veils on their faces,
   Their footsteps can scarcely be heard;
They pass through the Valley, like virgins
   Too pure for the touch of a word!

Do you ask me the place of the Valley,
   Ye hearts that are harrowed by Care?
It lieth afar, between mountains,
   And God and His angels are there;
And one is the dark mount of Sorrow,
   And one the bright mountain of Prayer.

MARY, VIRGIN AND MOTHER

By E. Seton

Oh, Virgin Joy of all the world art thou,
  In whose white, fragrant steps the countless throng
  On souls elect doth follow God with song:
Creation's Queen, whose bright and holy brow
The multitude of Saints, like stars, endow
  With changeful splendors, flashing far and strong:
  The Maid unshadow'd by the primal wrong:
God's Lily, chosen in His shrine to bow.

All these thy glories are, and still a grace
  More high, more dread, and yet more sweet and fair
    Doth bind thy royal brows, O Mary blest.
God called thee Mother; yea, His sacred face
  The tender likeness of thine own doth wear.
    And thou art ours—we trust Him for the rest.

THE WIND ON THE HILLS

By Dora Sigerson

Go not to the hills of Erin
  When the night winds are about;
Put up your bar and shutter,
  And so keep the danger out.

For the good-folk whirl within it,
  And they pull by the hand,
And they push you by the shoulder,
  Till you move to their command.

THE WIND ON THE HILLS

And lo! you have forgotten
  What you have known of tears,
And you will not remember
  That the world goes full of years;

A year there is a lifetime,
  And a second but a day;
And an older world will greet you
  Each morn you come away.

Your wife grows old with weeping,
  And your children one by one
Grow grey with nights of watching,
  Before your dance is done.

And it will chance some morning
  You will come home no more;
Your wife sees but a withered leaf
  In the wind about the door.

And your children will inherit
  The unrest of the wind;
They shall seek some face elusive,
  And some land they never find.

When the wind is loud, they sighing
  Go with hearts unsatisfied,
For some joy beyond remembrance,
  For some memory denied.

And all your children's children,
  They cannot sleep or rest,
When the wind is out in Erin
  And the sun is in the West.

BELIEVE AND TAKE HEART

By John Lancaster Spalding

What can console for a dead world?
We tread on dust which once was life;
To nothingness all things are hurled:
What meaning in a hopeless strife?
        Time's awful storm
        Breaks but the form.

Whatever comes, whatever goes,
Still throbs the heart whereby we live;
The primal joys still lighten woes,
And time which steals doth also give.
        Fear not, be brave:
        God can thee save.

The essential truth of life remains,
Its goodness and its beauty too,
Pure love's unutterable gains,
And hope which trills us through and through
        God has not fled,
        Souls are not dead.

Not in most ancient Palestine,
Nor in the lightsome air of Greece,
Were human struggles more divine,
More blessed with guerdon of increase:
        Take thou thy stand
        In the workers' band.

Hast then no faith? Thine is the fault:—
What prophets, heroes, sages, saints,
Have loved, on thee still makes assault,
Thee with immortal things acquaints.
      On life then seize:
      Doubt is disease.

AVE MARIA BELLS

By Charles Warren Stoddard

At dawn, the joyful choir of bells,
  In consecrated citadels,
Flings on the sweet and drowsy air
A brief, melodious call to prayer;
  For Mary, Virgin meek and lowly,
  Conceived of the Spirit Holy,
As the Lord's angel did declare.

At noon, above the fretful street,
  Our souls are lifted to repeat
The prayer, with low and wistful voice:
"According to thy word and choice,
  Though sorrowful and heavy laden,
  So be it done to thy Handmaiden";
Then all the sacred bells rejoice.

At eve with roses in the west,
  The daylight's withering bequest,
Ring, prayerful bells, while blossom bright
The stars, the lilies of the night:
  Of all the songs the years have sung us,
  "The Word made Flesh had dwelt among us,"
Is still our ever-new delight.

STIGMATA

By Charles Warren Stoddard

In the wrath of the lips that assail us,
  In the scorn of the lips that are dumb,
The symbols of sorrow avail us,
  The joy of the people is come.
They parted Thy garments for barter,
  They follow Thy steps with complaint;
Let them know that the pyre of the martyr
  But purges the blood of the saint!

They have crucified Thee for a token,
  For a token Thy flesh crucified
Shall bleed in a heart that is broken
  For love of the wound in Thy side;
In pity for palms that were pleading,
  For feet that were grievously used,
There is blood on the brow that is bleeding
  And torn, as Thy brow that was bruised!
By Thee have we life, breath, and being;
  Thou hast knowledge of us and our kind;
Thou hast pleasure of eyes that are seeing,
And sorrow of eyes that are blind;
By the seal of the mystery shown us—
  The wound that with Thy wounds accord—
O Lord, have mercy upon us!
  Have mercy upon us, O Lord!

THE BELLS OF SAN GABRIEL

BY CHARLES WARREN STODDARD

(The Mission of San Gabriel Archangel, near Los Angeles,
founded in 1771, was, for a time, the most flourishing
mission in California)

THINE was the corn and the wine,
  The blood of the grape that nourished;
The blossom and fruit of the vine
  That was heralded far away.
When the wine and fig-tree flourished,
The promise of peace and of glad increase
  Forever and ever and aye.
What then wert thou, and what art now?
  Answer me, O, I pray!

  And every note of every bell
    Sang Gabriel! rang Gabriel!
  In the tower that is left the tale to tell
    Of Gabriel, the Archangel.

Oil of the olive was thine;
  Flood of the wine-press flowing,
Blood of the Christ was the wine—
  Blood of the Lamb that was slain.
Thy gifts were fat of the kine
  Forever coming and going
Far over the hills, the thousand hills—
  Their lowing a soft refrain.
What then wert thou, and what art now?
  Answer me once again!

And every note of every bell
Sang Gabriel! rang Gabriel!
In the tower that is left the tale to tell
Of Gabriel, the Archangel.

Seed of the corn was thine—
　Body of Him thus broken
And mingled with blood of the vine—
　The bread and the wine of life.
Out of the good sunshine
　They were given to thee as a token—
The body of Him, and the blood of Him,
　When the gifts of God were rife.
What then wert thou, and what art now?
　After the weary strife?

And every note of every bell
Sang Gabriel! rang Gabriel!
In the tower that is left the tale to tell
Of Gabriel the Archangel.

Where are they now, O bells?
　Where are the fruits of the Mission?
Garnered, where no one dwells,
　Shepherd and flock are fled.
O'er the Lord's vineyard swells
　The tide that with fell perdition
Sounded their doom and fashioned their tomb
　And buried them with the dead.
What then wert thou, and what art now?
　The answer is still unsaid.

> And every note of every bell
> Sang Gabriel! rang Gabriel!
> In the tower that is left the tale to tell
> Of Gabriel, the Archangel.

Where are they now, O tower!
  The locusts and wild honey?
Where is the sacred dower
  That the bride of Christ was given?
Gone to the wielders of power,
  The misers and minters of money;
Gone for the greed that is their creed—
  And these in the land have thriven.
What then wert thou, and what art now,
  And wherefore hast thou striven?

> And every note of every bell
> Sang Gabriel! rang Gabriel!
> In the tower that is left the tale to tell
> Of Gabriel, the Archangel.

THE POOR

By Speer Strahan, C.S.C.

The poor I saw at the cloister gate
  Mutely beg with their patient eyes
An alms, for the love of Him who sate
  And supped with the poor in human guise.

And there were monks saw the nails' deep scars
  In the shrunken hands that reached for bread,
Who heard a Voice from beyond the stars
  In the broken thanks of them they fed.

I, too, at the gates of God each day
  Seek for an alms of strength and grace,
Beggar am I that wait and pray
  To feast my soul on His beauteous Face.

THE PROMISED COUNTRY

By Speer Strahan, C.S.C.

Fair must that promised country be
Whose streams rise from eternity
And One doth lead upon that way
Whose footfalls are the paths of day.

Nor lurking fear pursues them there,
As forward in the morning air
With Him the blessed ransomed go,
Their garments washen white as snow.

Alas! my days are very dim
That look up to the Seraphim.
Ah, Lord, some dawning may I be
One of that shining company!

HOLY COMMUNION

By Speer Strahan, C.S.C.

Disguised He stands without in the street;
Far come is He on heavy feet.
O heart of mine, open thy gate;
For darkness falls, and it is late!

Lord of the heaven's fairest height,
Homeless in the traveler's night,
Begging my hearth, my board, my cup,
That I, not He, may richly sup.

O soul of mine, the board begin,
And let this wondrous Beggar in!

STARS OF CHEER

Caroline D. Swan

The silent Christmas stars shine cool and clear
  Above a world of mingled joy and woe;
  On peaceful cottage homes, with thanks aglow
For royal bounty of the grape-crowned year;
And on red fields of blood, where many a tear
  Is wiped away by Death, a gentle foe,
  More merciful than they who bade it flow.
Shine, silver stars, rain down your blessed cheer!

Comfort the mourner with your Angel song!
The Christ-Child reigns. Behold His tiny hand
  Upraised in benediction warm and sweet!
O'er every joy and every bitter wrong
  The Babe of Bethlehem hath supreme command;
    Come, worship, kings and peoples, at His feet!

CHRIST AND THE PAGAN

By John B. Tabb

I had no God but these,
The sacerdotal Trees,
And they uplifted me.
"I hung upon a tree."

The sun and moon I saw,
And reverential awe
Subdued me day and night.
"I am the perfect light."

Within a lifeless Stone—
All other gods unknown—
I sought Divinity.
"The Corner-Stone am I."

For sacrificial feast
I slaughtered man and beast,
Red recompense to gain.
"So I, a Lamb, was slain.

*"Yea; such My hungering Grace
That where ev'r My face
Is hidden, none may grope
Beyond eternal Hope."*

OUT OF BOUNDS

By John B. Tabb

A little Boy of heavenly birth,
  But far from home to-day,
Comes down to find His ball, the Earth,
  That Sin has cast away.
O comrades, let us one and all
Join in to get Him back His ball!

FATHER DAMIEN

By John B. Tabb

O God, the cleanest offering
  Of tainted earth below,
Unblushing to Thy feet we bring—
  "A leper white as snow!"

RECOGNITION

By John B. Tabb

When Christ went up to Calvary,
  His crown upon His head,
Each tree unto its fellow-tree
  In awful silence said:
"Behold the Gardener is He
Of Eden and Gethsemane!"

"IS THY SERVANT A DOG?"

By John B. Tabb

So *must* he be, who in the crowded street,
Where shameless Sin and flaunting Pleasure meet,
Amid the noisome footprints finds the sweet
Faint vestige of Thy feet.

LILIUM REGIS

By Francis Thompson

O Lily of the King, low lies thy silver wing,
  And long has been the hour of thine unqueening;
And thy scent of Paradise on the night-wind spends its sighs,
  Nor any take the secrets of its meaning.
O Lily of the King, I speak a heavy thing,
  O patience, most sorrowful of daughters!
Lo, the hour is at hand for the troubling of the land,
  And red shall be the breaking of the waters.

Sit fast upon thy stalk, when the blast shall with thee talk,
  With the mercies of the King for thine awning,
And the Just understand that thine hour is at hand,
  Thine hour at hand with power in the dawning.
When the nations lie in blood, and their kings a broken brood,
  Look up, O most sorrowful of daughters!
Lift up thy head and hark what sounds are in the dark,
  For His feet are coming to thee on the waters.

O Lily of the King, I shall not see that sing,
    I shall not see the hour of thy queening!
But my Song shall see, and wake like a flower that
    dawn-winds shake,
    And sigh with joy the odours of its meaning.
O Lily of the King, remember then the thing
    That this dead mouth sang; and thy daughters,
As they dance before His way; sing there on the Day
    What I sang when night was on the waters!

TO THE ENGLISH MARTYRS

By Francis Thompson

Rain, rain on Tyburn tree,
Red rain a-falling;
Dew, dew on Tyburn tree,
Red dew on Tyburn tree,
And the swart bird a-calling.
The shadow lies on England now
Of the deathly-fruited bough:
Cold and black with malison
Lies between the land and sun;
Putting out the sun, the bough
Shades England now!

The troubled heavens so wan with care,
And burdened with the earth's despair
Shiver a-cold; the starved heaven
Has want, with wanting men bereaven.
Blest fruit of the unblest bough,
Aid the land that smote you, now!

That feels the sentence and the curse
Ye died if so ye might reverse.
When God was stolen from out man's mouth,

Stolen was the bread; then hunger and drouth
Went to and fro; began the wail,
Struck root the poor-house and the jail,
Ere cut the dykes, let through that flood,
Ye writ the protest with your blood;
Against this night—wherein our breath
Withers, and the toiled heart perisheth,—
Entered the *caveat* of your death.
Christ in the form of His true Bride,
Again hung pierced and crucified,
And groaned, "I thirst!" Not still ye stood,—
Ye had your hearts, ye had your blood;
And pouring out the eager cup,—
"The wine is weak, yet, Lord Christ, sup."
Ah, blest! who bathed the parched Vine
With richer than His Cana-wine,
And heard, your most sharp supper past:
"Ye kept the best wine to the last!"

Ah, happy who
That sequestered secret knew,
How sweeter than bee-haunted dells
The blosmy blood of martyrs smells!
Who did upon the scaffold's bed,
The ceremonial steel between you, wed
With God's grave proxy, high and reverend Death;
Or felt about your neck, sweetly,
(While the dull horde
Saw but the unrelenting cord)

TO THE ENGLISH MARTYRS

The Bridegroom's arm, and that long kiss
That kissed away your breath, and claimed you His.
You did, with thrift of holy gain,
Unvenoming the sting of pain,
Hive its sharp heather-honey. Ye
Had sentience of the mystery
To make Abaddon's hooked wings
Buoy you up to starry things;
Pain of heart, and pain of sense,
Pain the scourge, ye taught to cleanse;
Pain the loss became possessing;
Pain the curse was pain the blessing.

Chains, rack, hunger, solitude,—these,
Which did your soul from earth release,
Left it free to rush upon
And merge in its compulsive Sun.
Desolated, bruised, forsaken,
Nothing taking, all things taken,
Lacerated and tormented,
The stifled soul, in naught contented,
On all hands straitened, cribbed, denied,
Can but fetch breath o' the Godward side.
Oh, to me, give but to me
That flower of felicity,
Which on your topmost spirit ware
The difficult and snowy air
Of high refusal! and the heat
Of central love which fed with sweet
And holy fire i' the frozen sod
Roots that ta'en hold on God.

Unwithering youth in you renewed
Those rosy waters of your blood,—

The true *Fons Juventutis*, ye
Pass with conquest that Red Sea,
And stretch out your victorious hand
Over the Fair and Holy Land.
O by the Church's pondering art
Late set and named upon the chart
Of her divine astronomy,
Through your influence from on high
Long shed unnoted! Bright
New cluster in our Northern night,
Cleanse from its pain and undelight
An impotent and tarnished hymn,
Whose marish exhalations dim
Splendours they would transfuse! And thou
Kindle the words which blot thee now,
Over whose sacred corse unhearsed
Europe veiled her face, and cursed
The regal mantle grained in gore
Of genius, freedom, faith, and More!

Ah, happy Fool of Christ, unawed
By familiar sanctities,
You served your Lord at holy ease!
Dear Jester in the Courts of God——
In whose spirit, enchanting yet,
Wisdom and love together met,
Laughed on each other for content!
That an inward merriment,
An inviolate soul of pleasure,
To your motions taught a measure
All your days; which tyrant king,
Nor bonds, nor any bitter thing,
Could embitter or perturb;

TO THE ENGLISH MARTYRS

No daughter's tears, nor, more acerb,
A daughter's frail declension from
Thy serene example, come
Between thee and thy much content.
Nor could the last sharp argument
Turn thee from thy sweetest folly;
To the keen *accolade* and holy
Thou didst bend low a sprightly knee,
And jest Death out of gravity
As a too sad-visaged friend;
So, jocund passing to the end
Of thy laughing martyrdom;
And now from travel art gone home
Where, since gain of thee was given,
Surely there is more mirth in heaven!

Thus, in Fisher and in thee,
Arose the purple dynasty,
The anointed Kings of Tyburn tree;
High in act and word each one:
He that spake—and to the sun
Pointed—"I shall shortly be
Above yon fellow," He too, he
No less high of speech and brave,
Whose word was: "Though I shall have
Sharp dinner, yet I trust in Christ
To have a most sweet supper." Priced
Much by men that utterance was
Of the doomed Leonidas,—
Not more exalt than these, which note
Men who thought as Shakespeare wrote.
  But more lofty eloquence
Than is writ by poet's pens

Lives in your great deaths: O these
Have more fire than poesies!
And more ardent than all ode,
The pomps and raptures of your blood!
By that blood ye hold in fee
This earth of England; Kings are ye:
And ye have armies—Want, and Cold,
And heavy Judgments manifold
Hung in the unhappy air, and Sins
That the sick gorge to heave begins,
Agonies and Martyrdoms,
Love, Hope, Desire, and all that comes
From the unwatered soul of man
Gaping on God. These are the van
Of conquest, these obey you; these,
And all the strengths of weaknesses,
That brazen walls disbed. Your hand,
Princes, put forth to the command,
And levy upon the guilty land
Your saving wars; on it go down,
Black beneath God's and heaven's frown;
Your prevalent approaches make
With unsustainable grace, and take
Captive the land that captived you;
To Christ enslave ye and subdue
Her so bragged freedom: for the crime
She wrought on you in antique time,
Parcel the land among you; reign,
Viceroys to your sweet Suzerain!
Till she shall know
This lesson in her overthrow:
Hardest servitude has he
That's jailed in arrogant liberty;

And freedom, spacious and unflawed,
Who is walled about with God.

THE HOUND OF HEAVEN

By Francis Thompson

I FLED Him, down the nights and down the days;
  I fled Him down the arches of the years;
I fled Him down the labyrinthine ways
  Of my own mind; and in the midst of tears
I hid from Him, and under running laughter.
      Up vistaed hopes I sped;
      And shot, precipitated,
  Adown Titanic glooms of chasmed fears,
From those strong Feet that followed, followed after.
      But with unhurrying chase,
      And unperturbed pace,
  Deliberate speed, majestic instancy,
      They beat—and a Voice beat
      More instant than the Feet—
  "All things betray thee, who betrayest Me."

      I pleaded, outlaw-wise,
By many a hearted casement, curtained red,
  Trellised with intertwining charities;
(For, though I knew His love Who followed,
      Yet was I sore adread
Lest, having Him, I must have naught beside);
But, if one little casement parted wide,
  The gust of His approach would clash it to.
Fear wist not to evade, as Love wist to pursue.

Across the margent of the world I fled,
   And troubled the gold gateway of the stars,
   Smiting for shelter on their clanged bars;
      Fretted to dulcet jars
And silvern chatter the pale ports o' the moon.
I said to dawn, Be sudden; to eve, Be soon;
   With thy young skiey blossoms heap me over
      From his tremendous Lover!
Float thy vague veil about me, lest He see!
   I tempted all His servitors, but to find
My own betrayal in their constancy,
In faith to Him their fickleness to me,
   Their traitorous trueness, and their loyal deceit.
To all swift things for swiftness did I sue;
   Clung to the whistling mane of every wind.
      But whether they swept, smoothly fleet,
   The long savannahs of the blue;
      Or whether, Thunder-driven,
   They clanged his chariot 'thwart a heaven
Plashy with flying lightnings round the spurn o' their
   feet:—
   Fear wist not to evade as Love wist to pursue.
      Still with unhurrying chase,
      And unperturbed pace,
   Deliberate speed, majestic instancy,
      Came on the following Feet,
      And a Voice above their beat—
"Naught shelters thee, who wilt not shelter Me."

I sought no more that after which I strayed
   In face of man or maid;
But still within the little children's eyes
   Seems something, something that replies;

They at least are for me, surely for me!
I turned me to them very wistfully;
But, just as their young eyes grew sudden fair
    With dawning answers there,
Their angel plucked them from me by the hair.
"Come then, ye other children, Nature's—share
With me" (said I) "your delicate fellowship;
        Let me greet you lip to lip,
        Let me twine with you caresses,
            Wantoning
        With our Lady-Mother's vagrant tresses,
            Banqueting
        With her in her wind-walled palace,
        Underneath her azured dais,
        Quaffing, as your taintless way is,
            From a chalice
Lucent-weeping out of the dayspring."
        So it was done:
I in their delicate fellowship was one—
Drew the bolt of Nature's secrecies.
I knew all the swift importings
        On the wilful face of skies;
        I knew how the clouds arise
        Spumed of the wild sea-snortings;
            All that's born or dies
        Rose and drooped with—made them shapers
Of mine own moods, or wailful or divine—
        With them joyed and was bereaven.
        I was heavy with the even,
        When she lit her glimmering tapers
        Round the day's dead sanctities.
        I laughed in the morning's eyes.
I triumphed and I saddened with all weather,

THE HOUND OF HEAVEN

    Heaven and I wept together,
And its sweet tears were salt with mortal mine;
Against the red throb of its sunset-heart
    I laid my own to beat,
    And share commingling heat;
But not by that, by that, was eased my human smart
In vain my tears were wet on Heaven's grey cheek.
For ah, we know not what each other says
   These things and I; in sound *I* speak—
Their sound is but their stir, they speak by silences.
Nature, poor stepdame, cannot slake my drought;
   Let her, if she would owe me,
Drop yon blue bosom-veil of sky, and show me
   The breasts of her tenderness:
Never did any milk of hers once bless
     My thirsting mouth.
     Nigh and nigh draws the chase,
     With unperturbed pace,
   Deliberate speed, majestic instancy;
    And past those noised fleet—
    A Voice comes yet more fleet—
"Lo! naught contents thee who content'st not Me.

Naked I wait Thy love's uplifted stroke!
My harness piece by piece Thou hast hewn from me
   I am defenceless utterly.
   I slept, methinks, and woke,
And, slowly gazing, find me stripped in sleep.
In the rash lustihead of my young powers,
   I shook the pillaring hours
And pulled my life upon me; grimed with smears,
I stand amid the dust o' the mounded years—
My mangled youth lies dead beneath the heap.

My days have crackled and gone up in smoke,
Have puffed and burst as sun-starts on a stream.
    Yea, faileth now even dream
The dreamer, and the lute the lutanist;
Even the linked fantasies, in whose blossomy twist
I swung the earth a trinket at my wrist,
Are yielding; cords of all too weak account
For earth with heavy griefs so overplussed.
        Ah! is Thy love indeed
A weed, albeit an amaranthine weed,
Suffering no flowers except its own to mount?
        Ah! must—
    Designer infinite!—
Ah! must Thou char the wood ere Thou canst limn
    with it?
My freshness spent its wavering shower i' the dust;
And now my heart is as a broken fount,
Wherein tear-drippings stagnate, spilt down ever
      From the dank thoughts that shiver
Upon the sighful branches of my mind.
      Such is; what is to be?
The pulp so bitter, how shall taste the rind?
I dimly guess what Time in mists confounds;
Yet ever and anon a trumpet sounds
From the hid battlements of Eternity;
Those shaken mists a space unsettle, then
Round the half-glimpsed turrets slowly wash again
    But not ere him who summoneth
    I first have seen enwound
With glooming robes purpureal, cypress-crowned;
His name I know, and what his trumpet saith.
Whether man's heart or life it be which yields
    Thee harvest, must Thy harves fields
    Be dunged with rotten death?

Now of that long pursuit
   Comes on at hand the bruit;
That Voice is round me like a bursting sea:
   "And is thy earth so marred,
   Shattered in shard on shard?
Lo! all things fly thee, for thou fliest Me!
   Strange, piteous, futile thing,
Wherefore should any set thee love apart?
Seeing none but I makes much of naught" (He said)
"And human love needs human meriting:
   How hast thou merited—
Of all man's clotted clay the dingiest clot?
   Alack, thou knowest not
How little worthy of any love thou art!
Whom wilt thou find to love ignoble thee
   Save Me, save only Me?
All which I took from thee I did but take,
   Not for thy harms,
But just that thou might'st seek it in My arms.
   All which thy child's mistake
Fancies as lost, I have stored for thee at home:
   Rise, clasp My hand, and come!"

   Halts by me that footfall:
   Is my gloom, after all,
Shade of His hand, outstretched caressingly?
   Ah, fondest, blindest, weakest,
   "I am He Whom thou seekest!
Thou dravest love from thee, who dravest Me."

THE DREAD OF HEIGHT

By Francis Thompson

*"If ye were blind, ye should have no sin: but now ye say:
We see: your sin remaineth."*—John ix. 41

Not the Circean wine
Most perilous is for pain:
Grapes of the heaven's star-loaden vine,
Whereto the lofty-placed
Thoughts of fair souls attain,
Tempt with a more retributive delight,
And do disrelish all life's sober taste.

'Tis to have drunk too well
The drink that is divine,
Maketh the kind earth waste,
And breath intolerable.

Ah, me!
How shall my mouth content it with mortality?
Lo, secret music, sweetest music,
From distances of distance drifting its lone flight,
Down the arcane where Night would perish in night,
Like a god's loosened locks slips undulously:
Music that is too grievous of the height
For safe and low delight,
Too infinite
For bounded hearts which yet would girth the sea!
So let it be,
Though sweet be great, and though my heart be small:

So let it be,
O music, music, though you wake in me
No joy, no joy at all;
Although you only wake
Uttermost sadness, measure of delight,
Which else I could not credit to the height,
Did I not know,
Did I not know,
That ill is statured to its opposite;
And even of sadness so,
Of utter sadnes, make
Of extreme sad a rod to mete
The incredible excess of unsensed sweet,
And mystic wall of strange felicity.
So let it be,
Though sweet be great, and though my heart be small
And bitter meat
The food of Gods for men to eat;
Yea, John ate daintier, and did tread
Less ways of heat,
Than whom to their wind-carpeted
High banquet hall,
And golden love-feasts, the fair stars entreat.

But ah! withal,
Some hold, some stay,
O difficult joy, I pray,
Some arms of thine,
Not only, only arms of mine!
Lest like a weary girl I fall
From clasping love so high,
And lacking thus thine arms, then may
Most hapless I

THE DREAD OF HEIGHT

Turn utterly to love of basest rate;
For low they fall whose fall is from the sky.

Yea, who me shall secure
But I, of height grown desperate,
Surcease my wing, and my lost fate
Be dashed from pure
To broken writhings in the shameful slime:
Lower than man, for I dreamed higher,
Thrust down, by how much I aspire,
And damned with drink of immortality?
For such things be,
Yea, and the lowest reach of reeky Hell
Is but made possible
By foreta'en breath of Heaven's austerest clime.

These tidings from the vast to bring
Needeth not doctor nor divine,
Too well, too well
My flesh doth know the heart-perturbing thing;
That dread theology alone
Is mine,
Most native and my own;
And ever with victorious toil
When I have made
Of the delfic peaks dim escalade,
My soul with anguish and recoil
Doth like a city in an earthquake rock,
As at my feet the abyss is cloven then,
With deeper menace than for other men,
Of my potential cousinship with mire;
That all my conquered skies do grow a hollow mock,
My fearful powers retire,

No longer strong,
Reversing the shook banners of their song.

Ah, for a heart less native to high Heaven,
A hooded eye, for jesses and restraint,
Or for a will accipitrine to pursue!—
The veil of tutelar flesh to simple livers given,
Or those brave-fledging fervours of the Saint,
Whose heavenly falcon-craft doth never taint,
Nor they in sickest time their ample virtue mew.

TO MY GODCHILD—FRANCIS M. W. M.

By Francis Thompson

This labouring, vast, Tellurian galleon,
Riding at anchor off the orient sun,
Had broken its cable, and stood out to space
Down some froze Arctic of the aerial ways:
And now, back warping from the inclement main,
Its vapourous shroudage drenched with icy rain,
It swung into its azure roads again;
When, floated on the prosperous sun-gale, you
Lit, a white halcyon auspice, 'mid our frozen crew.

To the Sun, stranger, surely you belong,
Giver of golden days and golden song;
Nor is it by an all-unhappy plan
You bear the name of me, his constant Magian.
Yet, ah! from any other that it came,
Lest fated to my fate you be, as to my name.
When at the first those tidings did they bring,

My heart turned troubled at the ominous thing:
Though well may such a title him endower,
For when a poet's prayer implores a poet's power.
The Assisian, who kept plighted faith to three,
To Song, to Sanctitude, and Poverty,
(In two alone of whom most singers prove
A fatal faithfulness of during love!);
He the sweet Sales, of whom we scarcely ken
How God he could love more, he so loved men;
The crown and crowned of Laura and Italy;
And Fletcher's fellow—from these, and not from me,
Take you your name, and take your legacy!

Or, if a right successive you declare
When worms, for ivies, interwine my hair,
Take but this Poesy that now followeth
My clayey hest with sullen servile breath,
Made then your happy freedman by testating death.
My song I do but hold for you in trust,
I ask you but to blossom from my dust.
When you have compassed all weak I began,
Diviner poet, and ah! diviner man—
The man at feud with the perduring child
In you before song's altar nobly reconciled—
From the wise heavens I half shall smile to see
How little a world, which owned you, needed me.
If, while you keep the vigils of the night,
For your wild tears make darkness all too bright,
Some lone orb through your lonely window peeps,
As it played lover over your sweet sleeps,
Think it a golden crevice in the sky,
Which I have pierced but to behold you by!

And when, immortal mortal, droops your head,
And you, the child of deathless song, are dead;
Then, as you search with unaccustomed glance
The ranks of Paradise for my countenance,
Turn not your tread along the Uranian sod
Among the bearded counsellors of God;
For, if in Eden as on earth are we,
I sure shall keep a younger company:
Pass where beneath their ranged gonfalons
The starry cohorts shake their shielded suns,
The dreadful mass of their enridged spears:
Pass where majestical the eternal peers,
The stately choice of the great Saintdom, meet—
A silvern segregation, globed complete
In sandalled shadow of the Triune feet;
Pass by where wait, young poet-wayfarer,
Your cousined clusters, emulous to share
With you the roseal lightnings burning 'mid their hair
Pass the crystalline sea, the Lampads seven:—
Look for me in the nurseries of Heaven.

MICHAEL THE ARCHANGEL

By Katherine Tynan

Not woman-faced and sweet, as look
  The angels in the picture-book;
  But terrible in majesty,
More than an army passing by.

His hair floats not upon the wind
Like theirs, but curled and closely twined:

Wrought with his aureole, so that none
Shall know the gold curls from the crown.

His wings he hath put away in steel,
He goes mail-clad from head to heel;
Never moon-silver hath outshone
His breastplate and his morion.

His brows are like a battlement,
Beautiful, brave and innocent;
His eyes with fires of battle burn—
On his strong mouth the smile is stern.

His horse, the horse of Heaven, goes forth,
Bearing him off to South and North,
Neighing far off, as one that sees
The battle over distances.

His fiery sword is never at rest,
His foot is in the stirrup prest;
Through all the world where wrong is done
Michael the Soldier rideth on.

Michael, Commander! Angels are
That sound the trumpet and that bear
The banners by the Throne, where is
The King one nameth on his knees.

Angels there are of peace and prayers,
And they that go with wayfarers,
And they that watch the house of birth,
And they that bring the dead from earth,

And mine own Angel. Yet I see,
Heading God's army gloriously,
Michael Archangel, like a sun,
Splendid beyond comparison!

PLANTING BULBS

By Katherine Tynan

Setting my bulbs a-row
　In cold earth under the grasses,
Till the frost and the snow
　Are gone and the Winter passes—

Sudden a footfall light,
　Sudden a bird-call ringing;
And these in gold and in white
　Shall rise with a sound of winging

Airy and delicate all,
　All go trooping and dancing
At Spring's call and footfall,
　Airily dancing, advancing.

In the dark of the year,
　Turning the earth so chilly,
I look to the day of cheer,
　Primrose and daffodilly.

Turning the sods and the clay
　I think on the poor sad people
Hiding their dead away
　In the churchyard, under the steeple

All poor women and men,
  Broken-hearted and weeping,
Their dead they call on in vain,
  Quietly smiling and sleeping.

Friends, now listen and hear,
  Give over crying and grieving,
There shall come a day and a year
  When the dead shall be as the living.

There shall come a call, a footfall,
  And the golden trumpeters blowing
Shall stir the dead with their call,
  Bid them be rising and going.

Then in the daffodil weather
  Lover shall run to lover;
Friends all trooping together;
  Death and Winter be over.

Laying my bulbs in the dark,
  Visions have I of hereafter.
Lip to lip, breast to breast, hark!
  No more weeping, but laughter!

SHEEP AND LAMBS

By Katherine Tynan

All in the April evening,
  April airs were abroad;
The sheep with their little lambs
  Passed me by on the road.

The sheep with their little lambs
  Passed me by on the road;
All in the April evening
  I thought on the Lamb of God.

The lambs were weary, and crying
  With a weak, human cry.
I thought on the Lamb of God
  Going meekly to die.

Up in the blue, blue mountains
  Dewy pastures are sweet;
Rest for the little bodies,
  Rest for the little feet.

But for the Lamb of God
  Up on a hilltop green
Only a cross of shame
  Two stark crosses between.

All in the April evening,
  April airs were abroad;
I saw the sheep with their lambs,
  And thought on the Lamb of God.

THE MAKING OF BIRDS

By Katherine Tynan

God made Him birds in a pleasant humour;
  Tired of planets and suns was He.
He said: "I will add a glory to summer,
  Gifts for my creatures banished from Me!"

THE MAKING OF BIRDS

He had a thought and it set Him smiling
 Of the shape of a bird and its glancing head,
Its dainty air and its grace beguiling:
 "I will make feathers," the Lord God said.

He made the robin; He made the swallow;
 His deft hands moulding the shape to His mood,
The thrush and the lark and the finch to follow,
 And laughed to see that His work was good.

He Who has given men gift of laughter,
 Made in His image; He fashioned fit
The blink of the owl and the stork thereafter,
 The little wren and the long-tailed tit.

He spent in the making His wit and fancies;
 The wing-feathers He fashioned them strong;
Deft and dear as daisies and pansies,
 He crowned His work with the gift of song.

"Dearlings," He said, "make songs for my praises!"
 He tossed them loose to the sun and the wind,
Airily sweet as pansies and daisies;
 He taught them to build a nest to their mind.

The dear Lord God of His glories weary—
 Christ our Lord had the heart of a boy—
Made Him birds in a moment merry,
 Bade them soar and sing for His joy.

THE MAN OF THE HOUSE

By Katherine Tynan

Joseph, honoured from sea to sea,
This is your name that pleases me,
  "Man of the House."

I see you rise at the dawn and light
The fire and blow till the flame is bright.

I see you take the pitcher and carry
The deep well-water for Jesus and Mary.

You knead the corn for the bread so fine,
Gather them grapes from the hanging vine.

There are little feet that are soft and slow,
Follow you whithersoever you go.

There's a little face at your workshop door,
A little one sits down on your floor:

Holds His hands for the shavings curled,
The soft little hands that have made the world

Mary calls you: the meal is ready:
You swing the Child to your shoulder steady.

I see your quiet smile as you sit
And watch the little Son thrive and eat.

The vine curls by the window space,
The wings of angels cover the face.

Up in the rafters, polished and olden,
There's a Dove that broods and his wings are golden.

You who kept Them through shine and storm,
A staff, a shelter kindly and warm,

Father of Jesus, husband of Mary,
Hold us your lilies for sanctuary!

Joseph, honoured from sea to sea,
Guard me mine and my own roof-tree,
    "Man of the House"!

COELO ET IN TERRA

By Thomas Walsh

Earth is a jealous mother; from her breast
She will endure no separation long
From aught she bore;
So one by one
She claimeth evermore
The parent and the friend—
The loveliest and the best,
The meek, the faithful, and the strong,—
Till, link by golden link undone,
The very tomb that seems
To youth the dismal gulf of all that's fair,
Becomes the chosen hearthstone of our dreams.

The wonder-house of all most rare,
Most deathless, and most dear;
Where the bereaved heart,
Life's exile held apart,
Would turn for love-warmth and abiding cheer.
Yea,—earth can be so kind,—
Then ye that rule the wind,
Are ye of less appeal?
Ye spirits of the stars
And regions where the suns
Themselves as atoms wheel
Beneath your thundering cars?
Cerulean ones!—
Or goddesses, or saints,
Or demiurge, or Trinities,
Wherewith heaven highest faints!
Are ye less kind than these
Dim vaults of clay,
Ye boasts and fathers of the ancient day?
Thou god Avernian, Dis!—behold
What timid form and old
Adown thy purple gulf descends
Unto the arch of Death—(Grim friend of friends!
Be thou placated!) 'Tis a mother, see,
Takes her first step—a child—into eternity!
Leave her not fearful there
Who was of love entire,
So gentle and so fair!—
Thy majesty and dread withhold
For the high head and bold,—
Imperial Death, mock not thyself with ire!
Nay,—then it was not fear
That stayed her foot the while;

For now her lovely eyes,
Uncloudcd, brown,
Are lighted with their greeting smile—
The Hand awaited through the gloom
Is seen!—her whitened forehead lies
Upon the Shepherd's shoulder down—
Yea,—her own Jesus comes,—to lead
Unto the meadows where is Peace indeed!

EGIDIO OF COIMBRA—1597 A.D.

By Thomas Walsh

The rumor came to Frei Egidio
In cloistered Santa Cruz, that out of Spain
King Philip's secret courier had fared
With orders under seal suspending all
The statutes of Coimbra that controlled
The contests for the professorial chairs,
And ordering the Faculty to grant
Padre Francisco Suarez primacy
Among the masters theological.
And Frei Egidio, whose ancient name
Fonseca was relinquished when at court
It shone its brightest, who had ceaseless toiled
His score of years in cloister and in schools,
Unravelling knotty texts, disputing long
With monk and doctor of the Carmelites,
Dominicans and Trinitarians,
Consulting with the students, visiting,
Fawning and banqueting—himself and all
His faction in the University—

EGIDIO OF COIMBRA

Now in the iron mandate from Madrid
Saw failure blight his hopes, and Santa Cruz
Eclipsed, through imposition unforeseen
Of Suarez de Toledo—only half
A monk!—a fledgling doctor in the Schools!—
And Frei Egidio unsleeping schemed
To check the rising of this Spanish star
Within Coimbra,—and his henchmen went
Stealthy and sure to sow malignant seed
To choke the Hapsburg's new autocracy.
Stately was Frei Egidio, robust,
Swarthy and smooth his cheek; his raven locks
Piling about his tonsure in a crown.
Dark flashed his eye whene'er he rose to cast
His syllogistic spear across the lists,
Where many a mighty crest Minerva-crowned
Was forced to yield, or learnt the rapier thrust
Of his *distinguo* and *non-sequitur*.
Still more he shone when in procession moved
The doctors, masters, and licentiates,
With tufted caps, and rainbow gowns, and stoles,
And ring, and book across the steeps and squares,
While gallant youths pressed round on horse or foot
Holding his robe or stirrup through the town—
The *Catedratico da Vespera*.
But now this little shrivelled man sent out
From Salamanca,—Philip's paragon!—
To rule Coimbra in theology!—
One of Loyola's strange and restless band
In the Collegio de Jesus,—reproach
To every gorgeous doctor in the halls.
'Twas true he hid away within his house,
Came seldom to the festival or Acts.

Nor oft asserted his high presidence
O'er Frei Egidio—in craft or scorn,
It mattered not—for Frei Egidio
Would pluck him forth; no signet of the King
Could serve him here; the doctors of the Schools
Should learn how he, Fonseca, had been wronged.
With formal placards soon they smeared the walls
Of shrine and college, telling day and hour
And place, where Doutor Frei Egidio
Da Presentacao, of the Eremites
Of Sao Agostinho, titular
Da Vespera, would his conclusions hold
"De Voluntario et Involuntario"
Against all-comers, and imprimis there,
The Doutor Padre Suarez, titular
Da Prima of Coimbra, theologue
Of the *Collegia* and *Compania*
De Jesus. From near and far they came,
And took their stated rank, and filed
Into the Hall of Acts; the Chancellor
And Rector in their robes of silk, and fur,
And velvet, and great chains and seals of state;
The Bishop, and Inquisitor, and Dean,
And Chapter, in their purple; Canonists
In green; and Jurists in their scarlet gowns;
Frei Luiz of the Chair of Holy Writ,
In black and white of the Dominicans;
Frei Manoel of the Chair of Scotus, garbed
In white and brown of Carmel; titulars
In Peter Lombard and Durandus,—sons
Of Bernard, Francis and Saint Benedict.
When each in order of his ancientry
Was seated in the tribune, and below

Ranged the licentiates, and bachelors,
And, out beyond, the thousand students,—gay
In plumes and ruffs, or rags and disrepair,—
There entered Bacharel Frei Constantino
Citing the *obligations;* whereupon
Egidio began his argument
With exposition and arrangement clear,
And summary abrupt and crushing, as
His old experience in the courts had taught,—
So free in tone and doctrine that the throng
Swayed on their benches, beating noisily
Great tomes together like the roll of drums.
Then silence for Suarez's *quodlibet;*
As half-reluctant, without emphasis,
His cold unwavering voice proposed the plan
Of his objection,—When uproarious
Upon the instant, Frei Egidio
In tones of thunder shouted o'er the hall,—
"*Nego majorem!*"—the scholastic world's
Unmitigated insult! How would he,
Spain's boasted theologian, reply
To Portugal's? The Jesuits around
Suarez's rostrum marvelled, whispered, turned,
And hid their faces, when they saw him bowed
Silent a moment, ere descending, calm,
He led them home across the jeering town.
Then the mad acclamations; bells of shrine
And monastery on the hills; the sweep
Of robes prelatical, the cavalcade
Of gorgeous nobles into Santa Cruz;
The blare of trumpets, and the lanterns strung
Yellow beneath the moon; the beggar throngs;
The maskers down the lanes; the nightingales

And river-songs of students wafted far
Across Mondego's Hills of Loneliness
And Meditation where Coimbra slept.
Thus triumphed Frei Egidio. But high
In the Collegio de Jesus the blow
Was red on every cheek; the Rector rose
In the community and said: "Padre
Francisco, not in fifty years have we
In our Coimbra known such sore defeat;
Tell me, I pray, had you no thought to save
Your honor and the honor of our schools—
You, boast of Rome and Salamanca's halls,—
You, to whom all the dialectic arts
Have been as play—could you not parry, feint,
Or bait Egidio until some chance
Or newer turn might save your argument?"
Suarez bowed and answered: "Better far
That we be humbled than a great man fall
To utter shame and ruin! Had I told
Egidio there that in denying thus
My proposition he was challenging
A solemn canon, word for word, prescribed
At Constance by the Universal Church—
Fetch me the Book of Councils—he was lost."
Scarce was the secret spoken, ere it stole
In rumor through the novice-court, and thence
Below to Santa Cruz,—stole, like a cloud,
Black, ominous, across the starlit dome
Above the black *mosteiro,* where the moon
Revelled amid the sculptured lattices,—
The marble ropes and palms memorial
Of old Da Gama and his caravels,—
Upon the rose-paths and the trickling pools

Along the Cloister do Silencio.
There paced Fonseca, solitary guest
To catch the final crumbs, the laughter, far
Adown the stream, of lutes that mourned his feast,
When lo! a billet in his path!—"*Awake,—*"
He read,—"*at Constance 'twas decreed. Thy voice
Hath mocked the very words of Holy Church.*"—
No more,—yet in foreboding he made haste
To find his taper,—fumbled through the stacks
In dust and chill,—unclasped the folio
Liber Conciliorum,—saw his doom—
Perchance the rack and Secret Prisons—writ
Upon the parchment!—Silence, mocking lutes!
Come, rain! come, whirlwind, blot the lanterns out:
Now knew he their insidious subterfuge—
The slippery Pharisees—to undermine
Coimbra's last bright paragon,—they claimed
Another victim!—But his rage gave way
To grief; his scorn was all to blame; no scheme
Was theirs; Suarez spoke the Council's words
As duty bound him,—With the break of day
Came self-renouncement to Egidio;
And in amaze to greet his ashen face
The sacristan laid out for him the alb
And chasuble of Requiem; resigned,
Like some bowed reed the storm has swept by night,
He took the chalice, veiled it 'gainst his breast,
And 'mid the first faint glimmer down the nave
Crept forth unto his mystic Calvary.

SUPPLEMENTARY POEMS

CHARM AGAINST ENEMIES

(Translation by Lady Wilde)

THREE things are of the Evil One—
  An evil eye,
  An evil tongue,
  An evil mind;
Three things are of God, and these three are what Mary
    told her Son, for she heard them in heaven—
  The merciful word,
  The singing word,
  And the good word.
May the power of these three holy things be on all the
    men and women of Erin for evermore.

MAY THE SWEET NAME OF JESUS

(Translation by Eleanor Hull)

MAY the sweet name of Jesus
Be lovingly graven
In my heart's inmost haven.

O Mary, Blest Mother,
Be Jesus my Brother,
And I Jesu's lover.

A binding of love
That no distance can sever,
Be between us for ever,
  Yea, O my Saviour,
    For ever and ever.

A NIGHT PRAYER

(Translation by Eleanor Hull)

May the will of God be done by us,
May the death of the saints be won by us,
And the lights of the kingdom begun in us;
May Jesus the Child be beside my bed,
May the Lamb of mercy uplift my head,
May the Virgin her heavenly brightness shed
And Michael be steward of my soul!

THE STRAYING SHEEP

(Translation by Eleanor Hull)

Fair Jesu, guide Thy straying sheep
 Along the fragrant valleys,
And where the meadow-grass grows deep,
 Guard from the wild wolf's sallies;
No sickness unto death be theirs,
 But sickness unto healing,
Our sickness be for love to Thee,
 O King of all the living.

PRAYER BEFORE GOING TO SLEEP

(Translation by Eleanor Hull)

The cross of the angels
 On the bed where I lie;
The robe of the Kingdom,
 May it come very nigh;

O Glorious Virgin,
  My thousand loves thou,
My helpful supporter,
  My affection thou.
My woman-physician,
  Ill or well, thou,
My firm faithful helper
  In the Kingdom of graces, thou.
    O gentle Jesus,
    O Jesus, most gentle,
O Jesus Christ, have mercy upon us;
O glorious Virgin, pray thou also for us;
O Mother of God, O Bright Star of Knowledge,
O Queen of Paradise, watch thou and ward us,
The light of glory obtain from thy Child for us,
A sight of thy house, by thy great power's might, for us.
The Light of all lights, and a sight of the Trinity,
And the grace of long patience in days of adversity.

I REST WITH THEE, O JESUS

(Translation by Eleanor Hull)

I REST with Thee, O Jesus,
  And do Thou rest with me.
The oil of Christ on my poor soul,
The creed of the Twelve to make me whole,
  Above my head I see.
O Father, who created me,
O Son, who purchased me,
O Spirit Blest, who blesseth me,
  Rest ye with me.

THE SACRED TRINITY

(Translation by Eleanor Hull)

Three folds of the cloth, yet one only napkin is there,
Three joints in the finger, but still only one finger fair;
Three leaves of the shamrock, yet no more than one sham
  rock to wear.
Frost, snow-flakes and ice, all in water their origin share
Three Persons in God; to one God alone we make prayer

CONSECRATION

By Murdoch O'Daly, called Murdoch "the Scotchman" (Muiredach Albanach), on account of his affection for that country; born in Connaught towards the close of the twelfth century.

(Translation by Eleanor Hull)

How great the tale, that there should be,
In God's Son's heart, a place for me!
That on a sinner's lips like mine,
The cross of Jesus Christ should shine!

Christ Jesus bend me to Thy will,
My feet to urge, my griefs to still;
That even my flesh and blood may be
A temple sanctified to Thee.

No rest, no calm, my soul may win,
Because my body craves to sin;
Till Thou, dear Lord, Thyself impart
Peace to my head, light to my heart.

May consecration come from far,
Soft shining like the evening star!
My toilsome path make plain to me,
Until I come to rest in Thee.

THE THREE MUSICIANS

By Aubrey Beardsley

Along the path that skirts the wood,
The three musicians wend their way,
Pleased with their thoughts, each other's mood,
Franz Himmel's latest roundelay,
The morning's work, a new-found theme, their **breakfast**
    and the summer day.

One's soprano, lightly frocked
In cool, white muslin that just shows
Her brown silk stockings gaily clocked,
Plump arms and elbows tipped with rose,
And frills of petticoats and things, and **outlines as the**
    warm wind blows.

Beside her a slim, gracious boy
Hastens to mend her tresses' fall,
And dies her favour to enjoy,
And dies for *réclame* and recall
At Paris and St. Petersburg, Vienna and St. **James' Hall**.

The third's a Polish pianist
With big engagements everywhere,
A light heart and an iron wrist,

And shocks and shoals of yellow hair,
And fingers that can thrill on sixths and fill beginners
    with despair.

The three musicians stroll along
And pluck the ears of ripened corn,
Break into odds and ends of song,
And mock the woods with Siegfried's horn,
And fill the air with Gluck, and fill the tweeded tourist's
    soul with scorn.

The Polish genius lags behind,
And, with some poppies in his hand,
Picks out the strings and wood and wind
Of an imaginary band,
Enchanted that for once his men obey his beat and under-
    stand.

That charming cantatrice reclines
And rests a moment where she sees
Her château's roof that hotly shines
Amid the dusky summer trees,
And fans herself, half shuts her eyes and smooths her
    frock about her knees.

The gracious boy is at her feet,
And weighs his courage with his chance;
His fears soon melt in noonday heat.
The tourist gives a furious glance,
Red as his guide-book grows, moves on, and offers up a
    prayer for France.

MAN-CHILD

By Micheal Breathnach

Out of the fat lands
There is nothing born.
There is no pain
In plenitude,
And only sleep
In the flow of slow rivers
And in the red-ripe marrow
Of the fields.

There is agony
In the white murmuring
Of mountainy streams,
And one dark eve
A star will rise,
And in the hush
Of the music
Of Meadhbh's people,
Out of the womb of the West
Out of hungry Connacht,
Will be born
Another Goll,
To rivet the flaming ring
Of Eriu's four seas.

WID THADY'S PIPE BESIDE THE DOOR

By Madeline Bridges

Wid Thady's pipe beside the door,
   And Thady there, content and aisy—
Could wife or woman ask for more
   Barrin' she wor a fool—or crazy?
The queen could crave no blessin' higher
Than her good man, in comfort, nigh her.

Wid Thady's pipe beside the door,
   The hearth clean-swept, the praties bubblin'—
The childre playin' on the floor—
   Ah, what could make me heart be throublin'?
I'll smooth me hair an' take me knittin'—
A body might as well be sittin'!

Wid Thady's pipe beside the door—
   The friendly neighbors passin', callin',
Wid bits of talk and jokes galore—
   The quiet duskus round us fallin';
It's far to God me heart is strayin',
And many's the happy prayer I'm sayin'.

THE BOG-LANDS

By William A. Byrne

The purple heather is the cloak
God gave the bog-land brown,
But man has made a pall o' smoke
To hide the distant town.

THE BOG-LANDS

Our lights are long and rich in change,
Unscreened by hill or spire,
From primrose dawn, a lovely range,
To sunset's farewell fire.

Nor morning bells have we to wake
Us with their monotone.
But windy calls of quail and crake
Unto our beds are blown.

The lark's wild flourish summons us
To work before the sun;
At eve the heart's lone Angelus
Blesses our labour done.

We cleave the sodden, shelving bank
In sunshine and in rain,
That men by winter-fires may thank
The wielders of the slane.

Our lot is laid beyond the crime
That sullies idle hands;
So hear we through the silent time
God speaking sweet commands.

Brave joys we have and calm delight—
For which tired wealth may sigh—
The freedom of the fields of light,
The gladness of the sky.

And we have music, oh, so quaint!
The curlew and the plover,
To tease the mind with pipings faint
No memory can recover;

The reeds that pine about the pools
In wind and windless weather;
The bees that have no singing-rules
Except to buzz together.

And prayer is here to give us sight
To see the purest ends;
Each evening through the brown-turf light
The Rosary ascends.

And all night long the cricket sings,
The drowsy minutes fall—
The only pendulum that swings
Across the crannied wall.

Then we have rest, so sweet, so good,
The quiet rest you crave;
The long, deep bog-land solitude
That fits a forest's grave;

The long, strange stillness, wide and deep,
Beneath God's loving hand,
Where, wondering at the grace of sleep,
The Guardian Angels stand.

CIARAN, THE MASTER OF HORSES AND LANDS

By Joseph Campbell

Ciaran, the master of horses and lands,
Once had no more than the horn on his hands.

But Ciaran is rich now, and Ciaran is great,
And rides with the air of a squire of estate.

O Christ! and to see the man up on the back
Of a thoroughbred stallion, a bay or a black!

There's not a horsebreeder from Banna to Laoi
Can handle the snaffle as pretty as he!

And Ciaran, for all, has the wit of a child,
A heart just as soft, and an eye just as mild.

No maker of ballads puts curse at his door:
He handsels the singer, and harbours the poor.

For Ciaran, the master of horses and lands,
Once had no more than the horn on his hands.

I AM THE MOUNTAINY SINGER

By Joseph Campbell

I AM the mountainy singer,
And I would sing of the Christ
Who followed the paths thro' the mountains
To eat at the people's tryst.

He loved the sun-dark people
As the young man loves his bride,
And He moved among their thatches,
And for them was crucified.

And the people loved Him, also,
More than their houses or lands,
For they had known His pity
And felt the touch of His hands.

And they dreamed with Him in the mountains,
And they walked with Him on the sea,
And they prayed with Him in the garden,
And bled with Him on the tree.

Not ever by longing and dreaming
May they come to Him now,
But by the thorns of sorrow
That bruised His kingly brow.

I WILL GO WITH MY FATHER A-PLOUGHING

By Joseph Campbell

I WILL go with my father a-ploughing
To the green field by the sea,
And the rooks and the crows and the seagulls
Will come flocking after me.
I will sing to the patient horses
With the lark in the white of the air,
And my father will sing the plough-song
That blesses the cleaving share.

I will go with my father a-sowing
To the red field by the sea,
And the rooks and the gulls and the starlings
Will come flocking after me.

I will sing to the striding sowers
With the finch on the greening sloe,
And my father will sing the seed-song
That only the wise men know.

I will go with my father a-reaping
To the brown field by the sea,
And the geese and the crows and the children
Will come flocking after me.
I will sing to the tanfaced reapers
With the wren in the heat of the sun,
And my father will sing the scythe-song
That joys for the harvest done.

THE SHINING SPACES OF THE SOUTH

By Joseph Campbell

The shining spaces of the south,
The circle of the year, the sea,
The blowing rose, the maiden's mouth,
The love, the hate, the ecstasy,
The golden wood, the shadowed stream,
The dew, the light, the wind, the rain,
The man's desire, the woman's dream,
The bed embrace, the childing pain,
The sound of music heard afar,
The breathing grass, the broken sod,
The sun, the moon, the twilight star—
Do all proclaim the mind of God.
Then why should I, who am but clay,
Think otherwise, or answer nay?

WINE

By Francis Carlin

Wine to the weak and to those unsound;
  Ale to the strong and able;
But the Cup of Care must be passed around
  To every one at the table.

THE IRISH

By Francis Carlin

With a gentle Hand
  God made the Gael
For that fair land
  Of Innisfail,
By angels planned.

A child is he
  With an aged smile
Of mystery,
  In the oldest isle
Of an ancient sea.

And He Who made
  The Gael is kind
To the yew-tree's shade
  And the dusty wind,
Where the old are laid

In that strange land
   Of Innisfail,
By angels planned
   For the childish Gael
Who holds God's Hand.

ALCHEMY

By Francis Carlin

Because of the light of the moon,
   Silver is found on the moor;
And because of the light of the sun,
   There is gold on the walls of the poor.

Because of the light of the stars,
   Planets are found in the stream;
And because of the light of your eyes,
   There is love in the depths of my dream.

THE SOLAR ROAD

By Francis Carlin

From the start of Life
To the end of its strife
   There is many a weary league,
But the Road that runs
Among the Suns
   Shall cause us no fatigue.

HAMILCAR BARCA

By Sir Roger Casement

Thou that didst mark from Heircte's spacious hill
The Roman spears, like mist, uprise each morn,
Yet held, with Hesper's shining point of scorn,
Thy sword unsheathed above Panormus still;
Thou that wert leagued with nought but thine own will
Eurythmic vastness to that stronghold torn
From foes above, below, where, though forlorn,
Thou still hadst claws to cling and beak to kill—
Eagle of Eryx!—when the Ægatian shoal
Rolled westward all the hopes that Hanno wrecked,
With mighty wing, unwearying, didst thou
Seek far beyond the wolf's grim protocol,
Within the Iberian sunset faintly specked
A rock where Punic faith should bide its vow.

LOST YOUTH

By Sir Roger Casement

Weep not that you no longer feel the tide
High breasting sun and storm that bore along
Your youth in currents of perpetual song;
For in these mid-sea waters, still and wide,
A sleepless purpose the great deep doth hide.
Here spring the mighty fountains, pure and strong
That bear sweet change of breath to city throng,
Who, had the sea no breeze, would soon have died.

So, though the sun shines not in such a blue,
Nor have the stars the meaning youth devised,
The heavens are nigher, and a light shines through—
The brightness that nor sun nor stars sufficed,
And on this lonely waste we find it true
Lost youth and love not lost, are hid with Christ.

MAIRE MY GIRL

By John Keegan Casey

Over the dim blue hills
Strays a wild river,
Over the dim blue hills
Rests my heart ever.
Dearer and brighter than
Jewels and pearl,
Dwells she in beauty there,
Maire my girl.

Down upon Claris heath
Shines the soft berry,
On the brown harvest tree
Droops the red cherry.
Sweeter thy honey lips,
Softer the curl
Straying adown thy cheeks,
Maire my girl.

'Twas on an April eve
That I first met her;
Many an eve shall pass
Ere I forget her.

Since my young heart has been
Wrapped in a whirl,
Thinking and dreaming of
Maire my girl.

She is too kind and fond
Ever to grieve me,
She has too pure a heart
E'er to deceive me.
Were I Tyrconnell's chief
Or Desmond's earl,
Life would be dark, wanting
Maire my girl.

Over the dim blue hills
Strays a wild river,
Over the dim blue hills
Rests my heart ever;
Dearer and brighter than
Jewels or pearl,
Dwells she in beauty there,
Maire my girl.

THE FRET OF FATHER CARTY

After Last Mass on the Feast of All Saints

By Joseph I. C. Clarke

"Oh, wasn't he hard on poor sinners this mornin'?
  And his voice, begor! was no silver-tone flute
When he gave us," said Burke, "the 'third and last warnin',"
  With a taste and smell of blue sulphur to boot.
Arrah! what takes good Father Carty so quarely
  That he preaches of late so mortal crass?"

Said Shea, "It's surely the gettin' up early,
  And workin' and fastin' for ten o'clock mass."

"The priests," laughed Burke, "are for takin' it aisy
  As the Holy Father's four white mules.
But the bishops and cardinals drive them crazy
  For spires, marble statues, stained windows, and schools,
And soon as ever a mortgage is lifted,
  They must start out fresh for worry and fret.
If they don't, movrone, they are sure to be shifted
  To a Dago parish that's spanceled with debt.

"Still the life, I am sure, would suit me splendid:
  A snug, warm house with your nag at the door,
And then, when the ten o'clock mass was ended,
  To breakfast on bacon and chops galore."
"Yis," Shea snapped short, "you would ate, I'm thinkin',
  And there your most pious desires would stop.
When a man loves food like that, he is shrinkin'
  His soul to the size of a mutton chop.

"But, lad, if you lay, a ball in your shoulder,
  Blood-soaked and pain-racked and ravin' with thirst,
And a priest with cool words and something colder
  Was there on his knees beside you—the first;
And said as he soothed you, 'The good Lord thirsted
  And died on the cross for men like you,'
Then whispered: 'My son, the rebels were worsted!'
  You'd face your God with a smile or two.

"And here it's: 'Christen the child John Peter';
  'Please marry me, Father, to Tim McCann';
'Make Pat stop his swearin';' 'Make Julia neater';
  'Give the temperance pledge to my Turk of a man.'

And the vestrymen about debts pursue him.
 He's out upon sick-calls tender and bright;
All day all the woes of the poor drive through him;
 He hears their confessions till nine at night."

"Well, well," stammered Burke, "I was only funnin'"
 "Fun!" thundered Kelly. "Man hold your whist,
And think of the hour that the last fight's won in,
 And the priest's face there in the waverin' mist—
The face of a promise beyond the water
 That rolls to your feet without a sound.
Little help is mother or wife or daughter
 When you know that your soul is outward bound.

"He leaves the red blossoms of life to others,
 And his feet keep step to no earthly guide,
The poor far more than the rich his brothers,
 The Christ that he preaches has arms spread wide
So, if of a mornin' his temper's fretful,
 And whether he fast or whether he feast,
While he walks toward God, of himself forgetful,
 You can see the angel beside the priest."

BILL MANNING

By Joseph I. C. Clarke

WHERE is he gone, the queer little man,
 Who made and mended boots and shoes;
Who hammered the brogues and rushed the can,
And never finished and never began,
 While the lads were discussin' the news,
  Bill Manning?

Where is he? *Movrone!* One night at nine
  He put out the gas and moved away.
His trade was good, for he patched so fine,
You never could tell where it was on mine.
  He earned at least two dollars a day!
        Poor Manning.

I'm sorry he's gone. His Hole-in-the-Wall
  He made a sort of a Patriot's Club.
Night after night he'd lecture us all
To give cash or life at our country's call,
  And he barely cleared enough for his grub,
        Poor Manning.

He worked his days and half of his nights,
  But never managed to forge ahead.
The dead-beats knew poor Bill to rights:
They'd only to say they were Parnellites,
  And he'd mend their brogues and buy them bread,
        Poor Manning.

The begging nuns never called in vain;
  Why, he used to tip a Salvation lass!
He once brought a sick nigger out of the rain,
And filled him with beer to ease his pain,
  And he always was first at six o'clock mass,
        Poor Manning.

No wonder he bought his leather on tick.
  If a poor child came with a dime or two,
He'd say, and he thought it a splendid trick,
"I've put a Cork sole in your brogue, *avic*,"
  As he slipped a dollar inside the shoe,
        Poor Manning.

For Patrick's Day, he'd a grand tall hat,
  That no one saw for another year.
He talked of Emmet weeks after that,
And was proud that Sarsfield's name was Pat
  He couldn't say Ireland without a cheer,
        Poor Manning.

Some say he's gone for a soldier lad;
  Some say he's married the Widow Magee;
(I hope it's not true, for his sake, bedad!)
Some say he's dead (that's not half as bad),
  But wed or dead I'd give money to see
        Bill Manning.

FIRST BORN

By Frances O'Connell Corridan

I know the month, I know the week,
  I cannot guess the day,
But, Oh, it's sweet to be so sure
  Of Heart's Delight in May—

When all the dew-edged blossoms crown
  With joy my apple tree,
Amid the glory-time of Spring,
  You'll come from Heaven to me.

STRONG ARMS

By Frances O'Connell Corridan

"Soon—soon—soon" the prophet stars foretell,
  And Hope assuring whispers, "Have courage, all is well."
Suddenly I shiver with a thought as cold as snow—
  What if with that dear but anxious coming I should go?
Across the room you hasten, as if your heart had heard,
  You fold me in your warm strong arms without a single word;
Against your steady shoulder you press my tired head
  And I—once more wrapped in your love—am strangely comforted.

OF A DEAD POET

By Lord Alfred Douglas

Oft happening on some halting paraphrase
Of those high words that took from him their wings,
I call again to wistful communings,
The bitter sweet remembrance of past days,
When, like a lute-player that bends and plays,
He made the souls of men his gilded strings,
And plucked from them imperishable things,
And lured dull hours to walk enchanted ways.

O you that hold the puny hireling pen,
And drip weak venom in laborious blots,
Think you that in your shallow inky stream,
You can o'erwhelm the greatness of great men
Or drown immortal music? Wretched sots
Scrabbling on pillars of eternity.

A SUMMER STORM

By Lord Alfred Douglas

Alas! how frail and weak a little boat
I have sailed in. I called it Happiness,
And I had thought there was not storm nor stress
Of wind so masterful but it would float
Blithely in their despite; but lo! one note
Of harsh discord, one word of bitterness,
And a fierce overwhelming wilderness
Of angry waters chokes my gasping throat.
I am near drowned in this unhappy sea,
I will not strive, let me lie still and sink,
I have no joy to live. Oh! unkind love!
Why have you wounded me so bitterly?
That am as easily wounded as a dove
Who has a silver throat and feet of pink.

A PRAYER

By Lord Alfred Douglas

Often the western wind has sung to me,
There have been voices in the streams and meres,
And pitiful trees have told me, God, of Thee:
And I heard not. Oh! open Thou mine ears.

The reeds have whispered low as I passed by,
"Be strong, O friend, be strong, put off vain fears,
Vex not thy soul for doubts, God cannot lie":
And I heard not. Oh! open Thou mine ears.

There have been many stars to guide my feet,
Often the delicate moon, hearing my sighs,
Has rent the clouds and shown a silver street;
And I saw not. Oh! open Thou mine eyes.

Angels have beckoned me unceasingly,
And walked with me; and from the sombre skies
Dear Christ Himself has stretched out hands to me;
And I saw not. Oh! open Thou mine eyes.

A SONG

By Lord Alfred Douglas

Steal from the meadows, rob the tall green hills
   Ravish my orchard's blossoms, let me bind
A crown of orchard flowers and daffodils,
   Because my love is fair and white and kind.

To-day the thrush has trilled her daintiest phrases,
   Flowers with their incense have made drunk the air,
God has bent down to gild the hearts of daisies,
   Because my love is kind and white and fair.

To-day the sun has kissed the rose-tree's daughter,
   And sad Narcissus, Spring's pale acolyte,
Hangs down his head and smiles into the water,
   Because my love is kind and fair and white.

Crabbet Park, 1894.

GOOD NIGHT

By Bernard Isaac Durward

Our native cactus closes
Its hundred chalices,
Where wasps and wild bees hold their revelings
(With sheathed stings),
In nectar hid in gold.
  Another morning brings
New blossoms for one day,
Rich palaces
For tiny insect life as frail as they.
  The ruby-throated humming bird, that swings
Like a swift pendulum
Above his hidden mate, has flown away;
And all the songsters of the day are dumb.

  By love grown bold
Our constant summer guest,
The little pewee bird, reposes
Under the door-porch on her last year's nest,
By vine leaves screened.
Her name has told
The simple song she sings.

  With all her wealth, four soft brown little ones
(Two daughters and two sons),
Secure within the shelter of her wings
The patient peahen cowers in her coop,
Her Rajah with his splendid train adroop,

All smoothed and preened
And jewelled o'er with sapphire eyes
(When the emerald dies),
From his high perch above the streamlet blue,
Like guardian true,
Screams harsh his all well "Pavo!" thro' the air.

And there,
As fades the soft and dreamy light,
My dear one comes and says, "Good night!"
Good night!

TO MY FIRSTBORN

By Bernard Isaac Durward

Dear firstling of my little flock,
In tribute to the Master paid,
By what sweet streamlet dost thou feed?
What field, love-blest and beauteous made?
In what fair sunlight, ne'er to fade
Or shadow need?

With trembling breath and sinking heart,
Hard was it for a father's tongue
To bid thy dear young soul, "depart!"
How hard, can ne'er be said or sung,
Or from the soul of sorrow wrung
By mimic art.

TO MY FIRSTBORN

Again the dew is on thy feet—
Again appears the breaking morn—
Again thy lily body lies
All pallid, wasted and forlorn—
Again my heart with grief o'erworn
Within me dies!

O memory, break thy bitter wand!
O fancy, muffle up thy wings
And crouch within this gloomy hour,
Or waft me to the living springs
O'er which eternal glory flings
Its ceaseless shower!

There have the splendors claspèd thy soul
My son! O ever-blessèd Faith,
That steps between us and despair,
And lights the very shades of death,
Lift up my spirit from the breath
Of this dark lair!

From life's dim, dusty solitude
I yearn, my child, to see thy face!
O, when this flickering pulse is dumb,
As I to thee said, "Go in peace!"
By filial love and Jesus' grace,
To me say, "Come!"

MISSED AGAIN

By Rev. John T. Durward

By apt comparisons I thought to praise thee,
    In my great love;
And in immortal syllables to raise thee,
    Thy peers above.

I said, the lily gave thy form of grace,
    The rose thy hue;
The opal stone thy glow, and cloudless space
    The eyes of blue.

But flower and gem and gleaming sapphire vault
    As one aver;
Your work is vain, O bungler! you exalt
    Us, and not her.

THE OULD PLAID SHAWL

By Francis A. Fahy

Not far from old Kinvara, in the merry month of May,
When birds were singing cheerily, there came across my way,
As if from out the sky above an angel chanced to fall,
A little Irish *cailin* in an ould plaid shawl.

She tripped along right joyously, a basket on her arm;
And, oh! her face, and, oh! her grace, the soul of saint would charm;
Her brown hair rippled o'er her brow, but greatest charm of all
Was her modest blue eyes beaming 'neath her ould plaid shawl.

I courteously saluted her—"God save you, miss," says I;
"God save you, kindly sir," said she, and shyly passed me by;
Off went my heart along with her, a captive in her thrall,
Imprisoned in the corner of her ould plaid shawl.

Enchanted with her beauty rare, I gazed in pure delight,
Till round an angle of the road she vanished from my sight;
But ever since I sighing say, as I that scene recall,
"The grace of God about you and your ould plaid shawl."

I've heard of highway robbers that, with pistols and with knives,
Make trembling travellers yield them up their money or their lives,
But think of me that handed out my heart and head and all
To a simple little *cailin* in an ould plaid shawl!

Oh! graceful the mantillas that the signoritas wear,
And tasteful are the bonnets of Parisian ladies fair,
But never cloak or hood or robe, in palace, bow'r, or hall,
Clad half such witching beauty as that ould plaid shawl.

Oh! some men sigh for riches, and some men live for
  fame,
And some on history's pages hope to win a glorious name;
My aims are not ambitious, and my wishes are but small—
You might wrap them all together in an ould plaid shawl.

I'll seek her all through Galway, and I'll seek her all
  through Clare,
I'll search for tale or tidings of my traveller everywhere,
For peace of mind I'll never find until my own I call
That little Irish *cailin* in her ould plaid shawl.

TWO KISSES

By Mary Fleming

Two kisses! Only two remain
Forever etched upon my brain.
Two kisses! Only two, my dear;
After waiting many a year.

One for joy as well as pain;
And one that we may meet again.
One, for the present living day:
And one, that we may love alway.

THE DEAD AVIATOR

By Francis Hackett

So endlessly the gray-lipped sea
  Kept me within his eye,
And lean he licked his hollow flanks
  And followed up the sky.

I was the lark whose song was heard
When I was lost to sight,
I was the golden arrow loosed
To pierce the heart of night.

> I fled the little earth, I climbed
> Above the rising sun,
> I met the morning in a blaze
> Before my hour was gone.

I ran beyond the rim of space,
Its reins I flung aside,
Laughter was mine and mine was youth
And all my own was pride.

From end to end I knew the way,
I had no doubt nor fear,
The minutes were a forfeit paid
To fetch the landfall near.

> But all at once my heart I held,
> My carol frozen died,
> A white cloud laid her cheek to mine
> And wove me to her side.

Her icy fingers clasped my flesh,
Her hair drooped in my face,
And up we fell and down we rose
And twisted into space.

Laughter was mine and mine was youth,
I pressed the edge of life,
I kissed the sun and raced the wind,
I found immortal strife.

Out of myself I spent myself,
I lost the mortal share,
My grave is in the ashen plain,
My spirit in the air.

Good-bye, sweet pride of man that flew,
Sweet pain of man that bled,
I was the lark that spilled his heart,
The golden arrow sped.

> *So endlessly the gray-lipped sea*
> *Kept me within his eye,*
> *And lean he licked his hollow flanks*
> *And followed up the sky.*

FINEEN THE ROVER

By Robert Dwyer Joyce

An old castle towers o'er the billow
  That thunders by Cleena's green land,
And there dwelt as gallant a rover
  As ever grasped hilt by the hand.
Eight stately towers of the waters
  Lie anchored in Baltimore Bay,
And over their twenty score sailors,
  Oh! who but the Rover holds sway?
    Then, lo! for Fineen the Rover!
      Fineen O'Driscoll the free!
    Straight as the mast of his galley,
      And wild as the wave of the sea!

The Saxons of Cork and Moyallo,
  They harried his lands with their powers;
He gave them a taste of his cannon,
  And drove them like wolves from his towers.
And men of Clan London brought over
  Their strong fleet to make him a slave;
They met him by Mizen's wild highland
    And the sharks crunched their bones 'neath the wave
   Then, ho! for Fineen the Rover,
     Fineen O'Driscoll the free;
   With step like the red stag of Beara,
     And voice like the bold sounding sea.

Long time in that old battered castle,
  Or out on the waves with his clan,
He feasted and ventured and conquered,
  But ne'er struck his colours to man.
In a fight 'gainst the foes of his country
  He died as a brave man should die;
And he sleeps 'neath the waters of Cleena,
  Where the waves sing his *caoine* to the sky.
   Then, ho! for Fineen the Rover,
     Fineen O'Driscoll the free;
   With eye like the osprey's at morning,
     With smile like the sun on the sea.

THE LADY OF LIFE

By Tom Kettle

I sat with her, and spoke right goldenly
Of love and beauty, and because her hair
Brushed me, I plucked down Sirius like a pear,
To braid it, and had laughter for my fee;

Yea, suing her to heavier slavery,
Had all but plucked the fruitage of her lips,
When lo! inked clouds and absolute eclipse,
Courteous but unmistakable ennui.

Then did I mind me of the sorrow wailed
Thro' poets' books, and how the streaming torch
Of suns greater than Sirius had failed,
And as I shambled out the menials' door
I heard new feet sound in the statued porch
And salutations I had heard before.

PARNELL'S MEMORY

By Tom Kettle

TEARS will betray all pride, but when ye mourn him
Be it in soldier wise;
As for a captain who hath gently borne him,
And in the midnight dies.

Fewness of words is best; he was too great
For ours or any phrase.
Love could not guess nor the slipped hound of hate
Track that soul's secret ways.
Signed with a sign, unbroken, unrevealed,
His Calvary he trod.
So let him keep, where all world-wounds are healed,
The silences of God.

He taught us more, this best as it was last:
When comrades go apart
They shall go greatly, cancelling the past,
Slaying the kindlier heart.

Friendship and love, all clean things and unclean,
Shall be as drifted leaves,
Spurned by our Ireland's feet, that queenliest Queen
Who gives not but receives.

THE IRISH PEASANT GIRL

By Charles Joseph Kickham

She lived beside the Anner,
    At the foot of Slievna-man,
A gentle peasant girl,
    With mild eyes like the dawn;
Her lips were dewy rosebuds;
    Her teeth of pearls rare;
And a snow-drift 'neath a beechen bough
    Her neck and nut-brown hair.

How pleasant 'twas to meet her
    On Sunday, when the bell
Was filling with its mellow tones
    Lone wood and grassy dell

THE IRISH PEASANT GIRL

And when at eve young maidens
Strayed the river bank along,
The widow's brown-haired daughter
Was loveliest of the throng.

O brave, brave Irish girls—
We well may call you brave!—
Sure the least of all your perils
Is the stormy ocean wave,
When you leave our quiet valleys,
And cross the Atlantic's foam,
To hoard your hard-won earnings
For the helpless ones at home.

"Write word to my own dear mother—
Say, we'll meet with God above;
And tell my little brothers
I send them all my love;
May the angels ever guard them,
Is their dying sister's prayer"—
And folded in a letter
Was a braid of nut-brown hair.

Ah, cold and well-nigh callous,
This weary heart has grown
For thy helpless fate, dear Ireland,
And for sorrows of my own;
Yet a tear my eye will moisten,
When by Anner side I stray,
For the lily of the mountain foot
That withered far away.

MAIN STREET
(For S. M. L.)

By Joyce Kilmer

I LIKE to look at the blossomy track of the moon upon the sea,
But it isn't half so fine a sight as Main Street used to be
When it all was covered over with a couple of feet of snow,
And over the crisp and radiant road the ringing sleighs would go.

Now, Main Street bordered with autumn leaves, it was a pleasant thing,
And its gutters were gay with dandelions early in the Spring;
I like to think of it white with frost or dusty in the heat,
Because I think it is humaner than any other street.

A city street that is busy and wide is ground by a thousand wheels,
And a burden of traffic on its breast is all it ever feels:
It is dully conscious of weight and speed and of work that never ends,
But it cannot be human like Main Street, and recognise its friends.

There were only about a hundred teams on Main Street in a day,
And twenty or thirty people, I guess, and some children out to play.

And there wasn't a wagon or buggy, or a man or a girl or boy
That Main Street didn't remember, and somehow seem to enjoy.

The truck and the motor and trolley car and the elevated train
They make the weary city street reverberate with pain:
But there is yet an echo left deep down within my heart
Of the music the Main Street cobblestones made beneath a butcher's cart.

God be thanked for the Milky Way that runs across the sky,
That's the path that my feet would tread whenever I have to die.
Some folks call it a Silver Sword, and some a Pearly Crown,
But the only thing I think it is, is Main Street, Heaventown.

A BLUE VALENTINE

(For Aline)

By Joyce Kilmer

Monsignore,
Right Reverend Bishop Valentinus,
Sometime of Interamna, which is called Ferni,
Now of the delightful Court of Heaven,
I respectfully salute you,
I genuflect
And I kiss your episcopal ring.

A BLUE VALENTINE

It is not, Monsignore,
The fragrant memory of your holy life,
Nor that of your shining and joyous martyrdom,
Which causes me now to address you.
But since this is your august festival, Monsignore,
It seems appropriate to me to state
According to a venerable and agreeable custom,
That I love a beautiful lady.
Her eyes, Monsignore,
Are so blue that they put lovely little blue reflections
On everything that she looks at,
Such as a wall
Or the moon
Or my heart.

It is like the light coming through blue stained glass,
Yet not quite like it,
For the blueness is not transparent,
Only translucent.
Her soul's light shines through,
But her soul cannot be seen.
It is something elusive, whimsical, tender, wanton, infantile, wise
And noble.
She wears, Monsignore, a blue garment,
Made in the manner of the Japanese.
It is very blue—
I think that her eyes have made it more blue,
Sweetly staining it
As the pressure of her body has graciously given it form
Loving her, Monsignore,
I love all her attributes;
But I believe

That even if I did not love her
I would love the blueness of her eyes,
And her blue garment, made in the manner of the Japanese.

Monsignore,
I have never before troubled you with a request.
The saints whose ears I chiefly worry with my pleas are
    the most exquisite and maternal Brigid,
Gallant Saint Stephen, who puts fire in my blood,
    and your brother bishop, my patron,
The generous and jovial Saint Nicholas of Bari.
But, of your courtesy, Monsignore,
Do me this favour:
When you this morning make your way
To the Ivory Throne that bursts into bloom with roses
    because of her who sits upon it,
When you come to pay your devoir to Our Lady,
I beg you, say to her:
"Madame, a poor poet, one of your singing servants yet
    on earth,
Has asked me to say that at this moment he is especially
    grateful to you
For wearing a blue gown."

THE SINGING GIRL
(For the Rev. Edward F. Garesché, S. J.)

BY JOYCE KILMER

There was a little maiden
  In blue and silver drest,
She sang to God in Heaven
  And God within her breast.

It flooded me with pleasure,
   It pierced me like a sword,
When this young maiden sang: "My soul
   Doth magnify the Lord."

The stars sing all together
   And hear the angels sing,
But they said they had never heard
   So beautiful a thing.

Saint Mary and Saint Joseph,
   And Saint Elizabeth,
Pray for us poets now
   And at the hour of death.

TREES

(For Mrs. Henry Mills Alden)

By Joyce Kilmer

I THINK that I shall never see
A poem lovely as a tree.

A tree whose hungry mouth is prest
Against the earth's sweet flowing breast;

A tree that looks at God all day,
And lifts her leafy arms to pray;

A tree that may in Summer wear
A nest of robins in her hair;

Upon whose bosom snow has lain;
Who intimately lives with rain.

Poems are made by fools like me,
But only God can make a tree.

DAVE LILLY

By Joyce Kilmer

There's a brook on the side of Greylock that used to be full of trout,
But there's nothing there now but minnows; they say it's all fished out.
I fished there many a Summer day some twenty years ago,
And I never quit without getting a mess of a dozen or so.

There was a man, Dave Lilly, who lived on the North Adams road,
And he spent all his time fishing, while his neighbors reaped and sowed.
He was the luckiest fisherman in the Berkshire hills, I think.
And when he didn't go fishing he'd sit in the tavern and drink.

Well, Dave is dead and buried and nobody cares very much;
They have no use in Greylock for drunkards and loafers and such.

But I always liked Dave Lilly, he was pleasant as you could wish;
He was shiftless and good-for-nothing, but he certainly could fish.

The other night I was walking up the hill from Williamstown
And I came to the brook I mentioned, and I stopped on the bridge and sat down.
I looked at the blackened water with its little flecks of white
And I heard it ripple and whisper in the still of the Summer night.

And after I'd been there a minute it seemed to me I could feel
The presence of someone near me, and I heard the hum of a reel.
And the water was churned and broken, and something was brought to land
By a twist and flirt of a shadowy rod in a deft and shadowy hand.

I scrambled down to the brookside and hunted all about;
There wasn't a sign of a fisherman; there wasn't a sign of a trout.
But I heard somebody chuckle behind the hollow oak
And I got a whiff of tobacco like Lilly used to smoke.

It's fifteen years, they tell me, since anyone fished that brook;
And there's nothing in it but minnows that nibble the bait off your hook.

But before the sun has risen and after the moon has set
I know that it's full of ghostly trout for Lilly's ghost to
    get.

I guess I'll go to the tavern and get a bottle of rye
And leave it down by the hollow oak, where Lilly's ghost
    went by.
I meant to go up on the hillside and try to find his grave
And put some flowers on it—but this will be better for
    Dave.

THE GARDEN OF THE HOLY SOULS

(From "Hours of the Passion")

BY ELEANOR HAMILTON KING

IN Thy garden, in Thy garden, though the rain
  Fall, and the winds beat there,
And they stand unsheltered, piteous, in the storm,
  They who were once so fair,

In Thy garden of the souls, where Thou art gardener,
  Thou who was once so mild,
Now pruning down to naked stems and leafless
  The roses that ran wild,

Oh, Thy roses once waved in the wind so sweetly,
  Though thick with thorns beset;
In the morning sunshine opening, and at evening
  With cool dews wet.

In Thy garden, where Thou walkest as a warder,
  How poor, how small they stand;
Yet once their beauty, to the hearts that loved them,
  Lighted the living land.

In Thy garden, where no smile of Thine is granted
  Yet keep within Thy heart,
A place in Paradise for these transplanted,
  Still with Thee where Thou art,

In Thy garden, in Thy garden, where Thy roses
  Without a thorn are sweet,
And each poor branch in endless wreaths uncloses
  To kiss Thy feet.

LAMENT FOR THE POETS: 1916

By Francis Ledwidge

I heard the Poor Old Woman say:
"At break of day the fowler came,
And took my blackbirds from their songs
Who loved me well thro' shame and blame.

"Nor more from lovely distances
Their songs shall bless me mile by mile,
Nor to white Ashbourne call me down
To wear my crown another while.

"With bended flowers the angels mark
For the skylark the place they lie,
From there its little family
Shall dip their wings first in the sky.

"And when the first surprise of flight
Sweet songs excite, from the far dawn
Shall there come blackbirds loud with love,
Sweet echoes of the singers gone.

"But in the lonely hush of eve
Weeping I grieve the silent bills."
I heard the Poor Old Woman say
In Derry of the little hills.

HAD I A GOLDEN POUND

By Francis Ledwidge

Had I a golden pound to spend,
My love should mend and sew no more.
And I would buy her a little quern,
Easy to turn on the kitchen floor.

And for her windows curtains white,
With birds in flight and flowers in bloom,
To face with pride the road to town,
And mellow down her sunlit room.

And with the silver change we'd prove
The Truth of Love to life's own end,
With hearts the years could but embolden,
Had I a golden pound to spend.

A LAMENT

By Denis Florence MacCarthy

Youth's bright palace
Is overthrown,
With its diamond sceptre
And golden throne;
As a time-worn stone

A LAMENT

Its turrets are humbled,—
All hath crumbled
But grief alone!

Whither, oh! whither
Have fled away
The dreams and hopes
Of my early day?
Ruined and grey
Are the towers I builded;
And the beams that gilded—
Ah! where are they?

Once this world
Was fresh and bright,
With its golden moon
And its starry night;
Glad and light,
By mountain and river,
Have I blessed the Giver
With hushed delight.

Youth's illusions,
One by one,
Have passed like clouds
That the sun looked on.
While morning shone,
How purple their fringes!
How ashy their tinges
When that was gone!

As fire-flies fade
When the nights are damp,

As meteors are quenched
In a stagnant swamp—
Thus Charlemagne's camp,
Where the Paladins rally,
And the Diamond Valley,
And the Wonderful Lamp,

And all the wonders
Of Ganges and Nile,
And Haroun's rambles,
And Crusoe's isle,
And Princes who smile
On the Genii's daughters
'Neath the Orient waters
Full many a mile,

And all that the pen
Of Fancy can write,
Must vanish
In manhood's misty light—
Squire and Knight,
And damosels' glances,
Sunny romances
So pure and bright!

These have vanished,
And what remains?
Life's budding garlands
Have turned to chains—
Its beams and rains
Feed but docks and **thistles,**
And sorrow whistles
O'er desert plains!

GIRL OF THE RED MOUTH

By Martin MacDermott

Girl of the red mouth,
  Love me! Love me!
Girl of the red mouth,
  Love me!
'Tis by its curve, I know,
Love fashioneth his bow,
And bends it—ah, even so!
  Oh, girl of the red mouth, love me!

Girl of the blue eye,
  Love me! Love me!
Girl of the dew eye,
  Love me!
Worlds hang for lamps on high;
And thought's world lives in thy
Lustrous and tender eye—
  Oh, girl of the blue eye, love me!

Girl of the swan's neck,
  Love me! Love me!
Girl of the swan's neck,
  Love me!
As a marble Greek doth grow
To his steed's back of snow,
Thy white neck sits thy shoulder so,—
  Oh, girl of the swan's neck, love me!

Girl of the low voice,
  Love me! Love me!
Girl of the sweet voice,
  Love me!
Like the echo of a bell,—
Like the bubbling of a well—
Sweeter! Love within doth dwell,—
  Oh, girl of the low voice, love me!

LINES

By William H. Mallock

Homeless man goes, even on life's sunniest slope,
And yet between two homes he takes his way—
Between to-morrow, that's the home of Hope,
And Happiness, whose house is yesterday.

Yet, man, complain not. Thank your fates instead
And call them good before they bring you worse—
The days when Hope shall in her home lie dead
And Happiness forgotten fade in hers.

HUMAN LIFE

By William H. Mallock

Like smoke I vanish though I burn like flame,
I flicker in the gusts of wrong and right—
A shining frailty in the guise of might;
Before a nothing and behind a name.

DUST

By Sister Mary Angelita

Rich and strange thy history,
Essence of mortality,
Part and parcel of God's plan
When He molded earth and man,
Fabric of the quick and dead,
Framework of the earth we tread,
All the trails in all the lands
And the shifting brown sea sands;
Glowing in the wayside rose;
Sport of every wind that blows;
Spurned beneath our careless feet
As a thing for scorning meet,
High espousals thine,—the clod
Wedded to the breath of God.

Proudly hast thou played thy part,
Throbbed in mighty Caesar's heart,
Gleamed in Helen's peerless eyes,
Stirred the air with Sappho's sighs,
Made the marble breathe and glow
At the touch of Angelo,
Wielded the victorious blade
In the clasp of Joan, the maid
And o'er Dante's page divine
Traced each burning, deathless line

DUST

Solvent of humanity,
All things earthly come to thee;
Serf and monarch, fool and sage,
Golden youth and withered age,
Pomp of Nineveh and Tyre,
Court and temple, shaft and spire,
Stately Greece and lordly Rome,
Cobweb arch and bubble dome,
Live their day, and then return
To o'erflow thy brimming urn.
When the heavens, like a scroll,
At the voice of doom uproll,
When the earth and sky by fire
Melt in one vast funeral pyre,
Thou, O Dust, sole earthly thing,
To eternal life shalt spring;
Leap to clothe the ransomed soul
With a garment rich and whole,
Weaving round the blanching bone
Living vesture all its own,
Glowing flesh all firm and fair,
Ruddy lip and gleaming hair,
And the thrilling crimson stain
Of each artery and vein.
Then, transfigured, glorified,
Kingly spirit's lowborn bride,
Raised unto his high degree,
Thou shalt reign immortally
In the bodies of the just,—
Apotheosis of dust.

SIGNUM CUI CONTRADICETUR

By Sister Mary Angelita

Long months He lay within the womb,
    Prisoned from every lovely sight,
Wrapped round in darkness and in gloom,
    Who was the Light.

In a rude stable cold and dim,
    Maid Mary our Redeemer bore;
All doors were harshly closed to Him,
    Who was the Door.

Long time by silence did He teach,
    A helpless Infant, ere was heard
His first quaint, stammering baby speech,
    Who was the Word.

Three anguished days they strove to trace
    His childish footsteps gone astray.
Lost, in the crowded, alien place!—
    Who was the Way.

Meekly He did His parents' will:
    They gave commands, with secret awe,
And He was subject to them still,
    Who was the Law.

With wounded hands and feet and side,
    All mangled from the cruel strife,
He bowed His head and, shuddering, died.
    Who was the Life.

A WORD WITH A SKYLARK

By Mrs. Sarah M. B Piatt

If this be all, for which I've listened long,
    Oh, spirit of the dew!
You did not sing to Shelley such a song
    As Shelley sung to you.

Yet, with this ruined Old World for a nest,
    Worm-eaten through and through,—
This waste of grave-dust stamped with crown and crest,—
    What better could you do?

Ah me! but when the world and I were young,
    There was an apple-tree,
There was a voice came in the dawn and sung
    The buds awake—ah me!

Oh, Lark of Europe, downward fluttering near,
    Like some spent leaf at best,
You'd never sing again if you could hear
    My Blue-Bird of the West!

DEAR DARK HEAD

By William Rooney

O Dear Dark Head, bowed low in death-black sorrow,
    Let not they heart be trammelled in despair;
Lift, lift thine eyes unto the radiant morrow,
    And wait the light that surely shall break there.

What, though the grave hath closed above thy dearest,
  All are not gone that love thee, nor all fled;
And though thine own sweet tongue thou seldom hearest,
  Yet shall it ring again, O Dear Dark Head.

O Dear Dark Head that mourneth by thy waters,
    Crooning a *caoine* for the countless graves
Of valiant sons and brave true-hearted daughters,
    Waiting the angel's trump beneath the waves,
Take from each rising sun some ray to cheer thee,
    Some gleam of glory from each sunset red;
They bring an hour all close and closer near thee,
    That shall avenge these graves, O Dear Dark Head.

O! Dear Dark Head, though but the curlew's screaming
    Wakens the echoes of the hill and glen;
Yet shalt thou see once more the bright steel gleaming,
    Yet shalt thou hear again the tramp of men;
And though their fathers' fate be theirs, shall others
    With hearts as faithful still that pathway tread,
Till we have set, oh! mother dear of mothers,
    A nation's crown upon thy Dear Dark Head.

O Dear Dark Head, let not thy waiting daunt thee,
    The future if thou willest can be thine;
The past can summon up no shades to haunt thee,
    Of perjured faith or desecrated shrine;
Lift, lift thy heart then; for each year of mourning,
    Each sigh you breathed, every tear you shed,
There yet shall be a jewel bright adorning
    Thy mantle's myriad folds, O Dear Dark Head.

THE POET

By William Rooney

He walks amid the worldly, yet in his heart afar
   Back in the past he wanders or plunges into days
That suns have yet to look on, he sees the distant star
   Of Freedom's morning blaze.
He looks into the firelight, and lo! beholds the past;
   Cuchullain by the river looks towards the hosted foe,
And Ferdiah comes; their arms are round each other cast
   In grim resolve and woe!

He sees great Maedbh surrounded by knight and charioteer,
   Rurie and Keth he notes him amid the circling press;
The dust of combat rises—he hears the rolling cheer
   Soar, deepen, and grow less.

The winds bear him a message, the dusty summer days,
   The blossoms in the valleys, the tide upon the strands,
The reeds that by the rivers their slender forms upraise,
   All, all, he understands.

He's seen the gentle people trip o'er the moonlit dew,
   And heard their music stealing from out the green rath's heart;
He's listed to their laughter, and learnèd what they do,
   So he must dwell apart.

For they have waked a longing for all the long ago,
   And brought him dreams of Eirinn in æons yet to be;
They have his soul uplifted from sorrowing and woe,
   And willed that he may see!

The battle's breeze is round him, he marks the people's might
 Bear down oppression's legions, he feels the martial tread
Of Freedom shake the island, sees long dishonoured Right
 With rose-enwreathèd head.

And so he weaves his visions to stir the nation's soul,
 And sings his songs all hopeful to cheer the doubting on;
Though graves yawn on the pathway, though death wait in the goal,
 He knows what must be done!

FAR-AWAY

By George Sigerson

As chimes that flow o'er shining seas
 When Morn alights on meads of May,
Faint voices fill the western breeze
 With whisp'ring songs from Far-Away.
Oh, dear the dells of Dunanore,
 A home is odorous Ossory;
But sweet as honey, running o'er,
 The Golden Shore of Far-Away!

There grows the Tree whose summer breath
 Perfumes with joy the azure air;
And he who feels it fears not Death,
 Nor longer heeds the hounds of Care.

Oh, soft the skies of Seskinore,
    And mild is meadowy Mellaray;
But sweet as honey, running o'er,
    The Golden Shore of Far-Away!

There sings the Voice whose wondrous tune
Falls, like diamond-showers above
That in the radiant dawn of June
Renew a world of Youth and Love.
    Oh, fair the founts of Farranfore,
        And bright is billowy Ballintrae;
    But sweet as honey, running o'er,
        The Golden Shore of Far-Away!

Come, Fragrance of the Flowering Tree,
Oh, sing, sweet Bird, thy magic lay,
Till all the world be young with me,
And Love shall lead us far away.
    Oh, dear the dells of Dunanore,
        A home is odorous Ossory;
    But sweet as honey, running o'er,
        The Golden Shore of Far-Away!

THE CALLING

By George Sigerson

O sigh of the Sea, O soft lone-wandering sound,
Why callest thou me, with voice of all waters profound,
With sob and with smile, with lingering pain and delight,
With mornings of blue, with flash of thy billows at night?

The shell from the shore, though borne far away from
    thy side,
Recalls evermore the flowing and fall of thy tide,
And so, through my heart thy murmurs gather and grow—
Thy tides, as of old, awake in its darkness, and flow.

O Sigh of the Sea, from luminous isles far away,
Why callest thou me to sail the impassable way?
Why callest thou me to share the unrest of thy soul—
Desires that avail not, yearnings from pole unto pole?

Still call, till I hear no voice but the voice of thy love,
Till stars shall appear the night of my darkness above,
Till night to the dawn gives way, and death to new life—
Heart-full of thy might, astir with thy tumult and strife.

YOU AND I

By Timothy Daniel Sullivan

I know what will happen, sweet,
    When you and I are one;
Calm and bright and very fleet,
    All our days will run.
Fond and kind our words will be,
    Mixed no more with sighs;
Thoughts too fine for words we'll see
    Within each other's eyes.

Sweet, when you and I are one,
    Earth will bloom anew—
Brighter then the stars and sun,
    Softer than the dew.

Sweeter scents will then arise
  From the fields and flowers;
Holier calm will fill the skies
  In the midnight hours.

Music now unheard, unknown,
  Then will reach our ears;
Not a plaint in any tone,
  Not a hint of tears.
In a round of bliss complete
  All our days will run—
That is what will happen, sweet,
  When you and I are one.

THE ANCIENT RACE

By Rev. Michael Tormey

What shall become of the ancient race,
The noble Keltic island race?
Like cloud on cloud o'er the azure sky,
When winter storms are loud and high
Their dark ships shadow the ocean's face—
What shall become of the Keltic race?

What shall befall the ancient race—
The poor, unfriended, faithful race?
Where ploughman's song made the hamlet ring,
The hawk and the owlet flap their wing;
The village homes, oh, who can trace—
God of our persecuted race!

THE ANCIENT RACE

What shall befall the ancient race?
Is treason's stigma on their face?
Be they cowards or traitors? Go—
Ask the shade of England's foe;
See the gems her crown that grace;
They tell a tale of the ancient race.

They tell a tale of the ancient race—
Of matchless deeds in danger's face;
They speak of Britain's glory fed
With blood of Kelts, right bravely shed;
On India's spoil and Frank's disgrace—
Such tale they tell of the ancient race.

Then why cast out the ancient race?
Grim want dwelt with the ancient race,
And hell-born laws, with prison jaws;
And greedy lords, with tiger maws,
Have swallowed—swallow still apace—
The limbs and blood of the ancient race.

Will no one shield the ancient race?
They fly their fathers' burial place;
The proud lords with the heavy purse,
Their fathers' shame—their people's curse—
Demons in heart, nobles in face—
They dig a grave for the ancient race!

What shall befall the ancient race?
Shall all forsake their dear birthplace,
Without one struggle strong to keep
The old soil where their fathers sleep?
The dearest land on earth's wide space—
Why leave it so, O ancient race?

What shall befall the ancient race?
Light up one hope for the ancient race;
Oh, priest of God—Soggarth Aroon!
Lead but the way, we'll go full soon;
Is there a danger we will not face,
To keep old homes for the Irish race?

They shall not go, the ancient race—
They must not go, the ancient race!
Come, gallant Kelts, and take your stand—
And form a league to save the land;
The land of faith, the land of grace,
The land of Erin's ancient race!

They must not go, the ancient race!
They shall not go, the ancient race!
The cry swells loud from shore to shore,
From emerald vale to mountain hoar,
From altar high to market-place—
"THEY SHALL NOT GO, the ancient race!"

NIGHT

By Joseph Blanco White

MYSTERIOUS Night! When our first parent knew
Thee, from report divine, and heard thy name,
Did he not tremble for this lovely Frame,
This glorious canopy of Light and Blue?
Yet, 'neath a curtain of translucent dew,
Bathed in the rays of the great setting Flame,
Hesperus, with the Host of Heaven, came,
And lo! Creation widened on Man's view.

Who could have thought such darkness lay concealed
Within thy beams, O Sun! or who could find,
Whilst flower and leaf and insect stood revealed,
That to such countless orbs thou mad'st us blind!
Why do we then shun Death with anxious strife?
If Light can thus deceive, wherefore not Life?

SONNET ON HOLY WEEK

By Oscar Wilde

I wandered through Scoglietto's far retreat.
 The oranges on each o'erhanging spray
 Burned as bright lamps of gold to shame the day,
Some startled bird with fluttering wings and fleet
Made snow of all the blossoms, at my feet
 Like silver moons the pale narcissi lay:
 And the curved waves that streaked the great green bay
Laughed i' the sun, and life seemed very sweet.

Outside the young boy-priest passed singing clear,
 "Jesus the Son of Mary has been slain,
 O come and fill his sepulchre with flowers."
Ah, God! Ah, God! those dear Hellenic hours
 Had drowned all memory of Thy bitter pain,
 The Cross, the Crown, the Soldiers, and the Spear.

E TENEBRIS

By Oscar Wilde

Come down, O Christ, and help me! reach thy hand,
  For I am drowning in a stormier sea
  Than Simon on thy lake of Galilee:
The wine of life is spilt upon the sand,
My heart is as some famine-murdered land
  Whence all good things have perished utterly,
  And well I know my soul in Hell must lie
If I this night before God's throne should stand.
"He sleeps perchance, or rideth to the chase,
  Like Baal, when his prophets howled that name
  From morn till noon on Carmel's smitten height."
Nay, peace, I shall behold before the night,
  The feet of brass, the robe more white than flame,
  The wounded hands, the weary human face.

LE JARDIN DES TUILERIES

By Oscar Wilde

This winter air is keen and cold,
  And keen and cold this winter sun,
  But round my chair the children run
Like little things of dancing gold.

Sometimes about the painted kiosk
  The mimic soldiers strut and stride,
  Sometimes the blue-eyed brigands hide
In the bleak tangles of the bosk.

And sometimes, while the old nurse cons
   Her book, they steal across the square,
   And launch their paper navies where
Huge Triton writhes in greenish bronze.

And now in mimic flight they flee,
   And now they rush, a boisterous band—
   And, tiny hand in tiny hand,
Climb up the black and leafless tree.

Ah! cruel tree! if I were you,
   And children climbed me, for their sake
   Though it be winter I would break
Into spring blossoms white and blue.

AVE MARIA GRATIA PLENA

By Oscar Wilde

Was this His coming! I had hoped to see
   A scene of wondrous glory, as was told
   Of some great God who in a rain of gold
Broke open bars and fell on Danae:
Or a dread vision as when Semele
   Sickening for love and unappeased desire
   Prayed to see God's clear body, and the fire
Caught her brown limbs and slew her utterly:
With such glad dreams I sought this holy place,
   And now with wondering eyes and heart I stand
   Before this supreme mystery of Love:
Some kneeling girl with passionless pale face,
   An angel with a lily in his hand,
   And over both the white wings of a Dove.

Florence

JAPANESE CHERRIES

By Katherine Brégy

I carried a burden of bitterness
Into the park this afternoon.
My heart was heavy with dead dreams,
And tears unshed,
And disenchanted loyalties—
And the mortal tiredness had bored its way
Into my immortal soul. . . .
Then I saw a curving row of cherry trees
With plump pink blossoms laughing in the breeze,
As the setting sun smiled back at them.
I knew those fragile trees:
I recalled them, pitifully small and bare against the autumn
  sky,
Huddling together like frightened fawns against the wind,
Armored with ice against the beating winter rains.
And shame swept upon me
And courage and a singing peace:
From my heart cried out—
Shall a little alien tree be stronger and finer
Than your love?

SILENT SUFFERER

By John Gilland Brunini

If other men could clearly see your moon-white face
A chaliced flower, a coiling vine your hair,
Your breath such perfume as the swamp-winds bear
Drowsy with drugging death—if they could trace

Where in his life love's lightning ran its race,
Consuming all which he once held most fair—
Some portion of his anguish would you share,
Some sorrow that your nature was so base.

Were he than soul more animal which pained
Would fang the hand that dealt unwitting blows,
What vengeance might he not have mulled and rained
Down Damon's temple on your double woes?
Pray you may see again a greatness near
To his—no deed, no word, no tell-tale tear.

THE CONVERT

By Gilbert Keith Chesterton

After one moment when I bowed my head
And the whole world turned over and came upright,
And I came out where the old road shone white,
I walked the ways and heard what all men said,
Forests of tongues, like autumn leaves unshed,
Being not unlovable but strange and light;
Old riddles and new creeds, not in despite
But softly, as men smile about the dead.

The sages have a hundred maps to give
That trace their crawling cosmos like a tree,
They rattle reason out through many a sieve
That stores the sand and lets the gold go free:
And all these things are less than dust to me
Because my name is Lazarus and I live.

CELIBACY

By Austin Clarke

On a brown isle of Lough Corrib,
When clouds were bare as branch
And water had been thorned
By colder days, I sank
In torment of her side;
But still that woman stayed,
For eye obeys the mind.

Bedraggled in the briar
And grey fire of the nettle,
Three nights, I fell, I groaned
On the flagstone of help
To pluck her from my body;
For servant ribbed with hunger
May climb his rungs to God.

Eyelid stood back in sleep,
I saw what seemed an Angel:
Dews dripped from those bright feet.
But O, I knew the stranger
By her deceit and, tired
All night by tempting flesh,
I wrestled her in hair-shirt.

On pale knees in the dawn,
Parting the straw that wrapped me,
She sank until I saw

The bright roots of her scalp.
She pulled me down to sleep,
But I fled as the Baptist
To thistle and to reed.

The dragons of the Gospel
Are cast by bell and crook;
But fiery as the frost
Or bladed light, she drew
The reeds back, when I fought
The arrow-headed airs
That darken on the water.

SONG AGAINST SERVANTS

By Gertrude Jane Codd

It's right to have a little maid—
You often say I should—
With neat blue dress and apron,
With ways and manners good.

But don't you see, I like the touch
Of linen on the bed;
I like to plump the pillows up
Where you will lay your head.

I like to wash the china cups
And put them on the shelf;
I like to dust our little house
And straighten it myself.

It's fun to do the marketing
And get the things for tea,
To lay the plates and silver out
And food for you and me.

And when you knock upon the door
The happy way you do,
I want—*I* want to be the one
To open it for you.

QUO VADIS?

By Myles E. Connolly

Fare not abroad, O Soul, to win
   Man's friendly smile or favoring nod;
Be still, be strong, and seek within
   The Comradeship of God.

Beyond is not the journey's end,
   The fool goes wayfaring apart,
And even as he goes his Friend
   Is knocking at his heart.

NOX IGNATIANA

By James J. Daly, S.J.

His vigil was the stars; his eyes were bright
   With radiance of them. Mystically slow
   Was their processional, while far below
Rome's quick and dead slept—fellows in the night.

These very stars had marched in cryptic rite
   For Vergil in clear evenings long ago,
     Gliding, like motes, athwart the overflow
Of splendor from immortal tides of Light.

"What is this ant-life on a sphere of sand
   That it must drive, with ant-like cares, my soul
     Than all the stars together more sublime?"
So in the spacious night Ignatius planned
   His spacious morrows—centuries his scroll—
     Upon a background of Eternal Time.

UPON THIS ROCK

By James L. Duff

"Simon Bar-Jona, lovest thou Me?"
Three times the question, and three times I
Made the Master the same reply—
   And that was true.

"Thou wast with him, wast thou not?"
Three times the question, and three times I
Answered it with the selfsame lie—
   Then the cock crew.

"Simon Bar-Jona, lovest thou Me?"
This is the answer of Peter, the Rock:
Out of my love I shall feed Thy flock—
   Each sheep and each lamb.

"Thou wast with Him, wast thou not?"
This is the answer of Peter, the Rock:
No matter what enemies sneer and mock—
   I was and I am!

LONELINESS

By Father Edwin Essex

My soul has solitudes
Where no pace falls;
Thy silent trespassings
No man forestalls.

My soul has silences
No voice can break;
Only Thy hidden words
Its echoes wake.

But oh, the solitudes
Shouldst Thou not come!
The stricken silences,
When Thou art dumb!

A FLEDGLING ROBIN

By Leonard Feeney, S J.

Take us size for size and he
Is but a speck aside of me.
His gold-rimmed lip
Is but my finger tip;
His tiny throat—
A button on my coat!

Or take us age for age, and I
Am older immeasurably
By twenty years or so,
Three weeks ago
He was a wee, blue egg at rest
Under his mother's breast.

Or take us soul for soul; he knows
None of life's bitter, bitter woes,
No endless tears,
No agonizing fears,
No hopes of immortality
That ever try and trouble me.

Yet turn us both into a wood some May,
Some fresh, fair morn and listen all the day
How very deftly he
Creates more poetry
With three soft-gurgled notes, than I attain
By a whole life of pain!

GOOD LUCK

By Oliver Gogarty

Apples of gold the Hero dropt
As he was in the race outstript;
And Atalanta running stopt,
And all her lovely body dipt
A moment; but she lost her stride—
And had to go to bed a bride.

And was it not a cordial strong
By which the young Iseult was filled
With passion for a whole life long;
For that was what the juice instilled?
So he who kept the unwitting tryst
Was sure of love before he kissed.

But where can I get Western gold
Or posset of constraining fire?—
I who am fated to behold
Beauty outdistancing desire?
Aye; and to falter wonder-struck;
There's no good love without good luck!

NON DOLET

By Oliver Gogarty

Our friends go with us as we go
  Down the long path where Beauty wends,
Where all we love foregather; so
  Why should we fear to join our friends?

Who would survive them to outlast
  His children; to outwear his fame—
Left when the Triumph has gone past—
  To win from Age, not Time, a name?

Then do not shudder at the knife
  That Death's indifferent hand drives home
But with the strivers leave the strife,
  Nor after Caesar, skulk in Rome.

VERSE

By Oliver Gogarty

What should we know,
For better or worse,
Of the Long Ago,
Were it not for Verse:
What ships went down;
What walls were razed;
Who won the crown;
What lads were praised?
A fallen stone,
Or a waste of sands;
And all is known
Of Art-less lands.

But you need not delve
By the sea-side hills
Where the Muse herself
All Time fulfils,
Who cuts with his scythe
All things but hers;
All but the blithe
Hexameters.

THE WINDOVER

By Gerard Hopkins, S J.

I caught this morning morning's minion, kingdom of
    daylight's dauphin, dapple-dawn-drawn Falcon, in
    his riding
  Of the rolling level underneath him steady air, and
    striding
High there, how he rung upon the rein of a wimpling wing
In his ecstasy! then off, off forth on swing,
  As a skate's heel sweeps smooth on a bow-bend: the
    hurl and gliding
  Rebuffed the big wind. My heart in hiding
Stirred for a bird,—the achieve of, the mastery of the
    thing!

Brute beauty and valour and act, oh, air, pride, plume, here
  Buckle! AND the fire that breaks from thee then, a
    billion
Times told lovelier, more dangerous, O my chevalier!

  No wonder of it: shéer plód makes plough down sillion
Shine, and blue-bleak embers, ah my dear,
  Fall, gall themselves, and gash gold-vermillion.

PIED BEAUTY

By Gerard Hopkins, S.J.

Glory be to God for dappled things—
  For skies of couple-colour as a brinded cow;
    For rose-moles all in stipple upon trout that swim
Fresh-firecoal chestnut-falls; finches' wings;
  Landscape plotted and pieced—fold, fallow, and plough
    And áll trádes, their gear and tackle and trim.
All things counter, original, spare, strange;
  Whatever is fickle, freckled (who knows how?)
    With swift, slow; sweet, sour; adazzle, dim;
He fathers-forth whose beauty is past change:
        Praise him.

AT THE WEDDING MARCH

By Gerard Hopkins, S.J.

God with honour hang your head,
Groom, and grace you, bride, your bed
With lissome scions, sweet scions,
Out of hallowed bodies bred.

Each be other's comfort kind:
Déep, déeper than divined,
Divine charity, dear charity,
Fast you ever, fast bind.

Then let the march tread our ears:
I to him turn with tears
Who to wedlock, his wonder wedlock
Déals tríumph and immortal years.

TO A BAFFLED IDEALIST

By J. G. E. Hopkins

Because the upper and the nether stones
Of things that are, ground close and slew
That dreamer who was you;
Because the flowers your heart set in your mind,
So aptly ordered and so beautiful,
Were withered in the wind
That life sends hot and blighting over those
Who must dispose
A grand and God-like spirit in their kind;
You have turned inward-seeking and have cried
Out of your simple pride,
"See, Lord, how men are bitter and unsouled:
There is none just save me."
While we,
Expecting little, happen on the gold,
Seamy and tough of assay that runs through
The coarse ore of the mine-run that is Man,
Often enough to make our hearts grow glad
Out of humility,
Remembering that in Man are many men
Who live and die and hope for heaven, too.

LIGHT SHOES

By Patrick Kelly

He fixed his hat Kildare-side on
   And drew the door behind:
He danced a step to free his limbs
   And tripped it down the wind.
He gave a roar to show his sport
   And cried, "My work is done:
Farewell, Mayo, for I'm ready to go
   Around the world for fun."

He kissed his girl upon the mouth,
   She said, "Your eye is queer
And I'm afraid—O much afraid—
   I'm not your only dear."
He said, "My dear, I go from you
   That Fortune's kiss be won"—
And away he went and round the world,
   Around the world for fun.

He met an old man clear of Cong—
   "Good-bye, old man, good-bye."
The old man blinked and what did he do?
   Sat down on the road to cry.
The young man whistled and followed the road
   Straight into the morning sun—
"The curse o' the crows on all who fail
   To follow the road for fun."

Now here we sit too nice to stir,
   Afraid of the wind and rain.

While they're drinking deep in Santa Cruz
  The health of the King of Spain.
It's little would make me cut my stick
  Tho' my shoes they weigh a ton,
And kiss the girls I love, good-bye,
  And round the world for fun.

I SHALL NOT BE AFRAID

By Aline Kilmer

I shall not be afraid any more,
  Either by night or day;
What would it profit me to be afraid
  With you away?

Now I am brave. In the dark night alone,
  All through the house I go,
Locking the doors and making windows fast
  When sharp winds blow.

For there is only sorrow in my heart,
  There is no room for fear.
But how I wish I were afraid again,
  My dear, my dear!

OLIM MEMINISSE JUVABIT

By Aline Kilmer

Sometime it may be pleasing to remember
    The curls about your brow,
To talk about your eyes, your smile, your dearness,
    But it is anguish now.

Often I feel that I must speak and tell them
    Of all your golden ways,
How all the words you ever spoke were happy,
    Joy-filled your laughing days.

But though I miss you every empty moment
    Of all my longing years,
How can I speak about your thrilling beauty
    When all my thoughts are tears?

Sometime it may be pleasing to remember
    The curls about your brow,
The way you turned your head, your hands, your laughter
    But oh, not now, not now!

IF THIS OLD PLACE

By Mary Kolars

If this old place had held no grief before
No wild, unchildish woe wept out alone,
Where dirt turns into sand here by the shore
And bushes droop above the marking stone;

If memory were not made of things untender,
Could memory call the heart out of my breast?
O sorrow of a child, O dark befriender
By whom my lost comes back, my repossessed!

My far-off golden laughter has no reaping,
My far-off joy has not held these in keeping,—
The rock, the road beside the sandy shore;
But grief, once sown, can split the granite portal;
Youth's moment, incorruptible, immortal,
Is rendered back to me forevermore.

TO FEAR

By Clifford J. Laube

By this body's lonely ark
Through the daylight and the dark
You have kept your vigil well,
Archangelic sentinel.

Long ago in secret moods
Of my boyhood solitudes
Dimly I could feel the care
Of your hand upon my hair.

Limbs that ventured, rashly brisk,
Out upon the roads of risk,
Tamed their truant enterprise
To the caution in your eyes.

When these senses five caught fire
At the dawnrise of desire,
Touches of your frosty wing
Cooled their sullen smoldering.

Dark companion of my path,
Whisper still some hint of wrath
Lest these rebel fervors slip
Reins of grace and guardianship.

When this strength, less proudly nerved,
Droops, the dread subpoena served,
Stand beside me at my bier,
Bodyguard of holy fear.

AS ONE FINDING PEACE

By Sister M. Madeleva

The secret of the King possesses me
Unutterably.
I am a child to sudden woman grown
Who never yet has known
Invasion so imperious, so complete,
Blindly and madly sweet.
I am a bud to sudden blossom blown,
Intoxicate, replete
With fragrance most divinely not its own.
I am dew thirstily drunk up
Out of dawn's lifted cup.
I am my own impotent, daring self, plunged in a sea
Ecstatically!

AS ONE FINDING PEACE

O God, encompass me!
Be infinitely mine to hold, to bound me;
Absorb, consume, encompass and confound me;
Be in me and beneath me and above me;
O Father, love me, love me!
Tremendously be,
Strong God, my sea.

In ultimate joy upon this Lover's breast
I come to rest.
Peace, like a song,
Envelopes me;
Peace, like the night,
Folds me in conscious, beautiful delight.
Never has human love held me in tranquil thrall,
For not to human love does peace belong.
What if I be for the Lord God a wall,
Beauteous as cedar and as cedar strong;
What if I be a door, and sealed to all save Him,
Cunningly joined, guarded by flashing cherubim?
I am a door, a wall, tower of passionate strength
Around which multitudinously throng
Wild ecstasies, wild joys, unending blisses,
A God's caresses and a Father's kisses.

Presently let this rapture in profounder rapture cease;
A silver bulwark of wrought silence be,
My Father, since that I am come at length,
Captive and free,
Into Your presence as one finding peace.

AT WINTER'S END

By Sister M. Madeleva

Buds are backward and winter lingers
But you, the eager, the quick, the wary,
Have found the first gold fritillary,
The clustered, rose-pink lady-fingers.

You have found, too, with cautious hunting,
That tricky one, the elusive towhee,
The tanager, splendidly shy and showy,
The summer-minded lazuli bunting.

I come not back with April weather;
Winds cannot woo nor sun unbind me.
Much as you seek, you cannot find me;
We shall not have this spring together.

But we warm our hearts at no dying ember
Who can tell us how love is parted?
We are forever happy-hearted
Having one springtime to remember.

THE ROOT

By Francis Maguire

The fish are folded
In green seas;
Earth encircles
The shining trees;

Ivy clutches
With multiple art—
But God is a root
Around the heart.

Secret and silent,
He coils around,
Consuming the things
Of the dark ground.

He finds a fissure
Through which to crawl,
Or circles, circles,
A tragic wall.

A SONG OF WHITE AND RED

By Sister Mary Benvenuta, O.P.

White and ruddy is my Beloved:
  White of the Bread, red of the Wine,
White and ruddy, white and ruddy,
  Fruit of the corn-sheaf and the vine.

White and ruddy is my Beloved,
  White of the Flesh, red of the blood,
White and ruddy, white and ruddy,
  Red in the flower, white in the bud.

White and ruddy is my Beloved,
  White in the crib, red on the Rood,
White and ruddy, white and ruddy,
  God, my lover and my Food.

HAWKESYARD

(House of Studies for Dominican Novices)

BY SISTER MARY BENVENUTA, O. P.

THIS is the mew of God set high
   Beneath the heavens' windy rafter,
Whence all His falconry shall fly,
And, clean of wing and clear of eye,
   Make sport to wake the angels' laughter.
     Ah, birds of God,
   What prey shall ye bring home hereafter?

Here, hooded by His hand they sit,
   Nor fear the due monastic jesses
That leash them to His wrist, and knit
Their wills to His, as should befit
   The fledglings of His tendernesses,
     Who shall repay
   Some day, this spring-time of caresses.

AS ONE FINDING PEACE

BY SISTER MARY OF THE VISITATION

BECAUSE the Spirit of Delight has laid
His hand upon my lips, I may not tell
All that my heart has learned; because my eyes
Saw Beauty for one moment, unafraid,
I shall go singing through the very shade
Of death—yet never whisper what befell,
Nor ever show the ruddy wounds He made.

Whether the dart He used was tipped with flame
Or ice, I know not—I remember this:
One breathless word of unexpressive bliss,
The half unspoken utterance of a Name. . . .

Now by all paths where joys encompass me
Blindly I walk. These tears upon my face?
Think not of them, nor marvel there should be
A note of sadness in the songs I sing,
For all my former prowess is undone
Since I have stood one moment in a place
I may not name—and learned this secret thing:
The Spirits of Delight and Pain are One,
For both are Love. (Ineffably replete
With Pain, the heart that knows how Love is sweet,
And knowing, seeks, and blissfully has found.)
The Spirit of Delight has taught me this—
He that is called the blissful Paraclete.

HYMN TO THE GUARDIAN ANGEL

By J. Corson Miller

Perfection-bright Figure, daily with me sojourning,
Thy light invisible forging celestial shelter—
Lieutenant of God, from heights of love descended,
   See, I salute thee!

Pomegranates of wisdom drop from Thy fingers,
Fire from Thine eyes, seeding the soul's glory;
Prisoning the will in a starry liberation—
   Sentry of Sainthood!

Lo, I am sealed by the Blood and framed in the Image
Of One Who blew in my clay the breath of the Spirit—
Divine Messenger, now in supplication,
   I bow before Thee. . . .

Let me, who cringed before the dragon of evil,
Summoning Thee, draw the proud sword of repentance;
Then, armored and visored with virtue, Thou shalt behold
    me
   Statured in triumph.

HER FAIRNESS, WEDDED TO A STAR

By Edward J. O'Brien

Her fairness, wedded to a star,
Is fairer than all lilies are,
And flowers within her eyes more white
Than moonlight on an April night.

Her wonder like a wind doth sing,
Wedded to the heart of spring.
And April, dawning in her eyes,
Reflects the wonder of the skies.

Her beauty lights the April day
With radiance of her chastity,
And innocence doth slumber now
Upon her candid April brow.

THE POET

By Seumas O'Brien

From a mountain top a poet looked down
On the stone and mortar of the town.

Crowds were hurrying to and fro,
And few knew why they were doing so.

The houses were twenty times too high;
And fearless man had learned to fly.

He lashed himself to a spinning wheel,
And had two masters—gold and steel.

Everything that the poet could see
Once was not—and in time, won't be.

"Strange," said he, "though it may seem,
They and I are only a dream
A prophet had when Babylon
Wasn't yet a brick to sit upon."

ON A DEAD TEACHER
(To K K.)
By Gerald Raftery

Her deed and her name will be lost
In the deep earth;
She has labored and never counted the cost
That a dream was worth.

The children who learned from her silent lips
Will remember awhile
Till the shadows of earth at last eclipse
Her words and her smile.

And all will be lost but the rich uncountable things
When her name is gone
There will burn the torch that every poet sings
That she handed on.

ON MOVING INTO A SKYLIGHT ROOM

By Sister Rita Agnes

ARTISTICALLY weather-proof,
A slanting region of the roof
Inside adds one expanse the more
To ceiling, four walls, and a floor.
Thus from the endless stretch of space
Seven surfaces enclose this place.
Herein my feet may be restrained
And my inquiring self contained
For one-third of the hours of breath
Between now and arresting death.

The cars that night and day rush by
Are faintly heard by me on high,
As breakers of a distant sea
Which surges intermittently.
A bevelled skylight opened wide
Gives glimpse of blue at either side,

But O the trusty wall is stout!
It shuts all hilltop pictures out.
No autumn splendors notice win
Where every inch seems facing in,
And furnishings impression give
That I have turned contemplative.

Yet now with joy I see my mind
Can not by walls remain confined,
And this—my eyes' new continence—
Has finely stirred an inner sense,
While peace and quiet make more clear
The words of One divinely dear.
The sweet air enters, cool and free,
A symbol of ubiquity;
It finds me glad to have no doubts
The Lord still knows my whereabouts.

MARY SALOME, WIDOW

By Anne Ryan

With your head-cloth knotted and your shawl pinned tight
You come out of your house this day and close the silent
　　door.
You are alone,
Your life has faded.
The misery of your youth,
The lost abundance of your love,
And those nights in which the name, Salome, was given
　　you,

The waste and the murders and the chaos of your village,
    long ago settled by Caesar,
All has drifted away like a mist of tales which encircle
Another woman unknown to you.

It is not yet light.
Along the road the cypress, fluted in black,
Stand mourning still.
You carry your cup of ointment carefully nested in folds,
A neighbor, hurrying, grieving for the flogged, dishonored
    Dead.

Later: In the chapel of Dona Maria Forteza
They have given you a niche of silver
With a canopy strange and chirurgeresque,
While for your office, your name—
Always like the ringing of two bells—
Is displayed forever
Between figures from the Calvary
And a fragment of the Resurrection.

NEWMAN

By George N. Shuster

Men found you subtle, master, blending skeins
Of taut silk thinking with the golden weave
Prayer finds in God. A stormy epoch's eve
Stirred your vast silence, till in flaming strains
You spoke glory. Yet deeper radiance gains
Who, listening close, can the still note perceive
That fires your music's heart—a note to grieve
And gladden, bred of the desert and swift rains.

Beacon of mystery! Soul's eagle, whose eye
Tirelessly saw through earth's hoar shadowings
The Undimmed Sun! With you these new years cry
For lighted ways and the dear morning's dew.
Hearing your voice, we feebly scan the wings
That made the peaks of sainthood plain to you.

TO PAIN

By George Sterling

Sandalled with morning and with evening star,
  Draw near me, Lady of ascendant pain,
  Whose hair has touched me in the twilight rain,
Whose home is where unchanging faces are.
You wait me where immortal feet have trod,
  And in your voice is music not-to-be,
  And in your eyes the night of mystery,
Old as the silence on the lips of God.

There is no treason in your given word.
  Your love is past all love, all vain delights,
And holy is the music I have heard.
  'Tis not the Cytherean that shall lead
To stranger seas and unimagined heights,
  Nor stand in flame beside me at my need.

INTEMPESTIVA

By Henry Longan Stuart

Once more the lumbering earth heaves its chill flank
   Through tempered sun and blessedness of rain;
   Spring wears to summer; now forget thy pain,
With quickened pulse the quickening season thank.
Leave thy close room, that, couched 'mid grasses rank
   While a wood's warbled woes for thine complain,
   Nature thy wounded heart may salve again,
With simples that of old Antaeus drank.

But stir me not! My soul begins to tire,
   With loveless summer sated, and is grown
      Kin to the winter it was wont to hate.
For I could weep because they quench my fire,
   Flinging the windows open, and have strown
      Forgotten flowers on an empty grate.

AVOWAL

By A. M. Sullivan

Night is not darkness—
Not the utter dark
Before the words of Genesis
Were spoken
And the divine spark
Had broken
The chrysalis
Of the sun.

AVOWAL

Night is a loom for light—
The hand of One
Who chose the earth
Of all His whirling spheres
For the birth
Of Adam and his brood
Weaves a symbol of might
Upon the solitude.

Men have seen in the dark
Further than at noon,
Further than the fickle arc
Of the moon;
They have peered in the hive
Of the Pleiades,
Have seen the swarms that thrive
Below Orion's belt,
And felt
No terror at the burning bees
That dart and swerve
Out of the black
Path of the zodiac.

Night is not darkness—
But a luminous net
To catch the furious wings of doubt.
Fools break feather and pinion
As they thresh
Against the starry mesh
Seeking dominion
Of a world
From which Lucifer was hurled—

Lucifer, bearer of Light
Who streaked the night
In flame
And lost a lordly name.

PLENITUDE

By A. M. Sullivan

Summer is come. The beetle's wings
Glint in the sun, and the wild thrush sings.

The bees go roistering through the vale
And stagger back with their heather ale.

Nature, drowsing upon the Earth,
Sighs with the generous pangs of birth.

Fruit on the tree, and fruit in the womb
Of the woman who peers from the shuttered room

But Farmer John is worrying more
About the sow, and the ribboned boar,

And not the woman who counts the weeks
With the pallor of birth upon her cheeks.

Harvest is come. The barn is full;
The bleating ewes have lost their wool.

The old cow broods above her cud
Where the farmer spilled her bullock's blood.

The orchard and the arbor vine
Have brought him purple and amber wine,

But bitter the taste of the wine of life
That burns in the veins of the farmer's wife.

The cow gave a calf that sold for a groat,
The sow brought a profit in each little shoat;

He bargained the colt of his Percheron mare
For a second-hand auto down at the Fair.

All bore their tribute, excepting his bride
Who came to travail and quietly died.

Winter is come. The shivering crow
Clings to the cross in the mound of snow.

WOODLAND

By Sister Margaret Teresa, S.S.J.

No secular sound—this is the house of prayer.
Infinities of light and leaf
Stir, lift, hover brief,
Rest again—ritual
For a perpetual
Arcane of offering,
Self-gift of psalmèd King,
Tacit Emmanuel.

But tabernacle, where?
Then here, in self, in this inharmony.
O Holy One, teach me
What it is to be
Golden house, roof, lock and key for Deity!

CONSTANT

By Frederic Thompson

Constant running up the path
with her hair a streaming flame
made her sister stop and laugh
in the middle of the game:

in her pale blue dotted-Swiss
Constant seemed so strange and gay
with her skinny legs and wrists
flapping as she coursed in play.

Robins scattered from the apples,
cat-birds shrilled in locust trees;
where the sunlight fell in dapples,
sparrows, thrush and chicadees

quit the knee-high summer grasses,
scattered for the summer sky
wondering who this running lass is
like a screaming butterfly.

CONSTANT

Constant through the summer air
coursed the locust trees between
with a riband in her hair,
blue and gold against the green—

at the hilltop's shining blue
suddenly she vanished quite
passing down the slope from view,
in her hair unearthly light.

Now her laughing sister paused,
felt the sudden emptiness
and without much seeming cause
started crying in her dress.